The Latest
Ninja Foodi Cookbook
for Beginners and Advanced Users

---

999 Days Simple, Affordable and Delicious Recipes for Your Friends and Family

Frank Munger

Table of Contents

Chapter 6: Vegan & Vegetable 36

Chapter 7: Fish & Seafood 49

Chapter 8: Poultry 64

Chapter 9: Beef, Pork & Lamb 78

Chapter 10: Desserts 94

Chapter 1: Introduction

Introduction to the History of the Ninja Foodi

The Ninja Foodi is a multi-functional cooking appliance that has taken the culinary world by storm. Combining the functionalities of a pressure cooker, air fryer, and slow cooker, the Ninja Foodi revolutionizes the way we cook, making it easier and more efficient than ever before.

The idea of a versatile kitchen appliance like the Ninja Foodi can be traced back to the early 21st century when there was a growing demand for appliances that could handle multiple cooking tasks. With the advancement of technology and consumer desire for convenience, the Ninja Foodi was born.

Introduction to the Benefits of the Ninja Foodi

The Ninja Foodi offers a wide range of benefits that make it a must-have appliance for any kitchen. Firstly, its multi-functionality saves both time and counter space. With the ability to pressure cook, air fry, slow cook, and more, you can streamline your cooking process and reduce the number of appliances cluttering your kitchen.

Secondly, the Ninja Foodi promotes healthier cooking. The air fryer feature allows you to enjoy crispy and delicious meals with significantly less oil. Moreover, the pressure cooking function retains more nutrients in your food compared to traditional cooking methods.

Furthermore, the Ninja Foodi is perfect for busy individuals and families. With its programmable settings and intuitive controls, you can set it and forget it, allowing you to attend to other tasks while your meal cooks to perfection.

Introduction to the Features of the Ninja Foodi

The Ninja Foodi boasts an impressive array of features designed to enhance your cooking experience. Firstly, its pressure cooking function is a game-changer. It utilizes a combination of steam and pressure to cook food up to 70% faster than traditional methods. This feature is particularly useful for cooking tough cuts of meat or quickly preparing meals on busy weeknights.

Secondly, the air frying capability of the Ninja Foodi delivers crispy and golden-brown results without the need for excessive oil. This feature is ideal for creating guilt-free versions of your favorite fried foods.

Additionally, the slow cooking feature allows you to tenderize meats and develop rich flavors over an extended period. The Ninja Foodi also offers options for sautéing, steaming, baking, and roasting, providing endless possibilities for your culinary creations.

Introduction to Tips for Using the Ninja Foodi

To maximize your cooking experience with the Ninja Foodi, here are some essential tips:

1. Read the instruction manual thoroughly: Familiarize yourself with the functions and settings of the appliance to ensure safe and efficient usage.

2. Use appropriate cooking accessories: The Ninja Foodi comes with a variety of cooking accessories such as a reversible rack, pressure cooking lid, and air fryer basket. Utilize these accessories to achieve the best results for different cooking methods.

3. Experiment with recipes: The Ninja Foodi offers a world of culinary possibilities. Explore various recipes and experiment with different ingredients to unleash your creativity in the kitchen.

4. Adjust cooking times and temperatures: As with any cooking appliance, it may take some trial and error to find the perfect cooking times and temperatures for your favorite recipes. Be willing to adjust these settings based on your preferences and desired results.

Introduction to Cleaning and Maintenance of the Ninja Foodi

Proper cleaning and maintenance are crucial to keep your Ninja Foodi functioning optimally. Here are some tips to ensure its longevity:

1. Allow the appliance to cool down: Before cleaning, ensure the Ninja Foodi has cooled down completely to avoid any potential burns.

2. Remove and clean detachable parts: Take out any removable parts, such as the cooking pot, pressure cooking lid, and air fryer basket, and wash them with warm soapy water. Ensure thorough drying before reassembling.

3. Wipe the exterior: Use a damp cloth to clean the exterior of the Ninja Foodi. Be cautious not to immerse the base in water or any other liquid.

4. Regularly descale the appliance: Over time, mineral deposits may build up in the pressure release valve or the float valve. Follow the provided instructions to descale these components periodically.

Conclusion

The Ninja Foodi is a revolutionary kitchen appliance that combines the functionalities of multiple cooking appliances into one sleek and efficient device. Its history, benefits, features, usage tips, and maintenance guidelines make it an indispensable tool for anyone looking to streamline their cooking process and create delicious and healthy meals. Embrace the power of the Ninja Foodi and elevate your culinary skills to new heights.

Chapter 2: Measurement Conversions

BASIC KITCHEN CONVERSIONS & EQUIVALENTS

DRY MEASUREMENTS CONVERSION CHART
3 TEASPOONS = 1 TABLESPOON = 1/16 CUP
6 TEASPOONS = 2 TABLESPOONS = 1/8 CUP
12 TEASPOONS = 4 TABLESPOONS = 1/4 CUP
24 TEASPOONS = 8 TABLESPOONS = 1/2 CUP
36 TEASPOONS = 12 TABLESPOONS = 3/4 CUP
48 TEASPOONS = 16 TABLESPOONS = 1 CUP

METRIC TO US COOKING CONVER SIONS
OVEN TEMPERATURES
120 °C = 250 °F
160 °C = 320 °F
180° C = 360 °F
205 °C = 400 °F
220 °C = 425 °F

LIQUID MEASUREMENTS CONVERSION CHART
8 FLUID OUNCES = 1 CUP = 1/2 PINT = 1/4 QUART
16 FLUID OUNCES = 2 CUPS = 1 PINT = 1/2 QUART
32 FLUID OUNCES = 4 CUPS = 2 PINTS = 1 QUART = 1/4 GALLON
128 FLUID OUNCES = 16 CUPS = 8 PINTS = 4 QUARTS = 1 GALLON

BAKING IN GRAMS
1 CUP FLOUR = 140 GRAMS
1 CUP SUGAR = 150 GRAMS
1 CUP POWDERED SUGAR = 160 GRAMS
1 CUP HEAVY CREAM = 235 GRAMS

VOLUME
1 MILLILITER = 1/5 TEASPOON
5 ML = 1 TEASPOON
15 ML = 1 TABLESPOON
240 ML = 1 CUP OR 8 FLUID OUNCES
1 LITER = 34 FL. OUNCES

WEIGHT
1 GRAM = .035 OUNCES

100 GRAMS = 3.5 OUNCES
500 GRAMS = 1.1 POUNDS
1 KILOGRAM = 35 OUNCES

US TO METRIC COOKING CONVERSIONS
1/5 TSP = 1 ML
1 TSP = 5 ML
1 TBSP = 15 ML
1 FL OUNCE = 30 ML
1 CUP = 237 ML
1 PINT (2 CUPS) = 473 ML
1 QUART (4 CUPS) = .95 LITER
1 GALLON (16 CUPS) = 3.8 LITERS
1 OZ = 28 GRAMS
1 POUND = 454 GRAMS

BUTTER
1 CUP BUTTER = 2 STICKS = 8 OUNCES = 230 GRAMS = 8 TABLESPOONS

WHAT DOES 1 CUP EQUAL
1 CUP = 8 FLUID OUNCES
1 CUP = 16 TABLESPOONS
1 CUP = 48 TEASPOONS
1 CUP = 1/2 PINT
1 CUP = 1/4 QUART
1 CUP = 1/16 GALLON
1 CUP = 240 ML

BAKING PAN CONVERSIONS
1 CUP ALL-PURPOSE FLOUR = 4.5 OZ
1 CUP ROLLED OATS = 3 OZ 1 LARGE EGG = 1.7 OZ
1 CUP BUTTER = 8 OZ 1 CUP MILK = 8 OZ
1 CUP HEAVY CREAM = 8.4 OZ
1 CUP GRANULATED SUGAR = 7.1 OZ
1 CUP PACKED BROWN SUGAR = 7.75 OZ
1 CUP VEGETABLE OIL = 7.7 OZ
1 CUP UNSIFTED POWDERED SUGAR = 4.4 OZ

BAKING PAN CONVERSIONS
9-INCH ROUND CAKE PAN = 12 CUPS
10-INCH TUBE PAN =16 CUPS
11-INCH BUNDT PAN = 12 CUPS
9-INCH SPRINGFORM PAN = 10 CUPS
9 X 5 INCH LOAF PAN = 8 CUPS
9-INCH SQUARE PAN = 8 CUPS

Chapter 3: Snacks, Appetizers & Sides

Nutmeg Peanuts

Servings: 8
Cooking Time: 1.5 Hour
Ingredients:
- 3 cups peanuts in shells
- 1 tablespoon salt
- 4 cups of water
- ½ teaspoon nutmeg

Directions:
1. Combine the water, nutmeg, and salt together.
2. Stir the mixture well until salt is dissolved.
3. Transfer the water in the Ninja Foodi's insert.
4. Add peanuts in shells and Close the Ninja Foodi's lid.
5. Cook the dish on the "Pressure" mode for 90 minutes.
6. Once done, remove the peanuts from the Ninja Foodi's insert.
7. Let the peanuts cool before serving.

Nutrition:
- InfoCalories: 562; Fat: 36.8g; Carbohydrates: 8.57g; Protein: 28g

Green Vegan Dip

Servings: 4
Cooking Time: 20 Min
Ingredients:
- 10 ounces canned green chiles, drained with liquid reserved /300g
- 2 cups broccoli florets /260g
- ¼ cup raw cashews /32.5g
- ¼ cup soy sauce /62.5ml
- 1 cup water /250ml
- ¾ cup green bell pepper; chopped /98g
- ¼ tsp garlic powder /1.25g
- ½ tsp sea salt /2.5g
- ¼ tsp chili powder /1.25g

Directions:
1. In the cooker, add cashews, broccoli, green bell pepper, and water. Seal the pressure lid, choose Pressure, set to High, and set the timer to 5 minutes. Press Start. When ready, release the pressure quickly.
2. Drain water from the pot; add reserved liquid from canned green chilies, sea salt, garlic powder, chili powder, soy sauce, and cumin.
3. Use an immersion blender to blend the mixture until smooth; set aside in a mixing bowl. Stir green chilies through the dip; add your desired optional additions.

Honey Sriracha Chicken Wings

Servings: 4
Cooking Time: 30 Minutes
Ingredients:
- 1 tablespoon Sriracha hot sauce

- 1 tablespoon honey
- 1 garlic clove, minced
- ½ teaspoon kosher salt
- 16 chicken wings and drumettes
- Cooking spray

Directions:
1. Preheat the Ninja Foodi Deluxe Pressure Cooker to 360ºF .
2. In a large bowl, whisk together the Sriracha hot sauce, honey, minced garlic, and kosher salt, then add the chicken and toss to coat.
3. Spray the cooking pot with cooking spray, then place 8 wings in the pot. Close crisping lid. Select Roast and set time to 15 minutes. Press Start to begin. Turn halfway through the cooking time. Repeat this process with the remaining wings.
4. Remove the wings and allow to cool on a wire rack for 10 minutes before serving.

Seasoned Parsnip Fries

Servings: 4
Cooking Time: 15 Minutes
Ingredients:
- Nonstick cooking spray
- 1 lb. parsnips, cut in shoestrings 3" x ¼"
- 1 ½ tsp fresh thyme, chopped
- ½ tsp garlic powder
- ¼ tsp salt
- 1/8 tsp pepper

Directions:
1. Spray the fryer basket with cooking spray. Line a baking sheet with parchment paper.
2. Place the parsnip fries on the baking sheet and spray with cooking spray. Toss the fries and spray again.
3. Sprinkle the seasonings over fries and toss to coat well. Place fries in the basket, don't over crowd them. Place the basket in the cooker.
4. Add the tender crisp lid and set to air fry on 450°F. Cook fries, in batches, about 15 minutes or until golden brown, turning over halfway through cooking time. Serve.

Nutrition:
- InfoCalories 118,Total Fat 4g,Total Carbs 21g,Protein 1g,Sodium 157mg.

Zucchini Chips

Servings: 6
Cooking Time: 10 Minutes
Ingredients:
- Nonstick cooking spray
- 1/3 cup whole wheat bread crumbs
- ¼ cup parmesan cheese, reduced fat
- ½ tsp garlic powder

- 1/8 tsp cayenne pepper
- 3 tbsp. skim milk
- 1 zucchini, cut in 1/4-inch slices

Directions:
1. Spray the rack with cooking spray and place in the cooking pot.
2. In a medium bowl, combine bread crumbs, parmesan, garlic powder, and cayenne pepper.
3. Pour milk into a shallow dish.
4. Dip the zucchini first in the milk then the crumb mixture. Lay them in a single layer on the rack.
5. Add the tender-crisp lid and set to air fry on 400°F. Cook zucchini 10 minutes, or until crisp and lightly browned. Serve immediately.

Nutrition:
- InfoCalories 39,Total Fat 1g,Total Carbs 5g,Protein 2g,Sodium 111mg.

Pistachio Stuffed Mushrooms

Servings: 8
Cooking Time: 20 Minutes
Ingredients:
- 16 large mushrooms
- 1 tbsp. olive oil
- ½ onion, diced fine
- ¼ cup unsalted pistachios, chopped
- 1/3 cup pretzels, crushed
- 2 tbsp. sour cream, fat free
- 2 tbsp. fresh parsley, chopped
- ¼ tsp pepper
- 1/8 tsp hot pepper sauce

Directions:
1. Remove stems from mushrooms and dice them.
2. Set cooker to sauté on medium heat. Add oil and let it get hot.
3. Add the chopped mushrooms, onions, and pistachios and cook, until vegetables are tender, about 2-4 minutes. Transfer to a large bowl.
4. Add the remaining ingredients to the mushroom mixture and mix well.
5. Wipe out the cooking pot and add the rack to it. Select the air fryer function on 350°F.
6. Stuff the mushroom caps with the filling. Lay a sheet of parchment paper over the top of the rack and place mushrooms on it.
7. Add the tender-crisp lid and bake 20-25 minutes or until mushrooms are tender. Serve.
8. Preheat oven to 350 °F. Remove mushroom stems from caps; finely chop stems.

Nutrition:
- InfoCalories 84,Total Fat 4g,Total Carbs 11g,Protein 3g,Sodium 26mg.

The Kool Poblano Cheese Frittata

Servings:4
Cooking Time: 25 Minutes
Ingredients:
- 4 whole eggs
- 1 cup half and half
- 10 ounces canned green chilies
- ½ -1 teaspoon salt
- ½ teaspoon ground cumin
- 1 cup Mexican blend shredded cheese
- ¼ cup cilantro, chopped

Directions:
1. Take a bowl and beat eggs and a half and half

2. Add diced green chilis, salt, cumin and ½ cup of shredded cheese
3. Pour the mixture into 6 inches greased metal pan and cover with foil
4. Add 2 cups of water to the Ninja Foodi. Place trivet in the pot and place the pan in the trivet
5. Lock up the lid and cook on HIGH pressure for 20 minutes
6. Release the pressure naturally over 10 minutes
7. Scatter half cup of the cheese on top of your quiche and broil for a while until the cheese has melted. Enjoy!

Steak And Minty Cheese

Servings: 4
Cooking Time: 15 Min
Ingredients:
- 2 New York strip steaks
- 8 oz. halloumi cheese /240g
- 12 kalamata olives
- Juice and zest of 1 lemon
- Olive oil
- 2 tbsp chopped parsley /30g
- 2 tbsp chopped mint /30g
- Salt and pepper, to taste

Directions:
1. Season the steaks with salt and pepper, and gently brush with olive oil. Place into the Ninja Foodi, close the crisping lid and cook for 6 minutes (for medium rare) on Air Crisp mode at 350 °F or 177°C. When ready, remove to a plate and set aside.
2. Drizzle the cheese with olive oil and place it in the Ninja Foodi; cook for 4 minutes.
3. Remove to a serving platter and serve with sliced steaks and olives, sprinkled with herbs, and lemon zest and juice.

Chicken Lettuce Wraps

Servings: 6
Cooking Time: 30 Minutes
Ingredients:
- 8 ounces chicken fillet
- ¼ cup tomato juice
- 5 tablespoon sour cream
- 1 teaspoon black pepper
- 8 ounces lettuce leaves
- 1 teaspoon salt
- ½ cup chicken stock
- 1 teaspoon butter
- 1 teaspoon turmeric

Directions:
1. Chop the chicken fillet roughly and sprinkle it with sour cream, tomato juice, black pepper, turmeric, and salt.
2. Mix up the meat mixture. Put the chicken spice mixture in the Ninja Foodi's insert and add chicken stock.
3. Close the Ninja Foodi's lid and cook the dish in the "Sauté" mode for 30 minutes.
4. Once the chicken is done, remove it from the Ninja Foodi's insert and shred it well.
5. Add the butter and blend well. Transfer the shredded chicken to the lettuce leaves.
6. Serve the dish warm.

Nutrition:
- InfoCalories: 138; Fat: 7.4g; Carbohydrates: 12.63g; Protein: 6g

Butter-flower Medley

Servings: 10
Cooking Time: 15 Minutes
Ingredients:
- 3 cups butternut squash, peel & cut in 1-inch cubes
- 1 head cauliflower, separated into florets
- 2 cloves garlic
- 1 tbsp. skim milk
- ½ tsp onion powder
- ¼ tsp thyme
- 1/8 tsp salt
- 1/8 tsp black pepper
- 1 tbsp. butter
- 1 tbsp. parmesan cheese, reduced fat

Directions:
1. Add the squash, cauliflower, and garlic to the cooking pot. Pour in ½ cup water. Add the lid and select pressure cooking on high. Set the timer for 8 minutes.
2. When timer goes off use natural release to remove the lid. Drain the vegetables and place in a large bowl.
3. Add remaining ingredients, except parmesan, and beat until smooth.
4. Transfer the squash mixture back to the cooking pot and sprinkle top with parmesan cheese. Add the tender-crisp lid and select air fry on 400°F. Cook 5-6 minutes or until top is lightly browned. Serve.

Nutrition:
- InfoCalories 47,Total Fat 1g,Total Carbs 8g,Protein 2g,Sodium 68mg.

Candied Maple Bacon

Servings:12
Cooking Time: 20 Minutes
Ingredients:
- ½ cup maple syrup
- ¼ cup brown sugar
- Nonstick cooking spray
- 1 pound (454 g) (454 g) thick-cut bacon

Directions:
1. Place the Reversible Rack in the pot. Close the Crisping Lid. Preheat the unit by selecting Air Crisp, setting the temperature to 400°F , and setting the time to 5 minutes.
2. Meanwhile, in a small mixing bowl, mix together the maple syrup and brown sugar.
3. Once the Ninja Foodi has preheated, carefully line the Reversible Rack with aluminum foil. Spray the foil with cooking spray.
4. Arrange 4 to 6 slices of bacon on the rack in a single layer. Brush them with the maple syrup mixture.
5. Close the Crisping Lid. Select Air Crisp and set the temperature to 400°F . Set the time to 10 minutes, then select Start/Stop to begin.
6. After 10 minutes, flip the bacon and brush with more maple syrup mixture. Close the Crisping Lid, select Air Crisp, set the temperature to 400°F , and set the time to 10 minutes. Select Start/Stop to begin.
7. Cooking is complete when your desired crispiness is reached. Remove the bacon from the Reversible Rack and transfer to a cooling rack for 10 minutes. Repeat steps 4 through 6 with the remaining bacon.

Hungarian Cornmeal Squares

Servings: 4
Cooking Time: 55 Minutes
Ingredients:
- 1¼ cup (63 mL) water, divided
- 1 cup (250 mL) yellow cornmeal
- 1 cup (250 mL) yogurt
- 1 egg, beaten
- ½ cups sour cream
- 1 teaspoon baking soda
- 2 tablespoons safflower oil
- ¼ teaspoon salt
- 4 tablespoons plum jam

Directions:
1. Pour 1 cup of water in the cooking pot. Set a reversible rack in the pot. Spritz a baking pan with cooking spray.
2. Combine the cornmeal, yogurt, egg, sour cream, baking soda, ¼ cup of water, safflower oil, and salt in a large bowl. Stir to mix well.
3. Pour the mixture into the prepared baking pan. Spread the plum jam over. Cover with aluminum foil. Lower the pan onto the reversible rack.
4. Assemble pressure lid, making sure the pressure release valve is in the Seal position. Select Pressure and set to high . Set time to 55 minutes. Press Start to begin. Once cooking is complete, perform a quick pressure release, carefully open the lid.
5. Transfer the corn meal chunk onto a cooling rack and allow to cool for 10 minutes. Slice into squares and serve.

Dried Beet Chips

Servings:1
Cooking Time: 8 Hours
Ingredients:
- ½ beet, peeled and cut into ⅛-inch slices

Directions:
1. Arrange the beet slices flat in a single layer in the Cook & Crisp Basket. Place in the pot and close the Crisping Lid.
2. Press Dehydrate, set the temperature to 135ºF , and set the time to 8 hours. Select Start/Stop to begin.
3. When dehydrating is complete, remove the basket from the pot and transfer the beet chips to an airtight container.

Simple Broiled Baby Carrots

Servings: 4
Cooking Time: 2 Minutes
Ingredients:
- ½ pound (227 g) baby carrots, trimmed and scrubbed
- 1 tablespoon raisins
- ¼ cup (63 mL) orange juice
- 1 tablespoon red wine vinegar
- ½ tablespoon soy sauce
- ½ teaspoon mustard powder
- ¼ teaspoon cumin seeds
- ½ teaspoon shallot powder
- ½ teaspoon garlic powder
- 1 teaspoon butter, at room temperature
- ½ cup (125 mL) water
- 1 tablespoon sesame seeds, toasted

Directions:
1. Place all ingredients, except for the sesame seeds, in the cooking pot. Stir to mix well.
2. Assemble pressure lid, making sure the pressure release valve is in the Seal position. Select Pressure and set to high . Set time to 2 minutes. Press Start to begin.
3. Once cooking is complete, perform a quick pressure release. Carefully open the lid.
4. Transfer them into a large bowl, sprinkle the sesame seeds over and serve.

Dried Watermelon Jerky

Servings:1
Cooking Time: 12 Hours
Ingredients:
- 1 cup seedless watermelon (1-inch) cubes

Directions:
1. Arrange the watermelon cubes in a single layer in the Cook & Crisp Basket. Place the basket in the pot and close the Crisping Lid.
2. Press Dehydrate, set the temperature to 135ºF , and set the time to 12 hours. Select Start/Stop to begin.
3. When dehydrating is complete, remove the basket from the pot and transfer the jerky to an airtight container.

Crab Rangoon's

Servings: 15
Cooking Time: 20 Minutes
Ingredients:
- Nonstick cooking spray
- 8 oz. cream cheese, reduced fat, soft
- 1 tsp garlic powder
- 2 cups crab meat, chopped
- ¼ cup green onion, sliced thin
- 30 wonton wrappers

Directions:
1. Lightly spray the fryer basket with cooking spray.
2. In a medium bowl, beat cream cheese and garlic powder until smooth.
3. Stir in crab and onions and mix well.
4. Spoon a teaspoon of crab mixture in the center of each wrapper. Lightly brush edges with water and fold in half. Press edges to seal and lay in a single layer of the basket.
5. Add the tender-crisp lid and set to air fry on 350°F. Bake 15-20 minutes until crisp and golden brown, turning over halfway through cooking time. Serve immediately.

Nutrition:
- InfoCalories 236,Total Fat 3g,Total Carbs 15g,Protein 11g,Sodium 416mg.

Zucchini Egg Tots

Servings: 8
Cooking Time: 9 Minutes
Ingredients:
- 2 medium zucchinis
- 1 egg
- 1 teaspoon salt
- ½ teaspoon baking soda
- 1 teaspoon lemon juice
- 1 teaspoon basil
- 1 tablespoon oregano
- ⅓ cup oatmeal flour
- 1 tablespoon olive oil
- 1 teaspoon minced garlic
- 1 tablespoon butter

Directions:
1. Wash the zucchini and grate it. Beat the egg in a suitable mixing bowl and blend it using a whisk.
2. Add the baking soda, lemon juice, basil, oregano, and flour to the egg mixture.
3. Stir it carefully until smooth. Combine the grated zucchini and egg mixture together.
4. Knead the dough until smooth. Mix olive oil with minced garlic together.
5. Set the Ninja Foodi's insert to" Sauté" mode.

6. Add butter and transfer the mixture to the Ninja Foodi's insert. Melt the mixture.
7. Make the small tots from the zucchini dough and place them in the melted butter mixture.
8. Sauté the dish for 3 minutes on each side.
9. Once the zucchini tots are cooked, remove them from the Ninja Foodi's insert and serve.

Nutrition:
- InfoCalories: 64; Fat: 4.4g; Carbohydrates: 4.35g; Protein: 2g

Fried Beef Dumplings

Servings: 8
Cooking Time: 45 Min
Ingredients:
- 8 ounces ground beef /240g
- 20 wonton wrappers
- 1 carrot, grated
- 1 large egg, beaten
- 1 garlic clove, minced
- ½ cup grated cabbage /65g
- 2 tbsps olive oil /30ml
- 2 tbsps coconut aminos /30g
- ½ tbsp melted ghee /7.5ml
- ½ tbsp ginger powder /7.5g
- ½ tsp salt /2.5g
- ½ tsp freshly ground black pepper/2.5g

Directions:
1. Put the Crisping Basket in the pot. Close the crisping lid, choose Air Crisp, set the temperature to 400°F or 205°C, and the time to 5 minutes; press Start/Stop. In a large bowl, mix the beef, cabbage, carrot, egg, garlic, coconut aminos, ghee, ginger, salt, and black pepper.
2. Put the wonton wrappers on a clean flat surface and spoon 1 tbsp of the beef mixture into the middle of each wrapper.
3. Run the edges of the wrapper with a little water; fold the wrapper to cover the filling into a semi-circle shape and pinch the edges to seal. Brush the dumplings with olive oil.
4. Lay the dumplings in the preheated basket, choose Air Crisp, set the temperature to 400°F or 205°C, and set the time to 12 minutes. Choose Start/Stop to begin frying.
5. After 6 minutes, open the lid, pull out the basket and shake the dumplings. Return the basket to the pot and close the lid to continue frying until the dumplings are crispy to your desire.

Sweet Potato Fries

Servings: 4
Cooking Time: 20 Minutes
Ingredients:
- Nonstick cooking spray
- ½ tsp cumin
- ½ tsp chili powder
- ½ tsp pepper
- ½ tsp salt
- ¼ tsp cayenne pepper
- 2 sweet potatoes, peeled & julienned
- 1 tbsp. extra-virgin olive oil

Directions:
1. Lightly spray fryer basket with cooking spray.
2. In a small bowl, combine cumin, chili powder, pepper, salt, and cayenne pepper.

3.   Place potatoes in a large bowl and sprinkle spice mix and oil over them. Toss well to coat.
4.   Place the fries, in small batches, in the basket and place in the cooking pot.
5.   Add the tender-crisp lid and select air fryer on 425°F. Cook fries 15-20 minutes, until crispy on the outside and tender inside, turning halfway through cooking time. Serve immediately.

Nutrition:
- InfoCalories 86,Total Fat 3g,Total Carbs 13g,Protein 1g,Sodium 327mg.

Spicy Turkey Meatballs

Servings: 8
Cooking Time: 15 Minutes
Ingredients:
- 1 lb. lean ground turkey
- 1 onion, chopped fine
- ¼ cup shredded wheat cereal, crushed
- 2 egg whites
- ½ tsp garlic powder
- ½ tsp salt
- ¼ tsp pepper
- Nonstick cooking spray
- ¼ cup jalapeno pepper jelly

Directions:
1.   In a large bowl, combine all ingredients, except pepper jelly, and mix well. Form into 24 1-inch meatballs.
2.   Lightly spray the fryer basket with cooking spray. Place meatballs in a single layer in the basket, these will need to be cooked in batches.
3.   Add the basket to the cooking pot and secure the tender crisp lid. Set to air fry on 400°F. Cook meatballs 12-15 minutes, until no longer pink inside, turning halfway through cooking time.
4.   Place the pepper jelly in a medium, microwave safe bowl. Microwave in 30 second intervals until the jelly is melted.
5.   Toss cooked meatballs in the melted pepper jelly and serve immediately.
6.   In a medium bowl, combine the turkey, onion, cereal, egg whites, garlic powder, salt, and black pepper. Shape into 24 one-inch meatballs.

Nutrition:
- InfoCalories 113,Total Fat 5g,Total Carbs 6g,Protein 12g,Sodium 199mg.

Simple Cinnamon Popcorn

Servings: 2
Cooking Time: 1 Minute
Ingredients:
- 1 tablespoon coconut oil
- ¼ cup (63 mL) popcorn kernels
- ½ tablespoon ground cinnamon
- 3 tablespoons icing sugar

Directions:
1.   Press the Sauté button and melt the coconut oil in the cooking pot.
2.   Stir in the popcorn kernels and stir to cover. Cook for about a minute or until the popping slows down.
3.   Transfer the popped corn to a large bowl and toss with cinnamon and icing sugar to coat well. Serve immediately.

Wrapped Asparagus In Bacon

Servings: 6
Cooking Time: 30 Min
Ingredients:
- 1 lb. bacon; sliced /450g
- 1 lb. asparagus spears, trimmed /450g
- ½ cup Parmesan cheese, grated /65g
- Cooking spray
- Salt and pepper, to taste

Directions:
1.   Place the bacon slices out on a work surface, top each one with one asparagus spear and half of the cheese. Wrap the bacon around the asparagus.
2.   Line the Ninja Foodi basket with parchment paper. Arrange the wraps into the basket, scatter over the remaining cheese, season with salt and black pepper, and spray with cooking spray. Close the crisping lid and cook for 8 to 10 minutes on Roast mode at 370 °F or 188°C. If necessary, work in batches. Serve hot!

Rise And Shine Breakfast Casserole

Servings: 6
Cooking Time: 10 Minutes
Ingredients:
- 4 whole eggs
- 1 tablespoons milk
- 1 cup ham, cooked and chopped
- ½ cup cheddar cheese, shredded
- ¼ teaspoon salt
- ¼ teaspoon ground black pepper

Directions:
1.   Take a baking pan bowl, and grease it well with butter. Take a medium bowl and whisk in eggs, milk, salt, pepper and add ham, cheese, and stir. Pour mixture into baking pan and lower the pan into your Ninja Foodi
2.   Set your Ninja Foodi Air Crisp mode and Air Crisp for 325 degrees F for 7 minutes
3.   Remove pan from eggs and enjoy!

Turkey Scotch Eggs

Servings: 6
Cooking Time: 20 Min
Ingredients:
- 10 oz. ground turkey /300g
- 4 eggs, soft boiled, peeled
- 2 garlic cloves, minced
- 2 eggs, lightly beaten
- 1 white onion; chopped
- ½ cup flour /65g
- ½ cup breadcrumbs /65g
- 1 tsp dried mixed herbs /5g
- Salt and pepper to taste
- Cooking spray

Directions:
1.   Mix together the onion, garlic, salt, and pepper. Shape into 4 balls. Wrap the turkey mixture around each egg, and ensure the eggs are well covered.
2.   Dust each egg ball in flour, then dip in the beaten eggs and finally roll in the crumbs, until coated. Spray with cooking spray.
3.   Lay the eggs into your Ninja Foodi's basket. Set the temperature to 390 °F or 199°C, close the crisping lid and cook for 15 minutes. After 8 minutes, turn the eggs. Slice in half and serve warm.

Ultimate Layered Nachos

Servings: 4
Cooking Time: 18 Minutes
Ingredients:
- Cooking spray
- 8 (6-inch) corn tortillas, cut into sixths (like a pie)
- Kosher salt
- 8 ounces (227 g) Mexican-style cheese, shredded
- Refried Black Beans, for garnish (optional)
- Sliced pickled jalapeños, for garnish (optional)
- Diced red onion, for garnish (optional)
- Pitted and sliced black olives, for garnish (optional)
- Guacamole, for garnish (optional)
- Sour cream, for garnish (optional)
- Cilantro, for garnish (optional)
- Salsa, for garnish (optional)

Directions:
1. Spray the crisping basket with cooking spray, add the tortillas to the basket, and place in the Foodi's inner pot. Spray the tortillas liberally with cooking spray. Drop the Crisping Lid and set to Air Crisp at 390ºF for 15 minutes, or until the tortillas are brown and crispy.
2. Lift the lid and season the chips with salt. Remove the crisping basket and spray the bottom and sides of the Foodi's inner pot with cooking spray. Add a handful of cheese to the pot, then a handful of the chips, another handful of cheese, another handful of chips, and so on, making the last layer cheese.
3. Drop the Crisping Lid and set the Foodi to Bake/Roast at 375ºF for 3 minutes, or until cheese is melted throughout.
4. Lift the lid and carefully remove the inner pot from the Foodi. Flip the chips out and onto a platter. Add your choice of toppings and serve with plenty of salsa and your fave nacho accoutrements.

Cajun Shrimp And Asparagus

Servings: 4
Cooking Time: 3 Minutes
Ingredients:
- 1 cup (250 mL) water
- 1 pound (454 g) shrimp, peeled and deveined
- 1 bunch asparagus, trimmed
- ½ tablespoon Cajun seasoning
- 1 teaspoon extra virgin olive oil

Directions:
1. Pour the water in the cooking pot and place the reversible rack in pot. Put the shrimp and asparagus on the rack. Sprinkle with the Cajun seasoning and drizzle with the olive oil. Toss a bit.
2. Assemble pressure lid, making sure the pressure release valve is in the Seal position. Select Pressure and set to high . Set time to 3 minutes. Press Start to begin.
3. Once cooking is complete, do a quick pressure release. Carefully open the lid.
4. Remove from the cooker to a plate and serve.

Cheesy Tomato Bruschetta

Servings: 2
Cooking Time: 15 Min
Ingredients:
- 1 Italian Ciabatta Sandwich Bread
- 2 tomatoes; chopped
- 2 garlic cloves, minced
- 1 cup grated mozzarella cheese /130g
- Olive oil to brush
- Basil leaves; chopped
- Salt and pepper to taste

Directions:
1. Cut the bread in half, lengthways, then each piece again in half. Drizzle each bit with olive oil and sprinkle with garlic. Top with the grated cheese, salt, and pepper.
2. Place the bruschetta pieces into the Ninja Foodi basket, close the crisping lid and cook for 12 minutes on Air Crisp mode at 380 °F or 194°C. At 6 minutes, check for doneness.
3. Once the Ninja Foodi beeps, remove the bruschetta to a serving platter, spoon over the tomatoes and chopped basil to serve.

Cheesy Rutabaga And Bacon Bites

Servings: 8
Cooking Time: 5 Minutes
Ingredients:
- 1 cup (250 mL) water
- ½ pound (227 g) rutabaga, grated
- 7 ounces (198 g) Gruyère cheese, shredded
- 4 slices meaty bacon, chopped
- 3 eggs, lightly beaten
- 3 tablespoons almond flour
- 1 teaspoon shallot powder
- 1 teaspoon granulated garlic
- Sea salt and ground black pepper, to taste

Directions:
1. Pour the water in the cooking pot and insert a reversible rack.
2. Stir together the remaining ingredients in a bowl until well combined. Pour the mixture into a greased silicone pod tray and cover with a sheet of aluminum foil. Place it on top of the reversible rack.
3. Assemble pressure lid, making sure the pressure release valve is in the Seal position. Select Pressure and set to low . Set time to 5 minutes. Press Start to begin.
4. When the timer beeps, perform a quick pressure release. Carefully remove the lid.
5. Allow to cool for 5 minutes before serving.

Delicious Cocoa Almond Bites

Servings: 6
Cooking Time: 2 Hours
Ingredients:
- 3 cups of raw almonds
- 3 tablespoons coconut oil, melted
- Kosher salt
- ¼ cup Erythritol
- 1 tablespoon unsweetened cocoa powder
- 1 tablespoon ground cinnamon

Directions:
1. Add almonds coconut oil to the Ninja Foodi and stir until coated
2. Season with salt. Mix in Erythritol, cocoa powder, cinnamon, and cover
3. Cook on SLOW COOK MODE for 2 hours, making sure to stir every 30 minutes
4. Transfer nuts to a large baking sheet and spread them out to cool. Serve and enjoy!

Broccoli Turmeric Tots

Servings: 8
Cooking Time: 8 Minutes
Ingredients:
- 1-pound broccoli
- 3 cups of water
- 1 teaspoon salt
- 1 egg
- 1 cup pork rind
- ½ teaspoon paprika
- 1 tablespoon turmeric
- ⅓ cup almond flour
- 2 tablespoons olive oil

Directions:
1. Wash the broccoli and chop it roughly.
2. Put the broccoli in the Ninja Foodi's insert and add water.
3. Set the Ninja Foodi's insert to "Steam" mode and steam the broccoli for 20 minutes.
4. Remove the broccoli from the Ninja Foodi's insert and let it cool.
5. Transfer the broccoli to a blender. Add egg, salt, paprika, turmeric, and almond flour.
6. Blend the mixture until smooth. Add pork rind and blend the broccoli mixture for 1 minute more.
7. Pour the olive oil in the Ninja Foodi's insert.
8. Form the medium tots from the broccoli mixture and transfer them to the Ninja Foodi's insert.
9. Set the Ninja Foodi's insert to "Sauté" mode and cook for 4 minutes on each side.
10. Once the dish is done, remove the broccoli tots from the Ninja Foodi's insert.
11. Allow them to rest before serving.

Nutrition:
- InfoCalories: 147; Fat: 9.9g; Carbohydrates: 4.7g; Protein: 11.6g

Chicken And Vegetable Egg Rolls

Servings:16
Cooking Time: 10 Minutes Per Batch
Ingredients:
- 2 tablespoons sherry
- 2 tablespoons soy sauce
- 2 tablespoons beef broth
- 2 tablespoons cornstarch
- ½ teaspoon salt
- ½ teaspoon granulated sugar
- ½ teaspoon ground ginger
- 3 tablespoons canola oil
- 8 scallions, chopped
- ½ cup chopped mushrooms
- 3 cups shredded cabbage
- ½ cup shredded carrot
- ½ cup bean sprouts, washed
- 2 cups chopped cooked chicken
- 1 package egg rolls wrappers
- 1 egg, beaten
- Cooking spray
- Hot mustard, for dipping
- Sweet and sour sauce, for dipping

Directions:
1. In a small bowl, stir together the sherry, soy sauce, beef broth, cornstarch, salt, sugar, and ginger until combined and the sugar dissolves. Set aside.
2. Select SEAR/SAUTÉ and set temperature to HI. Select START/STOP to begin and allow to preheat for 5 minutes.
3. Add the canola oil to the cooking pot and allow to heat for 1 minute. Add the scallions and mushrooms and sauté for 2 to 3 minutes, stirring well, until the vegetables just begin to soften.
4. Add the cabbage, carrot, and bean sprouts, stirring to incorporate well. Decrease the temperature to MD:LO. Cook the vegetables for about 7 minutes, until cabbage and carrots are softened.
5. Stir in the chicken. Add the sauce and cook, stirring constantly, until the sauce thickens the filling, about 3 minutes. Select START/STOP to end the function. Transfer the filling to a bowl to cool. Wash the pot and return it to the cooker.
6. Place the Cook & Crisp Basket in the Foodi pot.
7. Select AIR CRISP, set the temperature to 390°F, and set the time to 5 minutes to preheat. Select START/STOP to begin.
8. Working one at a time, using a small silicone spatula, moisten the 4 sides of an egg roll wrapper with the beaten egg. Place 3 tablespoons of the filling on the center of the egg roll wrapper. Fold an edge over the mixture and tuck it under the point. Fold the edges in and continue rolling. Press the end point over the top of the roll to seal. Continue with the remaining wrappers and filling.
9. Place 3 egg rolls in the basket, making sure they don't touch each other. Coat the egg rolls in on cooking spray, then close the crisping lid.
10. Select AIR CRISP, set the temperature to 390°F, and set the time to 10 minutes. After 5 minutes, open the crisping lid, flip the egg rolls, and spritz the other side with cooking spray. Close the crisping lid and cook for the remaining 5 minutes.
11. Using tongs, carefully transfer the egg rolls to a wire rack to cool for least 6 minutes before serving.
12. Repeat step 8 with the remaining egg rolls. Keep in mind that the unit is already hot, which may decrease the cooking time. Monitor closely for doneness.
13. Serve with the hot mustard and sweet and sour sauce for dipping.

Nutrition:
- InfoCalories: 166,Total Fat: 6g,Sodium: 364mg,Carbohydrates: 20g,Protein: 9g.

Simple Treat Of Garlic

Servings: 4
Cooking Time: 5 Minutes
Ingredients:
- 1 tablespoon extra-virgin olive oil
- 2 garlic cloves, minced
- 2 large-sized Belgian endive, halved lengthwise
- ½ cup apple cider vinegar
- ½ cup broth
- Salt and pepper to taste
- 1 teaspoon cayenne pepper

Directions:
1. Set your Ninja Foodi to Saute mode and add oil, let the oil heat up
2. Add garlic and cook for 30 seconds unto browned
3. Add endive, vinegar, broth, salt, pepper, and cayenne
4. Lock lid and cook on LOW pressure for 2 minutes. Quick release pressure and serve. Enjoy!

Cheesy Garlic Pea Arancini

Servings: 6
Cooking Time: 45 Minutes
Ingredients:
- ½ cup extra-virgin olive oil, plus 1 tbsp.
- 1 small yellow onion, diced
- 2 garlic cloves, minced
- ½ cup white wine
- 5 cups chicken broth
- 2 cups arborio rice
- 1 cup frozen peas
- 1½ cups grated Parmesan cheese, plus more for garnish
- 1 tsp. freshly ground black pepper
- 1 tsp. sea salt
- 2 cups fresh bread crumbs
- 2 large eggs

Directions:
1. Preheat the pot by selecting Sear/Sauté. Select Start/Stop to begin. Preheat for 5 minutes.
2. In the preheated pot, add 1 tablespoon of oil and the onion. Cook until soft and translucent, stirring occasionally. Stir in the garlic and cook for 1 minute.
3. Place the wine, broth, and rice into the pot, stir to incorporate. Assemble the Pressure Lid, set the steamer valve to Seal.
4. Select Pressure. Set the time to 7 minutes. Press Start/Stop to begin.
5. After pressure cooking is finish, naturally release the pressure for 10 minutes, then turn the pressure release valve to the Vent position to quick release any remaining pressure. Remove the lid when the unit has finished releasing pressure carefully.
6. Add the frozen peas, Parmesan cheese, pepper and salt. Stir vigorously until the rice begins to thicken. Transfer the risotto to a large mixing bowl and allow it to cool.
7. At the same time, clean the pot. Stir together the bread crumbs and the remaining ½ cup of olive oil in a medium mixing bowl. Lightly beat the eggs in another mixing bowl.
8. Divide the risotto into 12 equal portions and shape each one into a ball. Dip each risotto ball in the beaten eggs, then dredge in the bread crumb mixture to coat well.
9. Arrange half of the arancini in the Crisp Basket in a single layer.
10. Close the Crisping Lid. Select Air Crisp, set the temperature to 400°F, and set the time to 10 minutes. Select Start/Stop to begin.
11. Repeat steps 9 and 10 to cook another half of arancini.

Stuffed Chicken Mushrooms

Servings:4
Cooking Time: 15 Minutes
Ingredients:
- 12 large fresh mushrooms, stems removed
- Stuffing
- 1 cup chicken meat, cubed
- ½ pound, imitation crabmeat, flaked
- 2 cups butter
- Garlic powder to taste
- 2 garlic cloves, peeled and minced

Directions:
1. Take a non-stick skillet and place it over medium heat, add butter and let it heat up
2. Stir in chicken and Saute for 5 minutes. Add for stuffing and cook for 5 minutes
3. Remove heat and let the chicken cool down. Divide filling into mushroom caps
4. Place stuffed mushroom caps in your Crisping basket and transfer basket to Foodi

5. Lock Crisping Lid and Air Crisp for 10 minutes at 375 degrees F. Serve and enjoy!

Chili-ranch Chicken Wings

Servings: 4
Cooking Time:28 Minutes
Ingredients:
- ½ cup water
- ½ cup hot pepper sauce
- 2 tablespoons unsalted butter, melted
- 1½ tablespoons apple cider vinegar
- 2 pounds frozen chicken wings
- ½ (1-ounce) envelope ranch salad dressing mix
- ½ teaspoon paprika
- Nonstick cooking spray

Directions:
1. Pour the water, hot pepper sauce, butter, and vinegar into the pot. Place the wings in the Cook & Crisp Basket and place the basket in the pot. Assemble the Pressure Lid, making sure the pressure release valve is in the Seal position.
2. Select Pressure and set to High. Set the time to 5 minutes. Select Start/Stop to begin.
3. When pressure cooking is complete, quick release the pressure by turning the pressure release valve to the Vent position. Carefully remove the lid when the unit has finished releasing pressure.
4. Sprinkle the chicken wings with the dressing mix and paprika. Coat with cooking spray.
5. Close the Crisping Lid. Select Air Crisp, set the temperature to 375°F, and set the time to 15 minutes. Select Start/Stop to begin.
6. After 7 minutes, open the Crisping Lid, then lift the basket and shake the wings. Coat with cooking spray. Lower the basket back into the pot and close the lid to resume cooking until the wings reach your desired crispiness.

White Bean Hummus

Servings: 8
Cooking Time: 8 Hours
Ingredients:
- 2 cups small white beans, soaked overnight
- 2 tbsp. pine nuts
- 1 tsp lemon zest, grated
- 1 tbsp. fresh lemon juice
- ¼ tsp garlic powder
- ¼ tsp salt

Directions:
1. Place beans with just enough water to cover them in the cooking pot. Add the lid and set to slow cooker function on low heat. Cook 8 hours, or until beans are tender.
2. Drain the beans, reserving some of the cooking liquid. Place beans in a food processor.
3. Wipe the cooking pot and set to sauté on low heat. Add the pine nuts and cook, stirring frequently, until lightly browned.
4. Add the lemon zest and juice, garlic powder, and salt to the beans. Pulse until almost smooth. If hummus is too thick, add reserved cooking liquid, a tablespoon at a time, until desired consistency.
5. Transfer hummus to a serving bowl and sprinkle with pine nuts. Serve.

Nutrition:
- InfoCalories 169,Total Fat 1g,Total Carbs 31g,Protein 12g,Sodium 81mg.

Shallots With Mushrooms

Servings: 7
Cooking Time: 30 Minutes
Ingredients:
- 9 ounces shallot
- 8 ounces mushrooms
- ½ cup chicken stock
- 1 tablespoon paprika
- ½ tablespoon salt
- ¼ cup cream
- 1 teaspoon coriander
- ½ cup dill, chopped
- ½ cup parsley
- 1 tablespoon Erythritol

Directions:
1. Slice the shallot and chop the mushrooms.
2. Combine the chicken stock, salt, paprika, cream, coriander, and Erythritol in a mixing bowl.
3. Blend the mixture well. Chop the dill and parsley.
4. Pour the cream mixture in the Ninja Foodi's insert.
5. Set the Ninja Foodi's insert to" Sauté" mode and add sliced shallot and chopped mushrooms.
6. Blend the mixture using a wooden spoon. Close the Ninja Foodi's lid and sauté the mixture for 30 minutes.
7. Chop the parsley and dill. Once the dish is done, transfer it to serving plates.
8. Sprinkle the cooked dish with the chopped parsley and dill.
9. Do not stir again before serving it.

Nutrition:
- InfoCalories: 52; Fat: 1g; Carbohydrates: 10.2g; Protein: 3g

Homemade Dried Mango

Servings: 2
Cooking Time: 8 Hours
Ingredients:
- ½ mango, peeled, pitted, and cut into ⅜-inch slices

Directions:
1. In a single layer in the Crisp Basket, add and flat the mango slices. Place the basket into the pot and close the Crisping Lid.
2. Press Dehydrate, set the temperature to 135°F, and set the time to 8 hours. Select Start/Stop to start.
3. Once dehydrating is complete, take the basket out from the pot and place the mango slices into an airtight container.

Garlic And Tomato "herbed" Chicken Thighs

Servings:4
Cooking Time: 5-7 Hours
Ingredients:
- 3 pounds boneless, skinless chicken thighs
- ½ cup low-sodium chicken broth
- 2 cups cherry tomatoes, halved
- 4 garlic cloves, minced
- 2 teaspoons garlic salt
- ¼ teaspoon ground white pepper
- 2 tablespoons fresh basil, chopped
- 2 tablespoons fresh oregano, chopped

Directions:
1. Add listed to your Ninja Foodi and gently stir. Lock lid and cook on SLOW COOK mode for 5-7 hours. Serve and enjoy!

Breaded Parmesan Arancini

Servings:6
Cooking Time: 28 Minutes
Ingredients:
- ½ cup extra-virgin olive oil, plus 1 tablespoon
- 1 small yellow onion, diced
- 2 garlic cloves, minced
- 5 cups chicken broth
- ½ cup white wine
- 2 cups arborio rice
- 1½ cups grated Parmesan cheese, plus more for garnish
- 1 cup frozen peas
- 1 teaspoon sea salt
- 1 teaspoon freshly ground black pepper
- 2 cups fresh bread crumbs
- 2 large eggs

Directions:
1. Select Sear/Sauté and set to Medium High. Select Start/Stop to begin. Allow the pot to preheat for 5 minutes.
2. Add 1 tablespoon of oil and the onion to the preheated pot. Cook until soft and translucent, stirring occasionally. Add the garlic and cook for 1 minute.
3. Add the broth, wine, and rice to the pot; stir to incorporate. Assemble the Pressure Lid, making sure the pressure release valve is in the Seal position.
4. Select Pressure and set to High. Set the time to 7 minutes. Press Start/Stop to begin.
5. When pressure cooking is complete, allow pressure to naturally release for 10 minutes, then quick release any remaining pressure by turning the pressure release valve to the Vent position. Carefully remove the lid when the unit has finished releasing pressure.
6. Add the Parmesan cheese, frozen peas, salt, and pepper. Stir vigorously until the rice begins to thicken. Transfer the risotto to a large mixing bowl and let cool.
7. Meanwhile, clean the pot. In a medium mixing bowl, stir together the bread crumbs and the remaining ½ cup of olive oil. In a separate mixing bowl, lightly beat the eggs.
8. Divide the risotto into 12 equal portions and form each one into a ball. Dip each risotto ball in the beaten eggs, then coat in the bread crumb mixture.
9. Arrange half of the arancini in the Cook & Crisp Basket in a single layer.
10. Close the Crisping Lid. Select Air Crisp, set the temperature to 400°F , and set the time to 10 minutes. Select Start/Stop to begin.
11. Repeat steps 9 and 10 to cook the remaining arancini.

Cheesy Smashed Sweet Potatoes

Servings: 4
Cooking Time: 70 Min
Ingredients:
- 2 slices bacon, cooked and crumbled
- 12 ounces baby sweet potatoes /360g
- ¼ cup shredded Monterey Jack cheese /32.5g
- ¼ cup sour cream /62.5ml
- 1 tbsp chopped scallions /15g
- 1 tsp melted butter /5ml
- Salt to taste

Directions:
1. Put the Crisping Basket in the pot and close the crisping lid. Choose Air Crisp, set the temperature to 350°F or 177°C, and the time to 5 minutes. Press Start/Stop to begin preheating.

2. Meanwhile, toss the sweet potatoes with the melted butter until evenly coated. Once the pot and basket have preheated, open the lid and add the sweet potatoes to the basket. Close the lid, Choose Air Crisp, set the temperature to 350°F or 177°C, and set the time to 30 minutes; press Start.

3. After 15 minutes, open the lid, pull out the basket and shake the sweet potatoes. Return the basket to the pot and close the lid to continue cooking. When ended, check the sweet potatoes for your desired crispiness, which should also be fork tender.

4. Take out the sweet potatoes from the basket and use a large spoon to crush the soft potatoes just to split lightly. Top with the cheese, sour cream, bacon, and scallions, and season with salt.

Gingered Butternut Squash

Servings: 6
Cooking Time: 15 Minutes
Ingredients:
- 8 cups butternut squash, peeled, seeded, & cut in 1-inch cubes
- 1 cup water
- ½ tsp salt
- 4 tbsp. butter
- ¼ cup half n half
- 3 tbsp. honey
- ½ tsp ginger
- ¼ tsp cinnamon

Directions:
1. Add the squash, water, and salt to the cooking pot, stir.
2. Add the lid and select pressure cooking on high. Set timer for 12 minutes. When the timer goes off, use quick release to remove the lid.
3. Drain the squash and place in a large bowl.
4. Add remaining ingredients. Set cooker to saute on medium heat. Cook until butter melts, stirring occasionally
5. Once the butter melts, pour the sauce over the squash and mash with a potato masher. Serve.

Nutrition:
- InfoCalories 198,Total Fat 9g,Total Carbs 31g,Protein 2g,Sodium 267mg.

Little Smokies With Grape Jelly

Servings: 4
Cooking Time: 2 Minutes
Ingredients:
- 3 ounces (85 g) little smokies
- 2 ounces (57 g) grape jelly
- ¼ teaspoon jalapeño, minced
- ¼ cup (63 mL) light beer
- ¼ cup (63 mL) chili sauce
- 1 tablespoon white vinegar
- ½ cup (125 mL) roasted vegetable broth
- 2 tablespoons brown sugar

Directions:
1. Place all ingredients in the cooking pot. Stir to mix.
2. Assemble pressure lid, making sure the pressure release valve is in the Seal position. Select Pressure and set to high . Set time to 2 minutes. Press Start to begin.
3. Once cooking is complete, perform a quick pressure release. Carefully open the lid.
4. Serve hot.

Cheesy Artichoke Dip

Servings: 10
Cooking Time: 15 Minutes
Ingredients:
- Nonstick cooking spray
- 2 13.75 oz. cans artichoke hearts, drain & chop
- 4 oz. green chilies, diced & drained
- 6 tbsp. mayonnaise
- 1 ½ cup cheddar cheese, grate fine

Directions:
1. Spray a small baking dish with cooking spray.
2. In a medium bowl, combine all ingredients, except ½ cup of cheese and mix well.
3. Spoon into prepared baking dish and top with cheese.
4. Place the rack in the cooker and set the dish on top. Add tender-crisp lid and select air fryer function on 350°F. Bake 15 minutes, or until hot and bubbly and cheese is nicely browned. Serve warm.

Nutrition:
- InfoCalories 109,Total Fat 6g,Total Carbs 8g,Protein 8g,Sodium 343mg.

Spinach Hummus

Servings: 12
Cooking Time: 1 Hr 10 Min
Ingredients:
- 2 cups spinach; chopped /260g
- ½ cup tahini /65g
- 2 cups dried chickpeas /260g
- 8 cups water /2000ml
- 5 garlic cloves, crushed
- 5 tbsp grapeseed oil /75ml
- 2 tsp salt; divided /10g
- 5 tbsp lemon juice /75ml

Directions:
1. In the pressure cooker, mix 2 tbsp oil, water, 1 tsp or 5g salt, and chickpeas. Seal the pressure lid, choose Pressure, set to High, and set the timer to 35 minutes. Press Start. When ready, release the pressure quickly. In a small bowl, reserve ½ cup of the cooking liquid and drain chickpeas.
2. Mix half the reserved cooking liquid and chickpeas in a food processor and puree until no large chickpeas remain; add remaining cooking liquid, spinach, lemon juice, remaining tsp salt, garlic, and tahini.
3. Process hummus for 8 minutes until smooth. Stir in the remaining 3 tbsp or 45ml of olive oil before serving.

South Of The Border Corn Dip

Servings: 8
Cooking Time: 2 Hours
Ingredients:
- 33 oz. corn with chilies
- 10 oz. tomatoes & green chilies, diced
- 8 oz. cream cheese, cubed
- ½ cup cheddar cheese, grated
- ¼ cup green onions, chopped
- ½ tsp garlic, diced fine
- ½ tsp chili powder

Directions:
1. Place all ingredients in the cooking pot and stir to mix.
2. Add the lid and set to slow cooking function on low heat. Set timer for 2 hours. Stir occasionally.

3. Dip is done when all the cheese is melted and it's bubbly. Stir well, then transfer to serving bowl and serve warm.

Nutrition:
- InfoCalories 225,Total Fat 13g,Total Carbs 24g,Protein 7g,Sodium 710mg.

Teriyaki Chicken Wings

Servings: 6
Cooking Time: 30 Min
Ingredients:
- 2 lb. chicken wings /900g
- 1 cup teriyaki sauce /250ml
- 1 tbsp honey /15ml
- 2 tbsp cornstarch 30g
- 2 tbsp cold water /30ml
- 1 tsp finely ground black pepper /5g
- 1 tsp sesame seeds /5g

Directions:
1. In the pot, combine honey, teriyaki sauce and black pepper until the honey dissolves completely; toss in chicken to coat. Seal the pressure lid, choose Pressure, set to High, and set the timer to 10 minutes. Press Start.
2. When ready, release the pressure quickly. Transfer chicken wings to a platter. Mix cold water with the cornstarch.
3. Press Sear/Sauté and stir in cornstarch slurry into the sauce and cook for 3 to 5 minutes until thickened. Top the chicken with thickened sauce. Add a garnish of sesame seeds, and serve.

Mini Crab Cakes

Servings: 9
Cooking Time: 10 Minutes
Ingredients:
- Nonstick cooking spray
- 2/3 cup Italian seasoned bread crumbs
- ½ cup egg substitute
- ½ red bell pepper, chopped fine
- ½ red onion, chopped fine
- 1 stalk celery, chopped fine
- 3 tbsp. lite mayonnaise
- 2 tsp fresh lemon juice
- ½ tsp salt
- ¾ tsp pepper
- 1 tsp dried tarragon
- 2 cans lump crabmeat, drained

Directions:
1. Lightly spray fryer basket with cooking spray.
2. In a large bowl, combine all ingredients, except crab, until combined. Gently fold in crab. Form into 36 patties. Place them in a single layer in the fryer basket without overcrowding them.

3. Add the tender-crisp lid and set to air fry on 350°F. Cook patties 3-5 minutes per side until golden brown. Repeat with remaining patties. Serve warm.

Nutrition:
- InfoCalories 96,Total Fat 2g,Total Carbs 8g,Protein 10g,Sodium 543mg.

Hot Crab Dip

Servings: 8
Cooking Time: 30 Minutes
Ingredients:
- 8 oz. cream cheese, fat free, soft
- ¼ lb. crabmeat, flaked
- ½ tsp fresh lemon juice
- ½ tsp onion powder
- 1 tbsp. fresh dill, chopped
- ¼ tsp garlic powder

Directions:
1. Set to air fryer on 350°F. Place the rack in the cooking pot.
2. In a medium bowl, combine all ingredients until smooth. Transfer to a small baking dish.
3. Place the dish on the rack and add the tender-crisp lid. Bake 30-35 minutes until heated through and lightly browned on top. Serve warm.

Nutrition:
- InfoCalories 78,Total Fat 1g,Total Carbs 8g,Protein 10g,Sodium 201mg.

Dried Tomatoes

Servings: 8
Cooking Time: 8 Hours
Ingredients:
- 5 medium tomatoes
- 1 tablespoon basil
- 1 teaspoon cilantro, chopped
- 1 tablespoon onion powder
- 5 tablespoon olive oil
- 1 teaspoon paprika

Directions:
1. Wash the tomatoes and slice them.
2. Combine the cilantro, basil, and paprika together and stir well.
3. Place the sliced tomatoes in the Ninja Foodi's insert and sprinkle them with the spice mixture.
4. Add olive oil and Close the Ninja Foodi's lid. Cook the dish on the "Slow Cook" mode for 8 hours.
5. Once done, the tomatoes should be semi-dry.
6. Remove them from the Ninja Foodi's insert.
7. Serve the dish warm or keep it in the refrigerator.

Nutrition:
- InfoCalories: 92; Fat: 8.6g; Carbohydrates: 3.84g; Protein: 1g

Chapter 4: Breakfast

Hearty Breakfast Skillet

Servings: 4
Cooking Time: 35 Minutes
Ingredients:
- ¼ cup walnuts
- 2 tbsp. olive oil
- ½ cup onion, chopped
- 4 cups Brussel sprouts, halved
- 2 cups baby Bella mushrooms, chopped
- ¼ tsp salt
- ¼ tsp pepper
- 1 clove garlic, diced fine
- 3 tbsp. chicken broth, low sodium
- 4 eggs
- ¼ cup parmesan cheese, grated

Directions:
1. Set to sauté on medium heat. Add walnuts and cook, stirring frequently, 3-5 minutes or until golden brown. Transfer to small bowl to cool.
2. Add oil and let it get hot. Once oil is hot, add onions and Brussel sprouts and cook 5 minutes, stirring occasionally.
3. Stir in mushrooms, salt, and pepper and cook 10-12 minutes until vegetables are tender. Add garlic and cook 1 minute more.
4. Pour in broth and cook until liquid has evaporated, about 3 minutes.
5. Make 4 "well" in vegetable mixture and crack an egg in each. Add tender-crisp lid and set to air fryer function on 350°F. Bake 8-10 minutes, or until whites are cooked through.
6. Chop the walnut and sprinkle over top with parmesan cheese and serve.

Nutrition:
- InfoCalories 261,Total Fat 18g,Total Carbs 14g,Protein 13g,Sodium 399mg.

Cranberry-raspberry Chia Oatmeal

Servings: 4
Cooking Time: 30 Min
Ingredients:
- 2 raspberries; sliced
- ½ cup dried cranberries, plus more for garnish /65g
- 2 cups old fashioned oatmeal /260g
- 3¾ cups water /938ml
- ¼ cup plain vinegar /62.5ml
- 1 tbsp cinnamon powder /5g
- ½ tsp nutmeg powder /2.5g
- ½ tsp vanilla extract /2.5ml
- ⅛ tsp salt /0.625g

- Honey; for topping

Directions:
1. Combine the oatmeal, water, vinegar, nutmeg, cinnamon, vanilla, cranberries, raspberries, and salt in the pot. Seal the pressure lid, hit Pressure, set to High, and set the timer to 11 minutes. Press Start/Stop to start cooking the oats.
2. When the timer has ended, perform a natural pressure release for 10 minutes, then a quick pressure release to let off any remaining pressure, and carefully open the lid. Stir the oatmeal, drizzle with honey and more dried cranberries, and serve immediately.

Spicy Red Shakshuka

Servings:6
Cooking Time: 18 Minutes
Ingredients:
- 2 red bell peppers, seeded, ribbed, and diced
- ½ medium yellow onion, diced
- 2 garlic cloves, minced
- 1 tablespoon tomato paste
- 1 (28-ounce / 794-g) can crushed tomatoes
- 2 tablespoons harissa
- 2 teaspoons ground cumin
- ¼ cup olive oil
- ½ teaspoon kosher salt
- 6 large eggs
- Pita or good-quality bread, for serving

Directions:
1. Place the bell peppers, onion, garlic, tomato paste, crushed tomatoes, harissa, cumin, olive oil, and ½ cup water in the Foodi's inner pot, stirring to combine. Lock on the Pressure Lid, making sure the valve is set to Seal, and set to Pressure on High for 5 minutes. When the timer reaches 0, quick-release the pressure and carefully remove the lid.
2. Set the Foodi to Sear/Saute on High, and cook until the vegetables have broken down and are kind of saucy, about 5 minutes. Turn off the Foodi and stir in the salt.
3. Crack 1 egg into a measuring cup, being careful not to break the yolk. Carefully pour the egg on top of the shakshuka. Repeat with the remaining eggs, spacing them evenly around the top.
4. Drop the Crisping Lid and set to Broil for 8 minutes, or until the whites are set. Serve immediately with pita or bread.

Chocolate Banana Muffins

Servings: 12
Cooking Time: 25 Minutes
Ingredients:
- 1 cup almond flour, sifted
- ½ tsp baking powder
- 1/8 tsp salt
- 2 eggs
- ¼ cup Stevia
- ½ tsp almond extract
- 3 bananas, mashed
- 2 tbsp. cocoa powder, unsweetened
- 1 tbsp. almonds, sliced

Directions:
1. Select bake function and heat cooker to 325°F. Line 2 6-cup muffin tins with liners.
2. In a large bowl, combine flour, baking powder, and salt.
3. Add remaining ingredients, except almonds, and beat until thoroughly combined.
4. Spoon into liners and top with sliced almonds.
5. Place muffin tin, one at a time, in the cooker and secure the tender-crisp lid. Bake 25-30 minutes or until muffins pass the toothpick test. Serve warm.

Nutrition:
- InfoCalories 87, Total Fat 5g, Total Carbs 19g, Protein 3g, Sodium 38mg.

Easy Cheesy Egg Bake

Servings: 4
Cooking Time: 27 Minutes
Ingredients:
- 4 eggs
- 1 cup milk
- 1 teaspoon sea salt
- 1 teaspoon freshly ground black pepper
- 1 cup shredded Cheddar cheese
- 1 red bell pepper, seeded and chopped
- 8 ounces ham, chopped
- 1 cup water

Directions:
1. In a medium mixing bowl, whisk together the eggs, milk, salt, and black pepper. Stir in the Cheddar cheese.
2. Place the bell pepper and ham in the Multi-Purpose Pan or an 8-inch baking pan. Pour the egg mixture over the pepper and ham. Cover the pan with aluminum foil and place on the Reversible Rack.
3. Pour the water into the pot. Place the rack with the pan in the pot in the lower position.
4. Assemble the Pressure Lid, making sure the pressure release valve is in the Seal position. Select Pressure and set to High. Set the time to 20 minutes. Select Start/Stop to begin.
5. When pressure cooking is complete, quick release the pressure by moving the pressure release valve to the Vent position. Carefully remove the lid when the unit has finished releasing pressure.
6. When cooking is complete, remove the pan from the pot and place it on a cooling rack. Let cool for 5 minutes, then serve.

Swiss Bacon Frittata

Servings: 6
Cooking Time: 23 Minutes
Ingredients:
- 1 small onion, chopped
- 1/2 lb. of raw bacon, chopped
- 1 lb. of frozen spinach
- 10 eggs
- 1 cup cottage cheese
- 1/2 cup half and half cream
- 1 tsp salt
- 1 cup shredded swiss cheese

Directions:
1. Preheat your Ninja Foodi for 5 minutes at 350 °F on Saute Mode.
2. Add bacon, and onion to the Foodi and saute for 10 minutes until crispy.
3. Stir in spinach and stir cook for 3 minutes.
4. Whisk eggs with cottage cheese, salt and half and half cream in a bowl.
5. Pour this mixture into the Ninja Foodi cooking pot.
6. Drizzle swiss cheese over the egg mixture.
7. Secure the Ninja Foodi lid and switch the Foodi to Bake/Roast mode for 20 minutes at 350 °F.
8. Serve warm.

Nutrition:
- InfoCalories 139; Total Fat 10.1g; Total Carbs 2.3g; Protein 10.1 g

Chicken Omelet

Servings: 2
Cooking Time: 16 Minutes
Ingredients:
- 1 teaspoon butter
- 1 small yellow onion, chopped
- ½ jalapeño pepper, seeded and chopped
- 3 eggs
- Black pepper and salt, as required
- ¼ cup cooked chicken, shredded

Directions:
1. Select the "Sauté/Sear" setting of Ninja Foodi and place the butter into the pot.
2. Press the "Start/Stop" button to initiate cooking and heat for about 2-3 minutes.
3. Add the onion and cook for about 4-5 minutes.
4. Add the jalapeño pepper and cook for about 1 minute.
5. Meanwhile, in a suitable, add the eggs, salt, and black pepper and beat well.
6. Press the "Start/Stop" button to pause cooking and stir in the chicken.
7. Top with the egg mixture evenly.
8. Close the Ninja Foodi's lid with a crisping lid and select "Air Crisp."
9. Set its cooking temperature to 355 °F for 5 minutes.
10. Press the "Start/Stop" button to initiate cooking.
11. Open the Ninja Foodi's lid and transfer the omelette onto a plate.
12. Cut into equal-sized wedges and serve hot.

Nutrition:
- InfoCalories: 153; Fat: 9.1g; Carbohydrates: 4g; Protein: 13.8g

Eggplant Breakfast

Servings: 4
Cooking Time: 10 Minutes.
Ingredients:
- 3 teaspoons Cajun seasoning
- 2 tablespoons lime juice

- 2 eggplants, cut into slices 1/2 inch
- 1/4 cup olive oil

Directions:
1. Coat the eggplant slices with the oil, lemon juice, and Cajun seasoning.
2. Take Ninja Foodi Grill, set it over your kitchen platform, and open the Ninja Foodi's lid.
3. Set the grill grate and close the Ninja Foodi's lid.
4. Select "Grill" mode and select the "MED" temperature.
5. Adjust the timer to 10 minutes and then press the "Start/Stop" button to initiate preheating.
6. Set the eggplant slices over the grill grate.
7. Close the Ninja Foodi's lid and cook for 5 minutes. Now open the Ninja Foodi's lid, flip the eggplant slices.
8. Close the Ninja Foodi's lid and cook for 5 more minutes.
9. Divide into serving plates.
10. Serve warm.

Nutrition:
- InfoCalories: 362; Fat: 11g; Carbohydrates: 16g; Protein: 8g

Cranberry Lemon Quinoa

Servings: 6
Cooking Time: 20 Minutes
Ingredients:
- 16 oz. quinoa
- 4 ½ cups water
- ½ cup brown sugar, packed
- 1 tsp lemon extract
- ½ tsp salt
- ½ cup cranberries, dried

Directions:
1. Add all ingredients, except the cranberries, to the cooker and stir to mix.
2. Secure the lid and select pressure cooking on high. Set timer for 20 minutes.
3. When timer goes off, use natural release for 10 minutes. Then use quick release and remove the lid.
4. Stir in cranberries and serve.

Nutrition:
- InfoCalories 284,Total Fat 4g,Total Carbs 56g,Protein 8g,Sodium 152mg.

Banana Bread French Toast

Servings: 4
Cooking Time:35 Minutes
Ingredients:
- VEGETARIAN

Directions:
1. In a medium mixing bowl, whisk together the eggs, milk, granulated sugar, vanilla, and cinnamon.
2. Grease the Multi-Purpose Pan or an 8-inch baking pan with cooking spray and arrange half the bread cubes in the pan in a single layer. Layer half the banana slices over the bread and sprinkle with 1 tablespoon of brown sugar.
3. Spread the cream cheese on top of the bread and bananas. Layer the remaining bread cubes on top of the cream cheese, layer the remaining banana slices on top of the bread, and sprinkle with the remaining 1 tablespoon of brown sugar.
4. Pour the egg mixture over the bread mixture, coating the bread completely.
5. Pour the water into the pot. Place the pan on the Reversible Rack, making sure the rack is in the lower

position, then place the rack with the pan in the pot. Assemble the Pressure Lid, making sure the pressure release valve is in the Seal position. Select Pressure and set to High. Set the time to 20 minutes. Select Start/Stop to begin.
6. When pressure cooking is complete, quick release the pressure by moving the pressure release valve to the Vent position. Carefully remove the lid when the pressure has finished releasing.
7. Top the French toast with the sliced butter, pecans (if using), and maple syrup.
8. Close the Crisping Lid. Select Bake/Roast, set the temperature to 390°F, and set the time to 5 minutes.
9. Check the doneness and add more time as needed until your desired crispiness is achieved. Serve immediately.

Cheesy Egg Bake With Ham

Servings: 4
Cooking Time: 27 Minutes
Ingredients:
- 1 cup milk
- 4 eggs
- 1 tsp. freshly ground black pepper
- 1 tsp. sea salt
- 1 cup shredded Cheddar cheese
- 8 ounces (227 g) ham, chopped
- 1 red bell pepper, seeded and chopped
- 1 cup water

Directions:
1. Add the milk, eggs, black pepper and salt in a medium mixing bowl, whisk them together. Add the Cheddar cheese and stir well.
2. In the Multi-Purpose Pan or an 8-inch baking pan, add the ham and bell pepper. Then pour the egg mixture over the ham and pepper. Use aluminum foil to cover the pan and place on the Reversible Rack.
3. In the pot, add the water. Place the rack with the pan in the pot.
4. Assemble the Pressure Lid, set the steamer valve to Seal. Select Pressure. Set the time to 20 minutes. Select Start/Stop to begin.
5. After pressure cooking is finish, move the pressure release valve to the Vent position to quick release the pressure. Remove the lid when the unit has finished releasing pressure carefully.
6. After cooking is finish, remove the pan from the pot and transfer it onto a cooling rack. Allow to cool for 5 minutes, and serve.

Banana Coconut Loaf

Servings: 8
Cooking Time: 35 Minutes
Ingredients:
- Nonstick cooking spray
- 1 ¼ cup whole wheat flour
- ½ cup coconut flakes, unsweetened
- 2 tsp baking powder
- ½ tsp baking soda
- ½ tsp salt
- 1 cup banana, mashed
- ¼ cup coconut oil, melted
- 2 tbsp. honey

Directions:

1. Select the bake function on heat cooker to 350°F. Spray an 8-inch loaf pan with cooking spray.
2. In a large bowl, combine flour, coconut, baking powder, baking soda, and salt.
3. In a separate bowl, combine banana, oil, and honey. Add to dry ingredients and mix well. Spread batter in prepared pan.
4. Secure the tender-crisp lid and bake 30-35 minutes or until loaf passes the toothpick test.
5. Remove pan from the cooker and let cool 10 minutes. Invert loaf to a wire rack and cool completely before slicing.

Nutrition:
- InfoCalories 201,Total Fat 11g,Total Carbs 26g,Protein 3g,Sodium 349mg.

Sweet Potato, Sausage, And Rosemary Quiche

Servings:6
Cooking Time: 38 Minutes
Ingredients:
- 6 eggs
- ¼ cup sour cream
- ½ pound ground Italian sausage
- 1 tablespoon fresh rosemary, chopped
- 2 medium sweet potatoes, cut into ½-inch cubes
- 2 teaspoons kosher salt
- ½ teaspoon freshly ground black pepper
- 1 store-bought refrigerated pie crust

Directions:
1. In a medium bowl, whisk together the eggs and sour cream until well combined. Set aside.
2. Select SEAR/SAUTÉ and set to HI. Select START/STOP to begin. Let preheat for 5 minutes.
3. Add the sausage and rosemary and cook, stirring frequently, for about 5 minutes. Add the sweet potatoes, salt, and pepper and cook, stirring frequently, for about 5 minutes. Transfer this mixture to a bowl.
4. Place the pie crust in the pan, using your fingers to gently push onto the bottom and sides of the pan. Place pan with pie crust on the Reversible Rack, making sure it is in the lower position. Place rack with pan in pot. Close crisping lid.
5. Select BAKE/ROAST, set temperature to 400°F, and set time to 8 minutes. Select START/STOP to begin.
6. Stir the sausage and sweet potatoes in to the egg mixture.
7. When cooking is complete, open lid and pour the egg mixture into the browned crust. Close crisping lid.
8. Select BAKE/ROAST, set temperature to 360°F, and set time to 15 minutes. Select START/STOP to begin.
9. When cooking is complete, carefully remove pan from pot. Let cool for 10 minutes before removing from pan.

Nutrition:
- InfoCalories: 344,Total Fat: 22g,Sodium: 743mg,Carbohydrates: 22g,Protein: 14g.

Vanilla Cinnamon Cashews

Servings: 4 To 6
Cooking Time: 10 Minutes
Ingredients:
- ½ cup water
- ¼ tsp. vanilla bean powder
- ½ cup unrefined whole cane sugar
- ¼ tsp. ground cinnamon

- 1½ cups raw cashews

Directions:
1. Use parchment paper to line the inner pot.
2. Add the water, vanilla bean powder, sugar and cinnamon in a small saucepan, stir them together over medium-low heat until the sugar is dissolved.
3. Stir in the cashews, press Sear/Sauté on High for 4 to 6 minutes, stirring continuously. Do not leave unattended, as the sugary liquid will begin to thicken and eventually stick to the cashews.
4. When all the liquid is gone, remove from the heat and evenly spread onto the Crisp Plate. Break apart the cashews to dry as individual pieces, or leave some together as clusters.

Breakfast Burrito Bake

Servings: 8
Cooking Time: 40 Minutes
Ingredients:
- 14 oz. pinto beans, drain & rinse
- 2 cups mild salsa
- 2 cups baby spinach, chopped
- 1 tsp cumin
- 1 tsp oregano
- Nonstick cooking spray
- 8 corn tortillas, gluten-free
- 1 ½ cups sharp cheddar cheese, grated
- 6 eggs
- ½ cup skim milk

Directions:
1. In a large bowl, combine the beans, salsa, spinach, cumin and oregano.
2. Spray an 8-inch baking dish with cooking spray.
3. Spread ¼ cup bean mixture in the bottom of the dish. Top with 4 tortillas, overlapping as necessary.
4. Top tortillas with half the remaining bean mixture and sprinkle with half the cheese.
5. On top of the cheese lay the remaining tortillas and cover with remaining bean mixture.
6. In a medium bowl, whisk together eggs and milk. Pour over casserole. Cover and refrigerate overnight.
7. Place the baking dish in the cooking pot and add the tender-crisp lid. Select air fryer function on 350°F. Bake 25-30 minutes, or until eggs are set and top starts to brown.
8. Sprinkle remaining cheese over the top and bake another 5 minutes until cheese melts. Let cool slightly before cutting and serving.

Nutrition:
- InfoCalories 277,Total Fat 12g,Total Carbs 27g,Protein 16g,Sodium 790mg.

Gooey Candied Bacon

Servings:6
Cooking Time: 22 Minutes
Ingredients:
- 1 pound (454 g) bacon strips
- 1 cup packed light brown sugar
- 1 teaspoon freshly ground black pepper

Directions:
1. Place all the bacon in the Foodi's inner pot along with 1 cup water. Lock on the Pressure Lid, making sure the valve is set to Seal, and set to Pressure on High for 2 minutes. When the timer reaches 0, quick-release the pressure and carefully remove the lid.

2. Add the brown sugar and the pepper and stir to dissolve the brown sugar.
3. Drop the Crisping Lid and set the Foodi to Air Crisp at 390ºF for 20 minutes, lifting the lid every 5 minutes to stir the bacon, until it is crisp and sticky.
4. Lift the lid and use tongs to remove the bacon. Separate it into strips on a rack and allow the bacon to cool to room temperature, about 10 minutes to achieve maximum stickiness.

Blueberry Oat Muffins

Servings: 7
Cooking Time: 18 Minutes
Ingredients:
- ½ cup rolled oats
- ½ cup frozen blueberries
- ¼ cup whole wheat pastry flour or white whole wheat flour
- ½ tbsp. baking powder
- ½ tsp. ground cardamom or ground cinnamon
- ⅛ tsp. kosher salt
- 2 large eggs
- ½ cup (120 ml) plain Greek yogurt
- 2 tbsps. pure maple syrup
- 2 tsps. extra-virgin olive oil
- ½ tsp. vanilla extract

Directions:
1. Stir together the flour, oats, cardamom, baking powder, and salt in a large bowl.
2. Whisk together the oil, maple syrup, eggs, yogurt, and vanilla in a medium bowl.
3. Add the egg mixture to oat mixture and stir to combine. Gently fold in the blueberries.
4. Scoop the batter into each egg bite mold.
5. Pour 1 cup of water into the Ninja pressure cooker. Put the egg bite mold on the wire rack and lower it into the pot carefully.
6. Close the pressure lid. Set the steamer valve toSeal, cook for 10 minutes.
7. Once cooking is complete, allow the pressure to release naturally for 10 minutes, then quick release any remaining pressure. Press Stop.
8. Lift the wire rack out of the pot and put on a cooling rack for 5 minutes. Invert the mold onto the cooling rack.
9. Serve the muffins warm or refrigerate.

Apple Walnut Quinoa

Servings: 2
Cooking Time: 15 Minutes
Ingredients:
- ½ cup quinoa, rinsed
- 1 apple, cored & chopped
- 2 cups water
- ½ cup apple juice, unsweetened
- 2 tsp maple syrup
- 1 tsp cinnamon
- ¼ cup walnuts, chopped & lightly toasted

Directions:
1. Set the cooker to sauté on med-low heat. Add the quinoa and apples and cook, stirring frequently, 5 minutes.
2. Add water and apple juice and stir to mix. Secure the lid and set to pressure cooking on high. Set timer for 10 minutes.

3. When timer goes off use quick release to remove the lid. Quinoa should be tender and the liquid should be absorbed, if not cook another 5 minutes.
4. When quinoa is done, stir in syrup and cinnamon. Sprinkle nuts over top and serve.
Nutrition:
- InfoCalories 348,Total Fat 12g,Total Carbs 54g,Protein 9g,Sodium 7mg.

Ham & Spinach Breakfast Bake

Servings: 6
Cooking Time: 30 Minutes
Ingredients:
- Nonstick cooking spray
- 10 eggs
- 1 cup spinach, chopped
- 1 cup ham, chopped
- 1 cup red peppers, chopped
- 1 cup onion, chopped
- 1 tsp garlic powder
- ½ tsp onion powder
- ¼ tsp salt
- ¼ tsp pepper
- 1 cup Swiss cheese, grated

Directions:
1. Select the bake function and heat cooker to 350°F. Spray the cooking pot with cooking spray.
2. In a large bowl, whisk eggs together.
3. Add remaining ingredients and mix well.
4. Pour into cooking pot and secure the tender-crisp lid. Cook 25-30 minutes, or until eggs are set and top has started to brown.
5. Let cool 5 minutes before serving.
Nutrition:
- InfoCalories 287,Total Fat 18g,Total Carbs 7g,Protein 23g,Sodium 629mg.

Sweet Potatoes & Fried Eggs

Servings: 4
Cooking Time:x
Ingredients:
- 2 large sweet potatoes, peel & cut in 1-inch cubes
- 1 tbsp. apple cider vinegar
- 1 ½ tsp salt, divided
- 3 tbsp. extra virgin olive oil, divided
- 1 cup red onion, chopped
- 1 cup green bell pepper, chopped
- 2 cloves garlic, diced fine
- ½ tsp pepper
- ½ tsp cumin
- ½ tsp paprika
- 4 eggs
- 2 tbsp. cilantro, chopped

Directions:
1. Add potatoes, vinegar, and one teaspoon salt to the cooking pot. Add just enough water to cover potatoes.
2. Secure the lid and set to pressure cooking on high. Set timer for 5 minutes. When timer goes off, use quick release to remove the lid. Potatoes should be slightly soft. Drain and set aside.
3. Add one tablespoon oil to the cooking pot and set to sauté function on medium heat. When oil is hot, add onions and bell pepper, cook about 5 minutes or until tender. Add

garlic and cook 1 minute more. Transfer to a bowl and keep warm.

4. Add remaining oil to the pot. When hot, add potatoes, remaining salt, pepper, cumin, and paprika and decrease heat to medium-low. Cook, stirring occasionally, until potatoes are nicely browned on the outside and tender.

5. Stir in the onion mixture and create 4 "wells" in the mixture. Crack an egg in each one.

6. Secure the tender-crisp lid and set to air fryer function on 350°F. Bake until whites are set. Sprinkle with cilantro and serve.

Nutrition:

- InfoCalories 239,Total Fat 15g,Total Carbs 18g,Protein 8g,Sodium 982mg.

Plum Breakfast Clafoutis

Servings: 4
Cooking Time: 60 Min
Ingredients:

- 2 large eggs
- ⅓ cup half and half /84ml
- ⅓ cup sugar /44g
- ½ cup flour /65g
- 1 cup plums; chopped /130g
- ⅔ cup whole milk /168ml
- 2 tbsps confectioners' sugar /30g
- ¼ tsp cinnamon /1.25g
- 2 tsp s butter, softened /30g
- ½ tsp vanilla extract /2.5ml
- Λ pinch of salt

Directions:

1. Grease four ramekins with the butter and divide the plums into each cup. Pour the milk, half and half, sugar, flour, eggs, cinnamon, vanilla, and salt in a bowl and use a hand mixer to whisk the Ingredients on medium speed until the batter is smooth, about 2 minutes. Pour the batter over the plums two-third way up.

2. Pour 1 cup of water into the inner pot. Fix the reversible rack at the bottom of the pot and put the ramekins on the rack. Lay a square of aluminium foil on the ramekins but don't crimp.

3. Put the pressure lid together and lock in Seal position. Choose Pressure, set to high, and set the time to 11 minutes; press Start.

4. When ready, perform a quick pressure release and carefully open the lid. Use tongs to remove the foil. Close the crisping lid and choose Bake/Roast. Adjust the temperature to 400°F or 205°C and the time to 6 minutes. Press Start to brown the top of the clafoutis.

5. Check after about 4 minutes to ensure the clafoutis are lightly browned; otherwise bake for a few more minutes. Remove the ramekins onto a flat surface. Cool for 5 minutes, and then dust with the confectioners' sugar. Serve warm.

Pecan Steel-cut Oats

Servings: 4
Cooking Time: 20 Minutes
Ingredients:

- 2 cups (320 g) steel-cut oats
- 3 cups (710 ml) water
- 1 (13.5-oz [400-ml, 383 g]) can full-fat coconut milk, divided
- ⅓ cup (80 ml) pure maple syrup, plus more to taste

- ½ tsp. sea salt
- ½ cup (56 g) toasted pecan pieces
- 2 tsps. (5 g) ground cinnamon (optional)

Directions:

1. Add the oats, water, 1 cup of the coconut milk, and the maple syrup and salt into the Ninja pressure cooker, combine them by quickly stirring the mixture. Lock the pressure lid and set the steamer vent to seal.

2. Choose Pressure, and cook for 4 minutes.

3. Use a natural release for 15 minutes, then release any remaining steam before removing the lid.

4. Once removing the lid, add the remaining coconut milk and additional maple syrup to taste.

5. Serve with the toasted pecans and sprinkle the cinnamon over if using.

Scramble Tofu With Turmeric

Servings:4
Cooking Time: 8 Minutes
Ingredients:

- 3 tablespoons peanut oil or vegetable oil
- ½ medium yellow onion, diced
- 1 garlic clove, minced
- 8 ounces(227 g) sliced button or cremini mushrooms
- 1 cup finely chopped cauliflower
- 2 teaspoons ground cumin
- 2 teaspoons ground turmeric
- 1 cup drained canned diced fire-roasted tomatoes
- 1 (14- to 16-ounce / 397- to 454-g) block firm tofu, drained
- 1 cup baby spinach leaves
- 1 cup drained canned chickpeas
- 2 teaspoons kosher salt
- Freshly ground black pepper, to taste

Directions:

1. Pour the oil into the Foodi's inner pot and set the Foodi to Sear/Saute on High to preheat for 4 minutes. Drop a piece of onion, when it sizzles in the oil, add all the onion and the garlic and cook until they begin to soften, about 3 minutes, stirring occasionally.

2. Add the mushrooms and cook until they begin to soften, about 3 more minutes, stirring occasionally.

3. Mix in the cauliflower, cumin, and turmeric and cook until aromatic, about 2 minutes, stirring occasionally.

4. Add the tomatoes and crumble the tofu into the pot. Lock on the Pressure Lid, making sure the valve is set to Seal, and set to Pressure on High for 0 minutes. When the timer reaches 0, turn off the Foodi and quick-release the pressure. Carefully remove the lid.

5. Stir in the spinach leaves and the chickpeas, vigorously mixing to break up the tofu even more. Add the salt and pepper to taste. Use a silicone slotted spoon to serve.

Bacon And Sausage Cheesecake

Servings: 6
Cooking Time: 25 Min
Ingredients:

- 8 eggs, cracked into a bowl
- 8 oz. breakfast sau sage; chopped /240g
- 4 slices bread, cut into ½ -inch cubes
- 1 large green bell pepper; chopped
- 1 large red bell pepper; chopped
- 1 cup chopped green onion /130g
- ½ cup milk /125ml

- 2 cups water /500ml
- 1 cup grated Cheddar cheese /130g
- 3 bacon slices; chopped
- 1 tsp red chili flakes /5g
- Salt and black pepper to taste

Directions:

1. Add the eggs, sausage chorizo, bacon slices, green and red bell peppers, green onion, chili flakes, cheddar cheese, salt, pepper, and milk to a bowl and use a whisk to beat them together.
2. Grease a bundt pan with cooking spray and pour the egg mixture into it. After, drop the bread slices in the egg mixture all around while using a spoon to push them into the mixture.
3. Open the Ninja Foodi, pour in water, and fit the rack at the center of the pot. Place bundt pan on the rack and seal the pressure lid. Select Pressure mode on High pressure for 6 minutes, and press Start/Stop.
4. Once the timer goes off, press Start/Stop, do a quick pressure release. Run a knife around the egg in the bundt pan, close the crisping lid and cook for another 4 minutes on Bake/Roast on 380 °F or 194°C.
5. When ready, place a serving plate on the bundt pan, and then, turn the egg bundt over. Use a knife to cut the egg into slices. Serve with a sauce of your choice.

Upside-down Broccoli And Cheese Quiche

Servings: 6
Cooking Time:20 Minutes
Ingredients:

- 8 eggs
- ½ cup milk
- 1 teaspoon sea salt
- 1 teaspoon freshly ground black pepper
- 1 cup shredded Cheddar cheese
- 1 tablespoon extra-virgin olive oil
- 1 yellow onion, chopped
- 2 garlic cloves, minced
- 2 cups thinly sliced broccoli florets
- 1 refrigerated piecrust, at room temperature

Directions:

1. Select Sear/Sauté and set to High. Select Start/Stop to begin. Allow the pot to preheat for 5 minutes.
2. In a large mixing bowl, whisk together the eggs, milk, salt, and pepper. Stir in the Cheddar cheese.
3. Put the oil, onion, and garlic in the preheated pot and stir occasionally for 5 minutes. Add the broccoli florets and sauté for another 5 minutes.
4. Pour the egg mixture over the vegetables and gently stir for 1 minute (this will allow the egg mixture to temper well and ensure that it cooks evenly under the crust).
5. Lay the piecrust evenly on top of the filling mixture, folding over the edges if necessary. Make a small cut in the center of the piecrust so that steam can escape during baking.
6. Close the Crisping Lid. Select Broil and set the time to 10 minutes. Select Start/Stop to begin.
7. When cooking is complete, remove the pot and place it on a heat-resistant surface. Let the quiche rest for 5 to 10 minutes before serving.

Mediterranean Quiche

Servings: 6
Cooking Time: 45 Minutes
Ingredients:

- Nonstick cooking spray
- 2 cups potatoes, grated
- ¾ cup feta cheese, fat free, crumbled
- 1 tbsp. olive oil
- 1 cup grape tomatoes, halved
- 3 cups baby spinach
- 2 eggs
- 2 egg whites
- ¼ cup skim milk
- ½ tsp salt
- ¼ tsp pepper

Directions:

1. Select bake function and heat to 375°F. Spray an 8-inch round pan with cooking spray.
2. Press the potatoes on the bottom and up sides of the prepared pan. Place in the cooker. Secure the tender-crisp lid and bake 10 minutes.
3. Remove pan from the cooker and sprinkle half the feta cheese over the bottom of the crust.
4. Set cooker to sauté function on medium heat. Add the oil and heat until hot.
5. Add the tomatoes and spinach and cook until spinach has wilted, about 2-3 minutes. Place over the feta cheese.
6. In a medium bowl, whisk together eggs, milk, salt, and pepper. Pour over spinach mixture and top with remaining feta cheese.
7. Place the pan back in the cooking pot and secure the tender-crisp lid. Set temperature to 375°F and bake 30 minutes or until eggs are completely set and starting to brown. Let cool 10 minutes before serving.

Nutrition:

- InfoCalories 145,Total Fat 8g,Total Carbs 12g,Protein 7g,Sodium 346mg.

Sour Cream Scrambled Eggs

Servings:2
Cooking Time: 9 Minutes
Ingredients:

- 6 large eggs, lightly beaten
- 3 tablespoons cold butter, cut into small pieces
- ½ teaspoon kosher salt
- Cooking spray
- 1 tablespoon sour cream
- Lemon wedges, for garnish
- Freshly ground black pepper, for garnish
- Chopped chives, for garnish

Directions:

1. Add the beaten eggs, butter, and salt to a medium bowl and stir to combine .
2. Generously coat the Foodi's inner pot with cooking spray. Drop the Crisping Lid and set the Foodi to Air Crisp at 390ºF for 9 minutes to preheat. After 1 minute, lift the lid and add the egg mixture. Drop the lid again and resume cooking, until eggs are fluffy and set.
3. When the timer reaches 0, lift the lid and stir in the sour cream. Serve the eggs with a lemon wedge, a sprinkle of pepper, and chives.

Cheddar Shrimp And Grits

Servings:4
Cooking Time: 22 Minutes
Ingredients:

- 3 tablespoons unsalted butter
- 1 cup Quaker Oats Quick 5-Minute Grits
- 2 garlic cloves, minced
- 1 teaspoon kosher salt, plus more as needed
- Freshly ground black pepper, to taste
- 2 cups whole milk
- ½ cup shredded cheddar cheese
- 2 tablespoons minced pickled jalapeño
- 12 ounces (340 g) frozen, peeled, and deveined raw extra jumbo shrimp (16–20 count)
- Cooking spray
- Chopped fresh chives, for garnish

Directions:

1. Set the Foodi to Sear/Saute on High. Add the butter to the inner pot and cook until melted, stirring the butter occasionally with a silicone spatula, about 4 minutes.
2. Add the grits, garlic, 1 teaspoon salt, and the pepper and allow to cook until the garlic begins to soften, about 3 minutes, stirring occasionally. Add 2 cups water and stir the grits once. Lock on the Pressure Lid, making sure the valve is set to Seal, and set to Pressure on High for 0 minutes. When the timer reaches 0, quick-release the pressure and carefully remove the lid.
3. Stir in the milk, cheese, and jalapeño. Insert the reversible rack in the high position.
4. In a bowl, spray both sides of the shrimp with cooking spray. Season with salt and pepper, then place the shrimp on the rack. Drop the Crisping Lid and set the Foodi to Broil for 10 minutes. After 5 minutes, lift the lid and flip the shrimp. Drop the lid and continue to cook until the shrimp are pink, about another 5 minutes. Set the shrimp aside.
5. Stir the grits and divide among 4 bowls. Top each bowl with a few shrimp, then sprinkle with chives and serve immediately.

Korean-style Spicy Chicken Stew

Servings: 6
Cooking Time: 20 Minutes
Ingredients:

- 2 pounds (907 g) bone-in chicken thighs
- 3 dried red chili peppers (optional)
- ¾ cup chicken stock
- ⅓ cup coconut aminos or tamari
- ⅓ cup rice wine
- 2 tbsps. gochujang (optional)
- 2 tsps. sesame oil
- 1 tsp. black pepper
- 1 tsp. sea salt (optional)
- 1 tsp. toasted sesame seeds, for garnish
- 4 cloves of garlic, crushed
- 1 medium onion, sliced
- 1 green bell pepper, sliced
- 1 (1-inch) piece ginger, peeled and sliced
- 3 scallions, cut into 2-inch pieces, chopped finely, reserve 1 tbsp, for garnish

Directions:

1. Turn on your Ninja pressure cooker and press Pressure, set the timer to 20 minutes.
2. Cut off the redundant skin and fat from the chicken thighs and then place the chicken thighs in the pot.
3. Set aside the chopped scallions and sesame seeds, blend the rest of the ingredients in a medium bowl and mix them well. Add gochujang, chili peppers or sea salt to fulfill your taste if needed.
4. Pour sauce on the chicken in the Ninja pressure cooker and mix well. Make sure the chicken thighs are well coated with the sauce.
5. Turn on your Ninja pressure cooker and then select Pressure, set the timer for 20 minutes. Close the pressure lid tightly and move the steamer valve to Seal.
6. After the cooking is complete, let the pot cool down naturally until the float valve drops down. Press Stop, and open the lid.
7. Stir occasionally, ladle out the chicken pieces in a bowl, garnish with the chopped scallions and sprinkle on sesame seeds. Then enjoy it in time.

Hard-boiled Breakfast Eggs

Servings: 9
Cooking Time: 8 Minutes
Ingredients:

- 9 large eggs

Directions:

1. Pour 1 cup of water into the Ninja pressure cooker and insert a rack. Gently make the eggs stand on the Reversible rack, fat ends down.
2. Close the pressure lid. Set the valve to Seal.
3. Select Pressure fand the time to 2 minutes.
4. Once cooking is complete, press Stop and allow the pressure to release naturally.
5. When the pin drops, unlock and remove the lid.
6. Use tongs to carefully remove the eggs from the pressure cooker. Peel or refrigerate the eggs when they are cool enough.

Pumpkin Steel Cut Oatmeal

Servings: 4
Cooking Time: 25 Min
Ingredients:

- ½ cup pumpkin seeds, toasted /65g
- 1 cup pumpkin puree /250ml
- 2 cups steel cut oats /260g
- 3 cups water /750ml
- 1 tbsp butter /15g
- 3 tbsp maple syrup /45ml
- ¼ tsp cinnamon /1.25g
- ½ tsp salt /2.5g

Directions:

1. Melt butter on Sear/Sauté. Add in cinnamon, oats, salt, pumpkin puree and water. Seal the pressure lid, choose Pressure, set to High, and set the timer to 10 minutes; press Start. When cooking is complete, do a quick release.
2. Open the lid and stir in maple syrup and top with toasted pumpkin seeds to serve.

Cranberry Vanilla Oatmeal

Servings: 6
Cooking Time: 8 Hours
Ingredients:

- Nonstick cooking spray
- 1 ½ cups steel cut oats
- 4 ½ cups water
- 1 ½ tsp cinnamon

- 2 ½ tsp vanilla
- 1 ½ cups cranberries, dried

Directions:
1. Spray the cooking pot with cooking spray.
2. Add the oats, water, cinnamon, and vanilla and stir to combine.
3. Secure the lid and set to slow cooker on low heat. Set timer for 8 hours.
4. When timer goes off stir in cranberries and serve.

Nutrition:
- InfoCalories 250,Total Fat 3g,Total Carbs 51g,Protein 7g,Sodium 2mg.

Cinnamon Roll Monkey Bread

Servings:8
Cooking Time: 20 Minutes
Ingredients:
- 4 eggs
- ¼ cup whole milk
- 1 teaspoon vanilla extract
- ½ teaspoon cinnamon
- Cooking spray
- 2 tubes refrigerated cinnamon rolls with icing, quartered

Directions:
1. In a medium bowl, whisk together the eggs, milk, vanilla, and cinnamon.
2. Lightly coat the pot with cooking spray, then place the cinnamon roll pieces in the pot. Pour the egg mixture over the dough. Close crisping lid.
3. Select BAKE/ROAST, set temperature to 350°F, and set time to 20 minutes. Select START/STOP to begin.
4. When cooking is complete, remove pot from unit and place it on a heat-resistant surface. Remove lid. Let cool for 5 minutes, then top with the icing from the cinnamon rolls and serve.

Nutrition:
- InfoCalories: 327,Total Fat: 12g,Sodium: 710mg,Carbohydrates: 46g,Protein: 7g.

Tex-mex Red Potatoes

Servings:6
Cooking Time: 29 Minutes
Ingredients:
- 3 pounds (1.4kg) baby red potatoes
- 1 tablespoon plus 1 teaspoon kosher salt
- Cooking spray
- 1 tablespoon sweet paprika
- Freshly ground black pepper

Directions:
1. Place the potatoes into the crisping basket and set the basket into the Foodi's inner pot. Add 1 tablespoon of the salt and 1 cup water to the pot. Lock on the Pressure Lid, making sure the valve is set to Seal, and set to Pressure on High for 4 minutes. When the timer reaches 0, quick-release the pressure and carefully remove the lid.
2. Remove the crisping basket and remove the inner pot from the Foodi. Discard the water remaining in the inner pot. Return the crisping basket to the inner pot and place the pot in the Foodi. Spray the potatoes heavily with cooking spray, gently tossing to make sure they are thoroughly coated. Season the potatoes with the remaining teaspoon salt, the paprika, and the pepper.
3. Drop the Crisping Lid and set the Foodi to Air Crisp at 390ºF for 25 minutes. Lift the lid and stir potatoes every 5 minutes with a silicone spoon or spatula, breaking them open slightly; spray them with more cooking spray so the interiors are also well coated. Cook until the potato skins are crisp and browned. Serve hot.

Broccoli, Ham, And Cheddar Frittata

Servings:6
Cooking Time: 40 Minutes
Ingredients:
- 1 head broccoli, cut into 1-inch florets
- 1 tablespoon canola oil
- Kosher salt
- Freshly ground black pepper
- 12 large eggs
- ¼ cup whole milk
- 1½ cups shredded white Cheddar cheese, divided
- 3 tablespoons unsalted butter
- ½ medium white onion, diced
- 1 cup diced ham

Directions:
1. Place Cook & Crisp Basket in the pot. Close crisping lid. Select AIR CRISP, setting temperature to 390°F, and set time to 5 minutes. Select START/STOP to begin preheating.
2. In a large bowl, toss the broccoli with the oil and season with salt and pepper.
3. Once unit is preheated, open lid and add the broccoli to basket. Close crisping lid.
4. Select AIR CRISP, set temperature to 390°F, and set time to 15 minutes. Select START/STOP to begin.
5. In a separate large bowl, whisk together the eggs, milk, and 1 cup of cheese.
6. After 7 minutes, open lid. Remove basket and shake the broccoli. Return basket to pot and close lid to continue cooking.
7. After 8 minutes, check the broccoli for desired doneness. When cooking is complete, remove broccoli and basket from pot.
8. Select SEAR/SAUTÉ and set to HI. Select START/STOP to begin.
9. After 5 minutes, add the butter. Melt for 1 minute, then add the onion and cook for 3 minutes, stirring occasionally.
10. Add the ham and broccoli and cook, stirring occasionally, for 2 minutes.
11. Add the egg mixture, season with salt and pepper, and stir. Close crisping lid.
12. Select BAKE/ROAST, set temperature to 400°F, and set time to 15 minutes. Select STOP/START to begin.
13. After 5 minutes, open lid and sprinkle the remaining ½ cup of cheese on top. Close lid to continue cooking.
14. When cooking is complete, remove pot from unit and let the frittata sit for 5 to 10 minutes before serving.

Nutrition:
- InfoCalories: 404,Total Fat: 30g,Sodium: 671mg,Carbohydrates: 10g,Protein: 27g.

Breakfast Farro With Walnuts And Berries

Servings: 6
Cooking Time: 17 Minutes
Ingredients:
- 1 cup farro, rinsed and drained
- 1 cup water
- 1 cup (240 ml) unsweetened almond milk

- 1½ cups fresh blueberries, raspberries, or strawberries
- 6 tbsps. chopped walnuts
- ¼ tsp. kosher salt
- ½ tsp. pure vanilla extract
- 1 tsp. ground cinnamon
- 1 tbsp. pure maple syrup

Directions:
1. Mix the farro, 1 cup water, almond milk, salt, cinnamon, vanilla, and maple syrup in the Ninja pressure cooker.
2. Close the pressure lid. Set the steamer valve to Seal.
3. Set Pressure and the time to 10 minutes.
4. Once cooking is complete, allow the pressure to release naturally for 10 minutes, then quick release any remaining pressure. Press Stop.
5. When the pin drops, unlock and remove the lid.
6. Stir the farro. Spoon into bowls and top each serving with berries and walnuts.

Carrot Cake Muffins

Servings: 12
Cooking Time: 30 Minutes
Ingredients:
- ¾ cup almond flour, sifted
- ½ cup coconut flour
- 1 tsp baking soda
- ½ tsp baking powder
- 1 tsp cinnamon
- ¼ tsp salt
- ¼ tsp cloves
- ¼ tsp nutmeg
- 2 eggs
- ½ cup honey
- 1 tsp vanilla
- ¼ cup coconut milk, unsweetened
- 2 tbsp. coconut oil, melted
- 1 banana, mashed
- 1 ½ cups carrots, grated

Directions:
1. Select the bake function and heat cooker to 350°F. Line 2 6-cup muffin tins with liners.
2. In a medium bowl, combine flours, baking soda, baking powder, cinnamon, salt, cloves, and nutmeg.
3. In a large bowl, beat eggs, honey, vanilla, and milk together until thoroughly combined.
4. Add the melted oil and mix well.
5. Add the banana and beat to combine. Stir in dry ingredients until mixed in. Fold in carrots.
6. Spoon into prepared muffin tins about ¾ full.
7. Place muffin tin, one at a time on the rack in the cooker and secure the tender-crisp lid. Bake 25-30 minutes, or until muffins pass the toothpick test.

Nutrition:
- InfoCalories 113,Total Fat 4g,Total Carbs 16g,Protein 1g,Sodium 196mg.

Banana Nut Muffins

Servings: 12
Cooking Time:x
Ingredients:
- 1 ½ cups flour
- 1 tsp baking powder
- 1 tsp baking soda
- ½ tsp salt

- ½ tsp cinnamon
- 1 egg
- 3 bananas, mashed
- ¾ cup Stevia
- 1/3 cup coconut oil, melted
- 1 tsp vanilla
- ½ cup walnuts, chopped

Directions:
1. Set cooker to air fryer function on 350°F. Line 2 6-cup muffin tins with paper liners.
2. In a medium bowl, combine flour, baking powder, baking soda, salt, and cinnamon.
3. In a large bowl, whisk together egg, banana, Stevia, oil, and vanilla until smooth.
4. Stir in dry ingredients just until combined. Fold in nuts and pour into prepared tins.
5. Add one at a time to the cooker and secure the tender-crisp lid. Bake 12-15 minutes or until muffins pass the toothpick test. Repeat.
6. Let cool in pan 10 minutes then transfer to wire rack to cool completely.

Nutrition:
- InfoCalories 174,Total Fat 10g,Total Carbs 34g,Protein 3g,Sodium 209mg.

Eggs And Mushrooms Casserole

Servings:4
Cooking Time: 18 Minutes
Ingredients:
- 1 tablespoon unsalted butter
- 2 medium shallots, minced
- 8 ounces (227 g) button mushrooms, sliced
- 1 teaspoon minced fresh thyme leaves
- 1 cup baby spinach leaves
- ½ teaspoon kosher salt
- Freshly ground black pepper, to taste
- 1 tablespoon plus 1 teaspoon finely chopped fresh chives
- 4 large eggs
- 4 slices Swiss cheese
- 4 pieces baguette, sliced on a bias
- Cooking spray
- Zest of ½ lemon

Directions:
1. Add the butter to the Foodi's inner pot and set to Sear/Saute on High. When the butter has melted, use a silicone spatula to "paint" the bottom of the pot with the butter. When the butter starts to foam, after about 5 minutes, add the shallots and cook until they begin to soften, about 3 minutes, stirring occasionally. Stir in the mushrooms and thyme, and cook until mushrooms begin to soften, about 7 minutes.
2. Add the spinach, stir, and allow to cook until the spinach begins to wilt, about 1 minute; mix in the salt, pepper to taste, and 1 tablespoon of the chives. Turn off the heat, stir, and divide the mixture among four 8-ounce ramekins, tamping the mixture down into the bottom of each ramekin. Wash the inner pot.
3. Crack the eggs and add one to each of the ramekins, being careful not to break the yolks.
4. Add ½ cup water to the Foodi's inner pot, insert the reversible rack in the low position, and carefully set the ramekins on the rack. Lock on the Pressure Lid, making sure the valve is set to Seal, and set to Pressure on Low for

3 minutes. When the timer reaches 0, quick-release the pressure and carefully remove the lid. Lay 1 slice of cheese on top of each egg.

5. Spray the baguette slices on both sides with cooking spray and arrange on top of the cheese in each ramekin. Drop the Crisping Lid and set to Broil for 5 minutes, or until the cheese is melted.

6. Combine the lemon zest with the remaining teaspoon of chives. Lift the lid and carefully remove the rack and ramekins. Sprinkle with the zest and chives. Serve warm.

Spinach Turkey Cups

Servings: 4
Cooking Time: 23 Minutes
Ingredients:
*   1 tablespoon unsalted butter
*   1-pound fresh baby spinach
*   4 eggs
*   7 ounces cooked turkey, chopped
*   4 teaspoons unsweetened almond milk
*   Black pepper and salt, as required

Directions:
1. Select the "Sauté/Sear" setting of Ninja Foodi and place the butter into the pot.
2. Press the "Start/Stop" button to initiate cooking and heat for about 2-3 minutes.

3. Add the spinach and cook for about 3 minutes or until just wilted.
4. Press the "Start/Stop" button to pause cooking and drain the liquid completely.
5. Transfer the spinach into a suitable and set aside to cool slightly.
6. Set the "Air Crisp Basket" in the Ninja Foodi's insert.
7. Close the Ninja Foodi's lid with a crisping lid and select "Air Crisp."
8. Set its cooking temperature to 355 °F for 5 minutes.
9. Press the "Start/Stop" button to initiate preheating.
10. Divide the spinach into 4 greased ramekins, followed by the turkey.
11. Crack 1 egg into each ramekin and drizzle with almond milk.
12. Sprinkle with black pepper and salt.
13. After preheating, Open the Ninja Foodi's lid.
14. Place the ramekins into the "Air Crisp Basket."
15. Close the Ninja Foodi's lid with a crisping lid and select "Air Crisp."
16. Set its cooking temperature to 355 °F for 20 minutes.
17. Press the "Start/Stop" button to initiate cooking.
18. Open the Ninja Foodi's lid and serve hot.

Nutrition:
*   InfoCalories: 200; Fat: 10.2g; Carbohydrates: 4.5g; Protein: 23.4g

Chapter 5: Soups & Stews

Tex-mex Chicken Tortilla Soup

Servings:8
Cooking Time: 20 Minutes
Ingredients:
- 1 tablespoon extra-virgin olive oil
- 1 onion, chopped
- 1 pound boneless, skinless chicken breasts
- 6 cups chicken broth
- 1 jar salsa
- 4 ounces tomato paste
- 1 tablespoon chili powder
- 2 teaspoons cumin
- ½ teaspoon sea salt
- ½ teaspoon freshly ground black pepper
- 1 pinch of cayenne pepper
- 1 can black beans, rinsed and drained
- 2 cups frozen corn
- Tortilla strips, for garnish

Directions:
1. Select SEAR/SAUTÉ and set to temperature to HI. Select START/STOP to begin. Let preheat for 5 minutes.
2. Place the olive oil and onions into the pot and cook, stirring occasionally, for 5 minutes.
3. Add the chicken breast, chicken broth, salsa, tomato paste, chili powder, cumin, salt, pepper, and cayenne pepper. Assemble pressure lid, making sure the pressure release valve is in the SEAL position.
4. Select PRESSURE and set to HI. Set time to 10 minutes. Select START/STOP to begin.
5. When pressure cooking is complete, allow pressure to naturally release for 10 minutes. After 10 minutes, quick release remaining pressure by moving the pressure release valve to the VENT position. Carefully remove lid when unit has finished releasing pressure.
6. Transfer the chicken breasts to a cutting board and shred with two forks. Set aside.
7. Add the black beans and corn. Select SEAR/SAUTÉ and set to MD. Select START/STOP to begin. Cook until heated through, about 5 minutes.
8. Add shredded chicken back to the pot. Garnish with tortilla strips, serve, and enjoy!

Nutrition:
- InfoCalories: 186,Total Fat: 4g,Sodium: 783mg,Carbohydrates: 23g,Protein: 19g.

Butternut Squash And Orzo Soup

Servings:8
Cooking Time: 28 Minutes
Ingredients:
- 4 slices uncooked bacon, cut into ½-inch pieces
- 12 ounces (340 g) butternut squash, peeled and cubed
- 1 green apple, cut into small cubes
- Kosher salt
- Freshly ground black pepper
- 1 tablespoon minced fresh oregano
- 2 quarts (1.8 kg) chicken stock
- 1 cup orzo

Directions:
1. Select SEAR/SAUTÉ and set temperature to HI. Select START/STOP to begin. Let preheat for 5 minutes.
2. Place the bacon in the pot and cook, stirring frequently, about 5 minutes, or until fat is rendered and the bacon starts to brown. Using a slotted spoon, transfer the bacon to a paper towel-lined plate to drain, leaving the rendered bacon fat in the pot.
3. Add the butternut squash, apple, salt, and pepper and sauté until partially soft, about 5 minutes. Stir in the oregano.
4. Add the bacon back into the pot along with the chicken stock. Bring to a boil for about 10 minutes, then add the orzo. Cook for about 8 minutes, until the orzo is tender. Serve.

Spicy Butternut Squash Apple Soup With Bacon

Servings: 8
Cooking Time: 28 Minutes
Ingredients:
- 12 ounces (340 g) butternut squash, peeled and cubed
- 2 quarts (64 ounces (1814g)) chicken stock
- 4 slices uncooked bacon, cut into ½-inch pieces
- 1 green apple, cut into small cubes
- Freshly ground black pepper
- 1 tbsp. minced fresh oregano
- 1 cup orzo
- Kosher salt

Directions:
1. Select the Saute mode, to preheat for 5 minutes.
2. Add bacon and cook until fat is rendered and the bacon starts to brown, stirring frequently. Transfer the bacon to a paper towel-lined plate with a slotted spoon, leaving the rendered bacon fat in the pot.
3. Add butternut squash, apple, salt, and pepper and sauté until partially soft. Add oregano and stir.
4. Add bacon, chicken stock into the pot. Simmer 10 minutes, then add the orzo and continue cooking for 8 minutes. Serve warm.

Loaded Potato Soup

Servings:6
Cooking Time: 30 Minutes
Ingredients:
- 5 slices bacon, chopped
- 1 onion, chopped
- 3 garlic cloves, minced
- 4 pounds Russet potatoes, peeled and chopped
- 4 cups chicken broth
- 1 cup whole milk
- ½ teaspoon sea salt
- ½ teaspoon freshly ground black pepper
- 1½ cups shredded Cheddar cheese
- Sour cream, for serving (optional)
- Chopped fresh chives, for serving (optional)

Directions:
1. Select SEAR/SAUTÉ and set to HI. Select START/STOP to begin. Let preheat for 5 minutes.
2. Add the bacon, onion, and garlic. Cook, stirring occasionally, for 5 minutes. Set aside some of the bacon for garnish.
3. Add the potatoes and chicken broth. Assemble pressure lid, making sure the pressure release valve is in the SEAL position.
4. Select PRESSURE and set to HI. Set time to 10 minutes, then select START/STOP to begin.
5. When pressure cooking is complete, quick release the pressure by moving the pressure release valve to the VENT position. Carefully remove lid when unit has finished releasing pressure.
6. Add the milk and mash the ingredients until the soup reaches your desired consistency. Season with the salt and black pepper. Sprinkle the cheese evenly over the top of the soup. Close crisping lid.
7. Select BROIL and set time to 5 minutes. Select START/STOP to begin.
8. When cooking is complete, top with the reserved crispy bacon and serve with sour cream and chives (if using).

Nutrition:
- InfoCalories: 468,Total Fat: 19g,Sodium: 1041mg,Carbohydrates: 53g,Protein: 23g.

Garlicy Roasted Cauliflower And Potato Soup

Servings: 6
Cooking Time: 30 Minutes
Ingredients:
- 8 garlic cloves, peeled
- 1 large cauliflower head, cut into small florets
- 2 russet potatoes, peeled and chopped into 1-inch pieces
- 1 yellow onion, coarsely chopped
- 1 celery stalk, coarsely chopped
- 1 tablespoon water, plus more as needed
- 6 cups no-sodium vegetable broth
- 2 thyme sprigs
- 2 teaspoons paprika
- ¼ teaspoon freshly ground black pepper
- 1 tablespoon chopped fresh rosemary leaves

Directions:
1. Use parchment paper to line the inner pot.
2. Use the aluminum foil to wrap the garlic cloves or place in a garlic roaster.

3. In Ninja Foodi, evenly spread with the potatoes and cauliflower. Place the wrapped garlic on the inner pot.
4. Press Roast and cook at 450°F for 15 to 20 minutes, or until the cauliflower is lightly browned.
5. Combine the onion and celery in Ninja Foodi, press Sear/Sauté and cook at 390ºF for 4 to 5 minutes, adding water, 1 tablespoon at a time, to prevent burning, until the onion starts to brown.
6. Pour in the vegetable broth and bring the soup to a simmer.
7. Add the roasted vegetables and thyme, garlic, paprika, and pepper. Bring the soup to a simmer, cover pressure lid and press Pressure and cook at 390ºF . for 10 minutes.
8. Remove and discard the thyme. Puree the soup with an immersion blender until smooth. Add some water if the soup is too thick, to the desired consistency.
9. Stir in the rosemary and serve.

Beef And Vegetable Stew

Servings: 6
Cooking Time: 46 Minutes
Ingredients:
- 2 tablespoons olive oil
- 2 pounds (907 g) beef stew cubes
- 1 medium sweet onion, peeled and diced
- 4 cloves garlic, peeled and minced
- 3 cups (750 mL) beef broth
- ½ cup (125 mL) dry red wine
- 1 (14.5-ounce / 411-g) can crushed tomatoes, undrained
- 2 medium carrots, peeled and diced
- 2 medium Russet potatoes, scrubbed and small-diced
- 1 stalk celery, chopped
- 2 tablespoons chopped fresh rosemary
- 1 teaspoon salt
- ½ teaspoon ground black pepper
- 2 tablespoons gluten-free all-purpose flour
- 4 tablespoons water
- ¼ cup (63 mL) chopped fresh Italian flat-leaf parsley

Directions:
1. Press the Sauté button and heat the oil. Add the beef and onion to the pot and sauté for 5 minutes, or until the beef is seared and the onion is translucent. Add the garlic and sauté for 1 minute.
2. Pour in the beef broth and wine and deglaze the pot by scraping up any bits from the sides and bottom of the pot.
3. Stir in the tomatoes with juice, carrots, potatoes, celery, rosemary, salt and pepper.
4. Assemble pressure lid, making sure the pressure release valve is in the Seal position. Select Pressure and set to high . Set time to 35 minutes. Press Start to begin. When the timer goes off, perform a natural pressure release for 10 minutes, then release any remaining pressure. Open the lid.
5. Create a slurry by whisking together the flour and water in a small bowl. Add the slurry to the pot. Select the Sauté mode and let simmer for 5 minutes, stirring constantly.
6. Ladle the stew into 6 bowls and serve topped with the parsley.

Garlicky Cumin Chickpea Soup

Servings: 4
Cooking Time: 30 Minutes
Ingredients:
- 1 tbsp. plus 1 tsp. kosher salt (or 2 tsps. fine salt), divided
- 1 pound (455 g) dried chickpeas
- 5 garlic cloves
- 1 tsp. cumin seeds
- 1 small onion, chopped
- 3 tbsps. olive oil, divided
- 6 cups water
- ¼ tsp. ground cumin
- 4 Italian or French bread slices
- Juice of 1 lemon (about 2 tbsps.)
- 2 tbsps. harissa (optional)
- ¼ cup Greek yogurt (optional)

Directions:
1. Dissolve 1 tablespoon of kosher salt in 1 quart of water in a large bowl. Place the chickpeas in the bowl and allow to soak at room temperature for 8 to 24 hours.
2. Peel and smash 4 garlic cloves. Peel and mince the remaining clove and set aside.
3. Drain and rinse the chickpeas. Add them into the Foodi inner pot. Then add the 4 smashed garlic cloves, the cumin seeds, onion, 1 tablespoon of olive oil, the remaining 1 teaspoon of kosher salt , and the water.
4. Lock the Pressure Lid into place, set the valve to Seal. Select Pressure, adjust the cook time to 6 minutes. Press Start.
5. Meanwhile, stir together the the minced garlic, remaining 2 tablespoons of olive oil, and the ground cumin in a small bowl. Spread this mixture over the bread slices.
6. When the cooking is complete, naturally release the pressure for 8 minutes, then quick release any remaining pressure. Open and remove the Pressure Lid carefully.
7. Taste the soup and adjust the seasoning. There should be plenty of broth, add more water if the texture is too thick. Stir in the lemon juice and harissa .
8. Put the Reversible Rack in the pot in the upper position. Place the bread slices on the rack.
9. Close the Crisping Lid and select Broil. Adjust the cook time to 7 minutes. Press Start.
10. Once the bread is crisp, remove the rack. Place a slice of bread in each of four bowls. Ladle over with the soup and garnish with a spoonful of yogurt .

Coconut And Shrimp Bisque

Servings:4
Cooking Time: 15 Minutes
Ingredients:
- ¼ cup red curry paste
- 2 tablespoons water
- 1 tablespoon extra-virgin olive oil
- 1 bunch scallions, sliced
- 1 pound medium shrimp, peeled and deveined
- 1 cup frozen peas
- 1 red bell pepper, diced
- 1 can full-fat coconut milk
- Kosher salt

Directions:
1. In a small bowl, whisk together the red curry paste and water. Set aside.

2. Select SEAR/SAUTÉ and set to MED. Select START/STOP to begin. Let preheat for 3 minutes.
3. Add the oil and scallions. Cook for 2 minutes.
4. Add the shrimp, peas, and bell pepper. Stir well to combine. Stir in the red curry paste. Cook for 5 minutes, until the peas are tender.
5. Stir in coconut milk and cook for an additional 5 minutes until shrimp is cooked through and the bisque is thoroughly heated.
6. Season with salt and serve immediately.
Nutrition:
- InfoCalories: 460,Total Fat: 32g,Sodium: 902mg,Carbohydrates: 16g,Protein: 29g.

Spanish Turkey Meatball Soup

Servings: 6 To 8
Cooking Time: 35 Minutes
Ingredients:
- 8 ounces (227 g) kale, stemmed and chopped
- 1 pound (455 g) ground turkey
- 1 slice hearty white sandwich bread, torn into quarters
- ¼ cup (60 ml) whole milk
- 1 ounce (28 g) Manchego cheese, grated (½ cup), plus extra for serving
- 5 tbsps. minced fresh parsley, divided
- ½ tsp. table salt
- 4 garlic cloves, minced
- 1 tbsp. extra-virgin olive oil
- 1 onion, chopped
- 1 red bell pepper, stemmed, seeded, and cut into ¾-inch pieces
- 2 tsps. smoked paprika
- ½ cup (120 ml) dry white wine
- 8 cups (1920 ml) chicken broth
- salt and pepper to taste

Directions:
1. Mash bread and milk together into paste with a fork in large bowl. Stir in 3 tablespoons parsley, Manchego, and salt until combined. Add turkey and knead mixture with your hands until well mixed. Roll 2-teaspoon-size pieces of pinched off mixture into balls and place on large plate , set aside.
2. In Ninja pressure cooker, select sauté function, heat oil until shimmering. Add onion and bell pepper and cook 5 to 7 minutes until softened and lightly browned. Stir in garlic and paprika and cook about 30 seconds until fragrant. Stir in wine, scraping up any browned bits, and cook about 5 minutes until almost completely evaporated. Stir in kale and broth, then gently submerge meatballs.
3. Lock lid and close pressure release valve. Select pressure function, cook for 3 minutes. Turn off and quick-release pressure. Carefully remove lid, letting steam escape away from you.
4. Stir in remaining parsley and season with salt and pepper. Serve with extra Manchego separately.

Garlicky Roasted Red Pepper And Tomato Soup

Servings: 4 To 6
Cooking Time: 11 Minutes
Ingredients:
- 1 tbsp. (15 ml) extra-virgin olive oil
- 2 (16-oz [455-g]) jars roasted red peppers, drained
- 1 (14.5-oz [411-g]) can fire-roasted diced tomatoes

- 1 yellow onion, diced
- 2 cloves garlic, grated
- 1 tbsp. (15 ml) sherry vinegar
- 2 cups (475 ml) water or vegetable stock
- 1 tsp. fresh lemon juice
- Salt
- Freshly ground black pepper
- 1 cup (237 ml) coconut milk
- Croutons, for topping (optional)

Directions:
1. Press sauté on the Ninja pressure cooker. Add the oil into the pot. Heat the oil for about 2 minutes, add the onion. Sauté for 2 minutes, or until translucent.
2. Press Stop and then stir in the garlic and vinegar. Mix in the roasted red peppers, tomatoes, water and lemon juice along with salt and pepper to taste.
3. In the sealed position, secure the pressure lid with the steam vent. Press Pressure. Adjust the time to 7 minutes.
4. Once the timer sounds, release the pressure quickly. Remove the lid. Add the coconut milk and stir. Puree the soup until smooth with an immersion blender. Seasoning with more salt and pepper and top with croutons, if using.

Chicken And Black Bean Enchilada Soup

Servings:8
Cooking Time: 30 Minutes
Ingredients:
- 1 tablespoon extra-virgin olive oil
- 1 small red onion, diced
- 2 (10-ounce / 283-g) cans fire-roasted tomatoes with chiles
- 1 (15-ounce / 425-g) can corn
- 1 (15-ounce / 425-g) can black beans, rinsed and drained
- 1 (10-ounce / 283-g) can red enchilada sauce
- 1 (10-ounce / 283-g) can tomato paste
- 3 tablespoons taco seasoning
- 2 tablespoons freshly squeezed lime juice
- 2 (8-ounce / 227-g) boneless, skinless chicken breasts
- Salt
- Freshly ground black pepper

Directions:
1. Select SEAR/SAUTÉ and set temperature to MD:HI. Select START/STOP to begin. Let preheat for 5 minutes.
2. Place the olive oil and onion in the pot. Cook until the onions are translucent, about 2 minutes.
3. Add the tomatoes, corn, beans, enchilada sauce, tomato paste, taco seasoning, lime juice, and chicken. Season with salt and pepper and stir. Assemble pressure lid, making sure the pressure release valve is in the SEAL position.
4. Select PRESSURE and set to HI. Set time to 9 minutes. Select START/STOP to begin.
5. When pressure cooking is complete, allow pressure to naturally release for 10 minutes. After 10 minutes, quick release remaining pressure by moving the pressure release valve to the VENT position. Carefully remove lid when unit has finished releasing pressure.
6. Transfer the chicken breasts to a cutting board. Using two forks, shred the chicken. Return the chicken back to the pot and stir. Serve in a bowl with toppings of choice, such as shredded cheese, crushed tortilla chips, sliced avocado, sour cream, cilantro, and lime wedges, if desired.

Curry Acorn Squash Soup

Servings: 6
Cooking Time: About 1 Hour
Ingredients:
- 1 acorn squash
- 2 garlic cloves, chopped
- 1 yellow onion, chopped
- 2 celery stalks, coarsely chopped
- 1 tbsp. water, plus more as needed
- 2 tbsps. whole wheat flour
- 2 cups no-sodium vegetable broth
- ½ tsp. dill
- 1 tsp. curry powder, plus more for seasoning
- ⅛ tsp. cayenne pepper
- 1 (14-ounce, 397 g) can full-fat coconut milk
- Chopped scallions, green parts only, for serving

Directions:
1. Cut the acorn squash in half lengthwise and scoop out the seeds and stringy center. Put the squash halves in the Ninja Foodi, cut-side down, and add enough water to come up about 1 inch all around.
2. Press Bake and cook at 350°F for 30 to 45 minutes, or until the squash can be easily pierced with a fork. Take the squash out from the inner pot and allow to cool for 10 minutes. Scoop out the soft flesh and set aside in a bowl.
3. Combine the garlic, onion, and celery in the Ninja Foodi, press Sear/Sauté on HIGH for 2 to 3 minutes, add the water, 1 tablespoon at a time, to prevent burning, until the onion is translucent but not browned.
4. Sprinkle over with the flour and stir to coat the vegetables.
5. Add the roasted squash, vegetable broth, dill, curry powder and cayenne pepper. Bring the mixture to a boil. Adjust to LOW, cover and cook for 10 minutes.
6. Pour in the coconut milk. Blend the soup until smooth with an immersion blender. Serve immediately or place in an airtight container and refrigerate for up to 1 week.
7. Place the scallions and a sprinkle of curry powder on the top and serve.

Haddock And Biscuit Chowder

Servings:8
Cooking Time: 30 Minutes
Ingredients:
- 5 strips bacon, sliced
- 1 white onion, chopped
- 3 celery stalks, chopped
- 4 cups chicken stock
- 2 Russet potatoes, rinsed and cut in 1-inch pieces
- 4 (6-ounce / 170-g) frozen haddock fillets
- Kosher salt
- ½ cup clam juice
- ⅓ cup all-purpose flour
- 2 (14-ounce / 397-g) cans evaporated milk
- 1 (14-ounce / 397-g) tube refrigerated biscuit dough

Directions:
1. Select SEAR/SAUTÉ and set to HI. Select START/STOP to begin. Let preheat for 5 minutes.
2. Add the bacon and cook, stirring frequently, for 5 minutes. Add the onion and celery and cook for an additional 5 minutes, stirring occasionally.
3. Add the chicken stock, potatoes, and haddock filets. Season with salt. Assemble pressure lid, making sure the pressure release valve is in the SEAL position.

4. Select PRESSURE and set to HI. Set time to 5 minutes. Select START/STOP to begin.
5. Whisk together the clam juice and flour in a small bowl, ensuring there are no flour clumps in the mixture.
6. When pressure cooking is complete, quick release the pressure by moving the pressure release valve to the VENT position. Carefully remove lid when unit has finished releasing pressure.
7. Select SEAR/SAUTÉ and set to MED. Select START/STOP to begin. Add the clam juice mixture, stirring well to combine. Add the evaporated milk and continue to stir frequently for 3 to 5 minutes, until chowder has thickened to your desired texture.
8. Place the Reversible Rack in the pot in the higher position. Place the biscuits on the rack; it may be necessary to tear the last biscuit or two into smaller pieces in order to fit them all on the rack. Close crisping lid.
9. Select BAKE/ROAST, set temperature to 350ºF , and set time to 12 minutes. Select START/STOP to begin.
10. After 10 minutes, check the biscuits for doneness. If desired, cook for up to an additional 2 minutes.
11. When cooking is complete, open lid and remove rack from pot. Serve the chowder and top each portion with biscuits.

Whole Farro And Leek Soup

Servings: 6 To 8
Cooking Time: 30 Minutes
Ingredients:
- 1 cup whole farro
- 1 tbsp. extra-virgin olive oil, plus extra for drizzling
- 3 ounces (85 g) pancetta, chopped fine
- 1 pound (455 g) leeks, ends trimmed, chopped, and washed thoroughly
- 1 celery rib, chopped
- 2 carrots, peeled and chopped
- ½ cup minced fresh parsley
- 8 cups (1920 ml) chicken broth, plus extra as needed
- salt and pepper to taste
- Grated Parmesan cheese

Directions:
1. Pulse farro in blender for about 6 pulses until about half of grains are broken into smaller pieces, set aside.
2. In Ninja pressure cooker, select sauté function, heat oil until shimmering. Add pancetta and cook 3 to 5 minutes until lightly browned. Stir in carrots, leeks, and celery and cook about 5 minutes until softened. Add broth, scraping up any browned bits, then stir in farro.

3. Lock lid and close pressure release valve. Choose pressure function and cook for 8 minutes. Turn off and quick-release pressure. Carefully remove lid, letting steam escape away from you.
4. Adjust consistency with extra hot broth if you like. Stir in parsley and season with salt and pepper. Drizzle each portion with extra oil and top with Parmesan. Serve.

Spanish Chorizo And Lentil Soup

Servings: 6 To 8
Cooking Time: 30 Minutes
Ingredients:
- 8 ounces (227 g) Spanish-style chorizo sausage, quartered lengthwise and sliced thin
- 1 large onion, peeled
- 1 tbsp. extra-virgin olive oil, plus extra for drizzling
- 2 carrots, peeled and halved crosswise
- 4 garlic cloves, minced
- 1½ tsp. smoked paprika
- 5 cups (1200 ml) water
- 1 pound (2¼ cups, 455 g) French green lentils, picked over and rinsed
- 4 cups (960 ml) chicken broth
- 1 tbsp. sherry vinegar, plus extra for seasoning
- 2 bay leaves
- 1 tsp. table salt
- ½ cup slivered almonds, toasted
- ½ cup minced fresh parsley
- salt and pepper to taste

Directions:
1. In Ninja pressure cooker, select sauté function, heat oil until shimmering. Add chorizo and cook 3 to 5 minutes until lightly browned. Stir in garlic and paprika and cook about 30 seconds until fragrant. Add water, scraping up any browned bits, then stir in lentils, bay leaves, vinegar, broth, and salt. Nestle carrots and onion into pot.
2. Lock lid and close pressure release valve. Choose pressure function and cook for 14 minutes. Turn off and quick-release pressure. Carefully remove lid, letting steam escape away from you.
3. Throw away bay leaves. Transfer onion and carrots to food processor with a slotted spoon and process about 1 minute until smooth, scraping down sides of bowl if you like. Stir vegetable mixture into lentils and season with pepper, salt, and extra vinegar. Drizzle each portion with extra oil, sprinkle with almonds and parsley and serve.

Chapter 6: Vegan & Vegetable

Vegan Split Pea Soup

Servings: 8
Cooking Time: 8 Hours
Ingredients:
- 16 oz. dried split peas
- 2 cups carrots, chopped
- 1 cup onion, chopped
- 1 cup celery, chopped
- 3 cups water
- ½ tsp salt
- ½ tsp pepper
- 4 cups vegetable broth, low sodium
- 1 bay leaf

Directions:
1. Place all ingredients in the cooking pot and stir to mix.
2. Add the lid and set to slow cook on low. Cook 8 hours or until peas are tender and soup has thickened.
3. Discard the bay leaf and serve immediately.

Nutrition:
- InfoCalories 225,Total Fat 1g,Total Carbs 42g,Protein 14g,Sodium 655mg.

Sour Cream & Onion Frittata

Servings: 6
Cooking Time: 15 Minutes
Ingredients:
- 1 lb. new potatoes, boiled peeled & sliced ¼-inch thick
- 1 ½ tbsp. olive oil
- 1 ½ tbsp. butter
- 1 onion, sliced thin
- 10 eggs
- ¾ cup cheddar cheese
- ½ tsp salt
- ¼ tsp pepper
- ½ cup sour cream

Directions:
1. Add oil and butter to the cooking pot and set to sauté on med-high heat.
2. Add the onions and cook 3-5 minutes until soft. Add the potatoes and cook until golden brown, about 5 minutes, stirring occasionally.
3. In a large bowl, beat eggs. Stir in cheese, salt and pepper. Pour over the onion mixture. Spoon sour cream over the eggs and swirl it evenly around the frittata. Reduce heat to medium and cook 2-4 minutes until edges are set, do not stir.
4. Add the tender-crisp lid and set to bake on 400°F. Bake frittata 10-12 minutes until eggs are completely set.
5. Use a knife to loosen the edges and invert onto a cutting board. Let cool slightly before serving.

Nutrition:
- InfoCalories 330,Total Fat 23g,Total Carbs 16g,Protein 15g,Sodium 248mg.

Delicious Beet Borscht

Servings:6
Cooking Time: 45 Minutes
Ingredients:
- 8 cups beets
- ½ cup celery, diced
- ½ cup carrots, diced
- 2 garlic cloves, diced
- 1 medium onion, diced
- 3 cups cabbage, shredded
- 6 cups beef stock
- 1 bay leaf
- 1 tablespoon salt
- ½ tablespoon thyme
- ¼ cup fresh dill, chopped
- ½ cup of coconut yogurt

Directions:
1. Add the washed beets to a steamer in the Ninja Foodi
2. Add 1 cup of water. Steam for 7 minutes
3. Perform a quick release and drop into an ice bath
4. Carefully peel off the skin and dice the beets
5. Transfer the diced beets, celery, carrots, onion, garlic, cabbage, stock, bay leaf, thyme and salt to your Instant Pot. Lock up the lid and set the pot to SOUP mode, cook for 45 minutes
6. Release the pressure naturally. Transfer to bowls and top with a dollop of dairy-free yogurt
7. Enjoy with a garnish of fresh dill!

Veggie Shepherd's Pie

Servings: 6
Cooking Time:22 Minutes
Ingredients:
- 1 tablespoon extra-virgin olive oil
- 1 onion, diced
- 16 ounces cremini mushrooms, sliced
- 6 carrots, diced
- 2 garlic cloves, minced
- 2 tablespoons tomato paste
- 2 cups vegetable broth
- 1 teaspoon dried thyme
- ¼ teaspoon dried rosemary
- 1 teaspoon sea salt
- 2 cups frozen peas
- 2 cups mashed potatoes

Directions:

1. Select Sear/Sauté and set to High. Select Start/Stop to begin. Allow the pot to preheat for 5 minutes.
2. Once preheated, add the oil, onion, mushrooms, and carrots. Sauté until the mushrooms have released their liquid and the onion is translucent, about 5 minutes. Add the garlic and tomato paste and sauté for 1 minute more.
3. Add the vegetable broth and season with the thyme, rosemary, and salt. Assemble the Pressure Lid, making sure the pressure release valve is in the Seal position.
4. Select Pressure and set to High. Set the time to 3 minutes, then select Start/Stop to begin. When pressure cooking is complete, quick release the pressure by moving the pressure release valve to the Vent position. Carefully remove the lid when the pressure has finished releasing.
5. Stir in the frozen peas, then spread the mixture in an even layer in the bottom of the pot. Spread the mashed potatoes evenly over the mixture. If desired, drag a fork over the potatoes to create a decorative topping.
6. Close the Crisping Lid. Select Broil and set the time to 5 minutes. Select Start/Stop to begin.
7. When cooking is complete, allow the shepherd's pie to rest for 10 minutes before serving.

Garganelli With Cheese And Mushrooms
Servings: 4
Cooking Time: 60 Min
Ingredients:
- 1 large egg
- 8 ounces garganelli /240g
- 8 ounces Swiss cheese, shredded /240g
- 1 recipe sautéed mushrooms
- 1 can full fat evaporated milk /360ml
- 1½ cups panko breadcrumbs /195g
- 1¼ cups water /312.5ml
- 2 tbsps chopped fresh cilantro /30g
- 3 tbsps sour cream /45ml
- 3 tbsps melted unsalted butter /45ml
- 3 tbsps grated Cheddar cheese /45g
- 1½ tsp s salt /7.5g
- 1½ tsp s arrowroot starch /7.5g

Directions:
1. Pour the garganelli into the inner pot, add half of the evaporated milk, the water, and salt. Seal the pressure lid, choose Pressure, set to High and the time to 4 minutes. Press Start.
2. In a bowl, whisk the remaining milk with the egg. In another bowl, combine the arrowroot starch with the Swiss cheese.
3. When the pasta has cooked, perform a natural pressure release for 3 minutes, then a quick pressure release and carefully open the lid. Pour in the milk-egg mixture and a large handful of the starch mixture. Stir to melt the cheese and then add the remaining cheese in 3 or 4 batches while stirring to melt. Mix in the mushrooms, cilantro, and sour cream.
4. In a bowl, mix the breadcrumbs, melted butter, and cheddar cheese. Then, sprinkle the mixture evenly over the pasta. Close the crisping lid. Choose Broil and adjust the time to 5 minutes. Press Start to begin crisping.
5. When done, the top should be brown and crispy, otherwise broil further for 3 minutes, and serve immediately.

Mushroom Goulash
Servings: 6
Cooking Time: 40 Minutes

Ingredients:
- 2 tbsp. olive oil, divided
- ½ onion, sliced thin
- 1 red bell pepper, chopped
- 2 lbs. mushrooms, chopped
- ½ tsp salt
- ¼ tsp pepper
- 14 oz. tomatoes, diced
- 2 cups vegetable broth, low sodium
- 1 tsp garlic powder
- 1 ½ tbsp. paprika
- 5 -6 sprigs fresh thyme

Directions:
1. Add half the oil to the cooking pot and set to sauté on med-high.
2. Add the onion and cook until they start to get soft, about 4 minutes. Add the red pepper and cook 3-5 minutes or until onions start to caramelize. Transfer to a plate.
3. Add the remaining oil to the pot and let it get hot. Add the mushrooms and cook until liquid is almost evaporated, stirring occasionally. Season with salt and pepper.
4. Add the peppers and onions back to the pot along with tomatoes, broth, garlic powder, paprika, and thyme, stir to mix well. Bring to a boil, cover, reduce heat to med-low and let simmer 20 minutes. Serve.

Nutrition:
- InfoCalories 115,Total Fat 5g,Total Carbs 14g,Protein 6g,Sodium 544mg.

Cheese Crusted Carrot Casserole
Servings: 6
Cooking Time: 40 Minutes
Ingredients:
- 1 ¼ lb. carrots, sliced
- Nonstick cooking spray
- ½ cup light mayonnaise
- ¼ cup onion, chopped fine
- 1 tsp horseradish
- ¼ cup cheddar cheese, reduced fat, grated
- 1 tbsp. whole wheat bread crumbs

Directions:
1. Add the carrots to the cooking pot with enough water to cover them. Set to sauté on high and bring to a boil. Reduce heat to med-low and simmer 7-9 minutes until carrots are tender-crisp. Drain.
2. Spray the cooking pot with cooking spray.
3. In a small bowl, combine mayonnaise, onion, and horseradish, mix well.
4. Return carrots to the cooking pot and spread mayonnaise mixture over the top. Sprinkle the cheese and bread crumbs over the top.
5. Add the tender-crisp lid and set to bake on 350°F. Bake 25-30 minutes until top is golden brown. Serve.

Nutrition:
- InfoCalories 121,Total Fat 7g,Total Carbs 12g,Protein 2g,Sodium 245mg.

Carrots Walnuts Salad
Servings: 4
Cooking Time: 15 Minutes
Ingredients:
- 4 carrots, roughly shredded
- ½ cup walnuts, sliced
- 3 tablespoons balsamic vinegar

- 1 cup chicken stock
- Black pepper and salt to the taste
- 1 tablespoon olive oil

Directions:
1. In your Ninja Foodi, mix the carrots with the vinegar and the other ingredients except for the walnuts.
2. Put the pressure cooking lid on and cook on High for 15 minutes.
3. Release the pressure quickly for 5 minutes, divide the mix between plates and serve with the walnuts sprinkled on top.

Nutrition:
- InfoCalories: 120; Fat: 4.5g; Carbohydrates: 5.3g; Protein: 1.3g

Winning Broccoli Casserole

Servings:4
Cooking Time: 6 Hours
Ingredients:
- 1 tablespoon extra-virgin olive oil
- 1 pound broccoli, cut into florets
- 1 pound cauliflower, cut into florets
- ¼ cup almond flour
- 2 cups of coconut milk
- ½ teaspoon ground nutmeg
- Pinch of fresh ground black pepper
- 1 and ½ cups cashew cream

Directions:
1. Grease the Ninja Foodi inner pot with olive oil. Place broccoli and cauliflower to your Ninja Foodi
2. Take a small bowl and stir in almond flour, coconut milk, pepper, 1 cup of cashew cream
3. Pour coconut milk mixture over vegetables and top casserole with remaining cashew cream
4. Cover and cook on SLOW COOK Mode for 6 hours. Server and enjoy!

Cabbage With Carrots

Servings: 4
Cooking Time: 20 Minutes
Ingredients:
- 1 Napa cabbage, shredded
- 2 carrots, sliced
- 2 tablespoons olive oil
- 1 red onion, chopped
- Black pepper and salt to the taste
- 2 tablespoons sweet paprika
- ½ cup tomato sauce

Directions:
1. Set the Foodi on Sauté mode, stir in the oil, heat it up, add the onion and sauté for 5 minutes.
2. Add the carrots, the cabbage and the other ingredients, toss.
3. Put the Ninja Foodi's lid on and cook on High for 15 minutes.
4. Release the pressure quickly for 5 minutes, divide everything between plates and serve.

Nutrition:
- InfoCalories: 140; Fat: 3.4g; Carbohydrates: 1.2g; Protein: 3.5 g

Vegetarian Stir Fry

Servings: 6
Cooking Time: 10 Minutes
Ingredients:

- 4 cloves garlic, chopped fine
- 2 tbsp. blue agave
- 1 tbsp. light soy sauce
- ¼ tsp ginger
- 1 tbsp. cornstarch
- 1 tsp sesame seeds
- 2 tsp olive oil
- 2 cups fresh broccoli florets
- ¼ lb. fresh snow peas, trimmed
- 1 red bell pepper, cut in ¼-inch strips
- 1 onion, cut in wedges

Directions:
1. In a small bowl, whisk together garlic, agave, soy sauce, ginger, and cornstarch until combined.
2. Set cooker to sauté on medium heat. Add sesame seeds and toast, stirring frequently, 2-3 minutes. Transfer to a plate.
3. Add the oil and increase the heat to med-high. Add broccoli, peas, bell pepper, and onion. Cook until tender-crisp, stirring occasionally, about 4-5 minutes.
4. Stir in the agave mixture and cook 2 minutes until sauce thicken. Serve immediately.

Nutrition:
- InfoCalories 58,Total Fat 2g,Total Carbs 8g,Protein 2g,Sodium 98mg.

Zucchinis Spinach Fry

Servings: 4
Cooking Time: 17 Minutes
Ingredients:
- 2 zucchinis, sliced
- 1-pound baby spinach
- ½ cup tomato sauce
- Black pepper and salt
- 1 tablespoon avocado oil
- 1 red onion, chopped
- 1 tablespoon sweet paprika
- ½ teaspoon garlic powder
- ½ teaspoon chilli powder

Directions:
1. Set the Foodi on Sauté, stir in the oil, heat it up, add the onion and sauté for 2 minutes.
2. Add the zucchinis, spinach, and the other ingredients Put the Ninja Foodi's lid on and cook on High for 15 minutes.
3. Release the pressure quickly for 5 minutes, divide everything between plates and serve.

Nutrition:
- InfoCalories: 130; Fat: 5.5g; Carbohydrates: 3.3g; Protein: 1g

Creamy Spinach Soup

Servings: 6
Cooking Time: 20 Minutes
Ingredients:
- Nonstick cooking spray
- 1 tsp garlic, chopped fine
- ½ cup green onions, sliced thin
- 3 ½ cups vegetable broth, low sodium
- 20 oz. fresh spinach, chopped
- 3 tbsp. cornstarch
- 3 cups skim milk
- ½ tsp nutmeg
- 1/8 tsp salt
- ½ tsp pepper

Directions:

1. Spray the cooking pot with cooking spray. Set to sauté on med-high heat.
2. Add the garlic and green onions and cook 3-4 minutes, stirring frequently, until soft. Stir in broth and spinach.
3. Add the lid and set to pressure cook on high. Set the timer for 8 minutes. When the timer goes off, use natural release to remove the pressure.
4. Set back to sauté on medium heat.
5. In a small bowl, whisk together cornstarch and milk until smooth. Stir into soup until combined. Add remaining ingredients and cook, stirring constantly, 6-8 minutes until soup has thickened. Serve immediately.

Nutrition:

- InfoCalories 95,Total Fat 1g,Total Carbs 16g,Protein 7g,Sodium 559mg.

Southwest Tofu Steaks

Servings: 4
Cooking Time: 30 Minutes
Ingredients:

- Nonstick cooking spray
- 1 pkg. firm tofu, drained & pressed
- 1 tbsp. chili powder
- 1 tsp cumin
- ½ tsp garlic powder
- 1 tsp paprika
- ½ tbsp. oregano
- ½ tbsp. ground coriander
- ½ tsp salt
- 3 tbsp. extra virgin olive oil
- 2 tbsp. water

Directions:

1. Line a baking sheet with foil. Spray fryer basket with cooking spray.
2. Slice tofu in half horizontally. Then slice each half horizontally again.
3. In a small bowl combine remaining ingredients and mix well. Spread mixture over both sides of tofu. Place on prepared pan and let sit 30-45 minutes.
4. Place tofu in fryer basket and add the tender-crisp lid. Set to air fry on 400°F. Cook tofu 30 minutes, turning over halfway through cooking time. Season with salt and pepper and serve immediately.

Nutrition:

- InfoCalories 219,Total Fat 18g,Total Carbs 6g,Protein 13g,Sodium 361mg.

Quinoa Pesto Bowls With Veggies

Servings: 2
Cooking Time: 30 Min
Ingredients:

- 1 cup quinoa, rinsed /130g
- 1 cup broccoli florets /130g
- ¼ cup pesto sauce /62.5ml
- 2 cups water /500ml
- ½ pound Brussels sprouts /225g
- 2 eggs
- 1 small beet, peeled and cubed
- 1 carrot, peeled and chopped
- 1 avocado, thinly sliced
- lemon wedges; for serving
- salt and ground black pepper to taste

Directions:

1. In the pot, mix water, salt, quinoa and pepper. Set the reversible rack to the pot over quinoa. To the reversible rack, add eggs, Brussels sprouts, broccoli, beet cubes, carrots, pepper and salt.
2. Seal the pressure lid, choose Pressure, set to High, and set the timer to 1 minute. Press Start. Release pressure naturally for 10 minutes, then release any remaining pressure quickly.
3. Remove reversible rack from the pot and set the eggs to a bowl of ice water. Peel and halve the eggs. Use a fork to fluff quinoa.
4. Separate quinoa, broccoli, avocado, carrots, beet, Brussels sprouts, eggs, and a dollop of pesto into two bowls. Serve alongside a lemon wedge.

Minty Radishes

Servings: 4
Cooking Time: 15 Minutes
Ingredients:

- 1-pound radishes, halved
- black pepper and salt
- 2 tablespoons balsamic vinegar
- 2 tablespoon mint, chopped
- 2 tablespoons olive oil

Directions:

1. In your Ninja Foodi's basket, combine the radishes with the vinegar and the other ingredients.
2. Cook on Air Crisp at 380 °F for 15 minutes.
3. Divide the radishes between plates and serve.

Nutrition:

- InfoCalories: 170; Fat: 4.5g; Carbohydrates: 7.4g; Protein: 4.6g

Spinach, Tomatoes, And Butternut Squash Stew

Servings: 6
Cooking Time: 65 Min
Ingredients:

- 2 lb. butternut squash, peeled and cubed /900g
- 1 can sundried tomatoes, undrained /450g
- 2 cans chickpeas, drained /450g
- 1 white onion; diced
- 4 garlic cloves, minced
- 4 cups baby spinach /520g
- 4 cups vegetable broth /1000ml
- 1 tbsp butter /15g
- ½ tsp smoked paprika /2.5g
- 1 tsp coriander powder /5g
- 1½ tsp s cumin powder /7.5g
- ½ tsp salt /2.5g
- ½ tsp freshly ground black pepper /2.5g

Directions:

1. Choose Sear/Sauté, set to Medium High, and the timer to 5 minutes; press Start/Stop to preheat the pot. Combine the butter, onion, and garlic in the pot. Cook, stirring occasionally; for 5 minutes or until soft and fragrant.
2. Add the butternut squash, vegetable broth, tomatoes, chickpeas, cumin, paprika, coriander, salt, and black pepper to the pot. Put the pressure lid together and lock in the Seal position.
3. Choose Pressure, set to High, and set the time to 8 minutes; press Start/Stop.
4. When the timer is done reading, perform a quick pressure release. Stir in the spinach to wilt, adjust the taste with salt and black pepper, and serve warm.

Pomegranate Radish Mix

Servings: 4
Cooking Time: 8 Minutes
Ingredients:
- 1-pound radishes, roughly cubed
- Black pepper and salt to the taste
- 2 garlic cloves, minced
- ½ cup chicken stock
- 2 tablespoons pomegranate juice
- ¼ cup pomegranate seeds

Directions:
1. In your Ninja Foodi, combine the radishes with the stock and the other ingredients.
2. Put the Ninja Foodi's lid on and cook on High for 8 minutes.
3. Release the pressure quickly for 5 minutes, divide everything between plates and serve.

Nutrition:
- InfoCalories: 133; Fat: 2.3g; Carbohydrates: 2.4g; Protein: 2g

Stir Fried Veggies

Servings: 6
Cooking Time: 5 Minutes
Ingredients:
- 1 tbsp. olive oil
- 2 bell peppers, cut in strips
- 1 cup sugar snap peas
- 1 cup carrots, sliced thin
- 1 cup mushrooms, sliced thin
- 2 cups broccoli, separate into small florets
- 1 cup baby corn
- ½ cup water chestnuts
- ¼ cup soy sauce
- 3 cloves garlic, chopped fine
- 3 tbsp. brown sugar
- 1 tsp sesame oil
- ½ cup vegetable broth
- 1 tbsp. cornstarch
- ¼ cup green onions, sliced

Directions:
1. Add oil to the cooking pot and set to saute on med-high heat.
2. Add bell pepper, peas, carrots, mushrooms, broccoli, corn, and water chestnuts. Cook, stirring frequently, 2-3 minutes until almost tender.
3. In a small bowl, whisk together soy sauce, garlic, brown sugar, sesame oil, broth, and cornstarch until combined.
4. Pour over vegetables and cook, stirring, until sauce has thickened. Spoon onto serving plates and garnish with green onions.

Nutrition:
- InfoCalories 150,Total Fat 5g,Total Carbs 26g,Protein 5g,Sodium 738mg.

Mushroom Risotto With Swiss Chard

Servings: 4
Cooking Time: 60 Min
Ingredients:
- 1 small bunch Swiss chard; chopped
- ½ cup sautéed mushrooms /65g
- ½ cup caramelized onions /65g
- ⅓ cup white wine /88ml
- 2 cups vegetable stock /500ml
- ⅓ cup grated Pecorino Romano cheese /44g
- 1 cup short grain rice /130g
- 3 tbsps ghee; divided /45g
- ½ tsp salt /2.5g

Directions:
1. Press Sear/Sauté and adjust to Medium. Press Start to preheat the inner pot. Melt 2 tbsps of ghee and sauté the Swiss chard for 5 minutes until wilted. Spoon into a bowl and set aside.
2. Use a paper towel to wipe out any remaining liquid in the pot and melt the remaining ghee. Stir in the rice and cook for about 1 minute.
3. Add the white wine and cook for 2 to 3 minutes, with occasional stirring until the wine has evaporated. Add in stock and salt; stir to combine.
4. Seal the pressure lid, choose Pressure; adjust the pressure to High and the cook time to 8 minutes; press Start. When the timer is done reading, perform a quick pressure release and carefully open the lid.
5. Stir in the mushrooms, swiss chard, and onions and let the risotto heat for 1 minute. Mix the cheese into the rice to melt, and adjust the taste with salt.Spoon the risotto into serving bowls and serve immediately.

Simple Molasses Glazed Carrots

Servings: 4
Cooking Time: 5 Minutes
Ingredients:
- 1 cup (250 mL) water
- 1 pound (454 g) baby carrots
- 2 tablespoons butter
- 1 tablespoon molasses
- ¼ teaspoon kosher salt
- ⅛ teaspoon white pepper
- ⅓ teaspoon cayenne pepper

Directions:
1. Pour the water in the cooking pot and place the reversible rack in pot. Put the carrots on the rack.
2. Assemble pressure lid, making sure the pressure release valve is in the Seal position. Select Steam and set time to 3 minutes. Press Start to begin.
3. Once cooking is complete, perform a quick pressure release. Carefully open the lid.
4. Discard the water and press the Sauté button. Add the butter to melt.
5. Stir in the cooked carrots, molasses, salt, white pepper, and cayenne pepper.
6. Sauté for about 2 minutes or until the carrots are well glazed and tender. Serve warm.

Aloo Gobi With Cilantro

Servings: 4
Cooking Time: 40 Min
Ingredients:
- 1 head cauliflower, cored and cut into florets
- 1 potato, peeled and diced
- 4 garlic cloves, minced
- 1 tomato, cored and chopped
- 1 jalapeño pepper, deseeded and minced
- 1 onion, minced
- 1 cup water /250ml
- 1 tbsp curry paste /15g
- 1 tbsp vegetable oil /15ml

- 1 tbsp ghee /15g
- 2 tsp cumin seeds /10g
- 1 tsp ground turmeric /5g
- ½ tsp chili pepper /2.5g
- salt to taste
- A handful of cilantro leaves; chopped

Directions:
1. Warm oil on Sear/Sauté. Add in potato and cauliflower and cook for 8 to 10 minutes until lightly browned; add salt for seasoning. Set the vegetables to a bowl.
2. Add ghee to the pot. Mix in cumin seeds and cook for 10 seconds until they start to pop; add onion and cook for 3 minutes until softened. Mix in garlic; cook for seconds.
3. Add in tomato, curry paste, chili pepper, jalapeño pepper, curry paste, and turmeric; cook for 3 to 5 minutes until the tomato starts to break down.
4. Return potato and cauliflower to the pot. Add water over the vegetables, add more salt if need be, and stir. Seal the pressure lid, choose Pressure, set to High, and set the timer to 4 minutes. Press Start. Release pressure naturally. Top with cilantro and serve.

Stuffed Portobello Mushrooms
Servings: 4
Cooking Time:28 Minutes
Ingredients:
- 4 large portobello mushrooms, stems and gills removed
- 2 tablespoons extra-virgin olive oil
- ½ cup cooked quinoa
- 1 tomato, seeded and diced
- 1 bell pepper, seeded and diced
- ¼ cup Kalamata olives, pitted and chopped
- ½ cup crumbled feta cheese
- Juice of 1 lemon
- ½ teaspoon sea salt
- ½ teaspoon freshly ground black pepper
- Minced fresh parsley, for garnish

Directions:
1. Place the Cook & Crisp Basket in the pot. Close the Crisping Lid. Preheat the unit by selecting Air Crisp, setting the temperature to 375°F, and setting the time to 5 minutes. Press Start/Stop to begin.
2. Coat the mushrooms with the oil. Open the Crisping Lid and arrange the mushrooms, open-side up, in a single layer in the preheated Cook & Crisp Basket.
3. Close the Crisping Lid. Select Air Crisp, set the temperature to 375°F, and set the time to 20 minutes. Select Start/Stop to begin.
4. In a medium mixing bowl, combine the quinoa, tomato, bell pepper, olives, feta cheese, lemon juice, salt, and black pepper.
5. Open the Crisping Lid and spoon the quinoa mixture evenly into the 4 mushrooms. Close the lid. Select Air Crisp, set the temperature to 350°F, and set the time to 8 minutes. Press Start/Stop to begin.
6. Garnish with fresh parsley and serve immediately.

Whole Roasted Broccoli And White Beans With Harissa, Tahini, And Lemon
Servings:4
Cooking Time: 30 Minutes
Ingredients:
- 2 cups water
- 2 small heads broccoli, cut in half

- 2 tablespoons unsalted butter
- ½ white onion, minced
- 2 garlic cloves, minced
- 1 can cannellini beans, rinsed and drained
- 1 can fire-roasted tomatoes and peppers
- 1 tablespoon spicy harissa
- Sea salt
- Freshly ground black pepper
- ¼ cup tahini
- ¼ cup walnuts, toasted and chopped
- Zest of 1 lemon
- Juice of 1 lemon

Directions:
1. Place Reversible Rack in pot, making sure it is in the lowest position. Pour the water into the pot and place the broccoli on the rack. Assemble the pressure lid, making sure the pressure release valve is in the SEAL position.
2. Select STEAM. Set time to 8 minutes. Select START/STOP to begin.
3. When steaming is complete, quick release the pressure by turning the pressure release valve to the VENT position. Carefully remove lid when unit has finished releasing pressure.
4. Remove rack and broccoli and set aside. Drain the remaining water from the pot and reinsert it in base.
5. Select SEAR/SAUTÉ and set to HI. Select START/STOP to begin. Let preheat for 5 minutes.
6. Add the butter to pot. Once melted, add the onions and garlic and cook for 3 minutes. Add the beans, tomatoes, harissa, and season with salt and pepper. Cook for 4 minutes.
7. Reinsert rack and broccoli. Close crisping lid.
8. Select AIR CRISP, set temperature to 390°F, and set time to 15 minutes. Select START/STOP to begin.
9. After 10 minutes, open lid and flip the broccoli. Close lid and continue cooking.
10. When cooking is complete, remove rack with broccoli from pot. Place the beans in serving dishes and top with the broccoli. Drizzle tahini over the broccoli and sprinkle with walnuts. Garnish with the lemon zest and juice and serve.

Nutrition:
- InfoCalories: 426,Total Fat: 25g,Sodium: 435mg,Carbohydrates: 39g,Protein: 15g.

Healthy Vegetable Broth
Servings: 3 Quarts
Cooking Time: 35 Minutes
Ingredients:
- 1 tbsp. vegetable oil
- 2 carrots, peeled and chopped
- 2 celery ribs, chopped
- 3 onions, chopped
- 4 scallions, chopped
- 15 garlic cloves, smashed and peeled
- 12 cups (2880 ml) water, divided
- ½ head cauliflower (1 pound, 455 g), cored and cut into 1-inch pieces
- 1 tomato, cored and chopped
- 3 bay leaves
- 8 sprigs fresh thyme
- 1 tsp. peppercorns
- ½ tsp. table salt

Directions:

1. In Ninja pressure cooker, Select Sauté function, heat oil until shimmering. Add scallions, onions, celery, carrots, and garlic and cook about 15 minutes until vegetables are softened and lightly browned. Add 1 cup water, scraping up any browned bits, then stir in remaining water, tomato, cauliflower, peppercorns, thyme sprigs, salt, and bay leaves.
2. Lock pressure lid and close pressure release valve. Select Pressure and cook for 1 hour. Turn off and let pressure release naturally for 15 minutes. Quick-release any remaining pressure and carefully remove lid, letting steam escape away from you.
3. Strain broth through colander into large container, without pressing on solids, throw away solids.

Sesame Radish

Servings: 4
Cooking Time: 15 Minutes
Ingredients:
*   2 leeks, sliced
*   ½ pound radishes, sliced
*   2 scallions, chopped
*   2 tablespoons black sesame seeds
*   1/3 cup chicken stock
*   1 tablespoon ginger, grated
*   1 tablespoon chives, minced

Directions:
1. In your Ninja Foodi, combine the leeks with the radishes and the other ingredients.
2. Put the Ninja Foodi's lid on and cook on High for 15 minutes more.
3. Release the pressure quickly for 5 minutes, divide everything between plates and serve.

Nutrition:
*   InfoCalories: 112; Fat: 2g; Carbohydrates: 4.2g; Protein: 2g

Bok Choy And Zoddle Soup

Servings: 6
Cooking Time: 35 Min
Ingredients:
*   1 lb. baby bok choy, stems removed /450g
*   2 zucchinis, spiralized
*   6 oz. Shitake mushrooms, stems removed and sliced to a 2-inch thickness /180g
*   2-inch ginger; chopped
*   2 cloves garlic, peeled
*   3 carrots, peeled and sliced diagonally
*   2 sweet onion; chopped
*   6 cups water /1500ml
*   2 tbsp sesame oil /30ml
*   2 tbsp soy sauce /30ml
*   2 tbsp chili paste /30g
*   Salt to taste
*   Sesame seeds to garnish
*   Chopped green onion to garnish

Directions:
1. In a food processor, add the chili paste, ginger, onion, and garlic; and process them until they are pureed. Turn on the Ninja foodi and select Sear/Sauté mode to High.
2. Pour in the sesame oil, once it has heated add the onion puree and cook for 3 minutes while stirring constantly to prevent burning. Add the water, mushrooms, soy sauce, and carrots.

3. Close the lid, secure the pressure valve, and select Pressure mode on High pressure for 5 minutes. Press Start/Stop.
4. Once the timer has ended, do a quick pressure release and open the lid. Add the zucchini noodles and bok choy, and stir to ensure that they are well submerged in the liquid.
5. Adjust the taste with salt, cover the pot with the crisping lid, and let the vegetables cook for 10 minutes on Broil mode.
6. Use a soup spoon to dish the soup with veggies into soup bowls. Sprinkle with green onions and sesame seeds. Serve as a complete meal.

Vegan Stuffed Peppers

Servings: 4
Cooking Time: 35 Minutes
Ingredients:
*   Nonstick cooking spray
*   2 bell peppers, halved lengthwise & cleaned
*   2 tbsp. olive oil
*   ½ cup onion, chopped
*   4 cloves garlic, chopped fine
*   2 tomatoes, chopped fine
*   ¼ tsp salt
*   ¼ cup fresh parsley, chopped
*   1/3 cup dry bread crumbs
*   2 tbsp. dry white wine
*   ¼ tsp pepper
*   2 tbsp. parmesan cheese

Directions:
1. Spray an 8x8-inch baking dish with cooking spray.
2. Fill the cooking pot halfway full with water. Set to sauté on high heat and bring to a boil.
3. Add the pepper halves and boil 4-5 minutes or until they start to soften. Drain and place peppers in cold water. Drain again.
4. Add oil to the cooking pot and set to medium heat. Add onion and garlic and cook just until onion has softened. Turn off heat and stir in remaining ingredients, except pepper and parmesan cheese, mix well.
5. Spoon the onion mixture into the peppers and place them in prepared dish. Sprinkle with parmesan cheese.
6. Place the rack in the cooking pot and add the peppers. Add the tender-crisp lid and set to bake on 350°F. Bake 35-40 minutes until filling is hot and peppers are tender. Serve immediately.

Nutrition:
*   InfoCalories 152,Total Fat 8g,Total Carbs 17g,Protein 4g,Sodium 285mg.

Crispy Cheese Lings

Servings: 4
Cooking Time: 15 Min
Ingredients:
*   4 cups grated cheddar cheese /520g
*   1 cup all-purpose flour /130g
*   1 tbsp baking powder /15g
*   1 tbsp butter /15g
*   1-2 tbsp water /30ml
*   ¼ tsp chili powder /1.25g
*   ¼ tsp salt, to taste /1.25g

Directions:
1. Mix the flour and the baking powder. Add the chili powder, salt, butter, cheese and 1-2 tbsp of water to the mixture.

2. Make a stiff dough. Knead the dough for a while. Sprinkle a tbsp or so of flour on the table. Take a rolling pin and roll the dough into ½ -inch thickness.

3. Cut the dough in any shape you want. Close the crisping lid and fry the cheese lings for 6 minutes at 370° °F or 188°C on Air Crisp mode.

Cheesy Corn Pudding

Servings: 6
Cooking Time: 3 Hours
Ingredients:
- 10 oz. corn, thawed & divided
- 1 cup milk
- 2 tbsp. flour
- ½ tsp cumin
- 1 tsp salt
- ¼ tsp pepper
- 3 eggs, lightly beaten
- 2 cups Monterey Jack cheese, grated
- 1 jalapeno pepper, seeded & chopped fine

Directions:
1. Add ¾ cup corn, milk, flour, cumin, salt, and pepper to a food processor or blender. Pulse until smooth.
2. Spray the cooking pot with cooking spray.
3. Pour the corn mixture into the pot then stir in remaining ingredients until combined.
4. Add the lid and set to slow cook on low. Cook 3 hours or until pudding is set. Serve hot.

Nutrition:
- InfoCalories 298,Total Fat 18g,Total Carbs 17g,Protein 17g,Sodium 707mg.

Steamed Artichokes With Lemon Aioli

Servings: 4
Cooking Time: 20 Min
Ingredients:
- 4 artichokes, trimmed
- 1 small handful parsley; chopped
- 1 lemon, halved
- 3 cloves garlic, crushed
- ½ cup mayonnaise /125ml
- 1 cup water /250ml
- 1 tsp lemon zest /5g
- 1 tbsp lemon juice /15ml
- Salt to taste

Directions:
1. On the artichokes cut ends, rub with lemon. Add water into the pot of pressure cooker. Set the reversible rack over the water,
2. Place the artichokes into the steamer basket with the points upwards; sprinkle each with salt. Seal lid and cook on High pressure for 10 minutes. Press Start. When ready, release the pressure quickly.
3. In a mixing bowl, combine mayonnaise, garlic, lemon juice, and lemon zest. Season to taste with salt. Serve with warm steamed artichokes sprinkled with parsley.

Roasted Vegetable Salad

Servings: 1
Cooking Time: 25 Min
Ingredients:
- 1 potato, peeled and chopped
- 1 cup cherry tomatoes/130g
- 1 carrot; sliced diagonally
- ½ small beetroot; sliced
- ¼ onion; sliced
- Juice of 1 lemon
- A handful of rocket salad
- A handful of baby spinach
- 2 tbsp olive oil /30ml
- 3 tbsp canned chickpeas /45g
- ½ tsp cumin /2.5g
- ½ tsp turmeric /2.5g
- ¼ tsp sea salt /1.25g
- Parmesan shavings

Directions:
1. Combine the onion, potato, cherry tomatoes, carrot, beetroot, cumin, seas salt, turmeric, and 1 tbsp olive oil, in a bowl. Place in the Ninja Foodi, close the crisping lid and cook for 20 minutes on Air Crisp mode at 370 °F or 188°C; let cool for 2 minutes.
2. Place the rocket, salad, spinach, lemon juice, and 1 tbsp olive oil, into a serving bowl. Mix to combine; stir in the roasted veggies.Top with chickpeas and Parmesan shavings.

Steamed Asparagus And Pine Nuts

Servings: 4
Cooking Time: 15 Min
Ingredients:
- 1 ½ lb. asparagus, ends trimmed /675g
- ½ cup chopped Pine Nuts /65g
- 1 cup water /250ml
- 1 tbsp butter /15g
- 1 tbsp olive oil to garnish/15ml
- Salt and pepper, to taste

Directions:
1. Open the Ninja Foodi, pour the water in, and fit the reversible rack at the bottom. Place the asparagus on the rack, close the crisping lid, select Air Crisp mode, and set the time to 8 minutes on 380 °F or 194°C. Press Start/Stop.
2. At the 4-minute mark, carefully turn the asparagus over. When ready, remove to a plate, sprinkle with salt and pepper, and set aside.
3. Select Sear/Sauté on your Ninja Foodi, set to Medium and melt the butter. Add the pine nuts and cook for 2-3 minutes until golden. Scatter over the asparagus the pine nuts, and drizzle olive oil.

Chorizo Mac And Cheese

Servings: 6
Cooking Time: 30 Min
Ingredients:
- 1 pound macaroni /450g
- 3 ounces chorizo; chopped /90g
- 2 cups milk /500ml
- 2 cups Cheddar cheese, shredded /260g
- 3 cups water /750ml
- 2 tbsp minced garlic /30g
- 1 tbsp garlic powder /15g
- salt to taste

Directions:
1. Put chorizo in the pot of your Foodi, select Sear/Sauté and stir-fry until crisp, about 5 minutes. Press Start. Set aside. Wipe the pot with kitchen paper. Add in water, macaroni, and salt to taste. Seal lid and cook on for 5 minutes High Pressure. Press Start.
2. When ready, release the pressure quickly. Stir in cheese and milk until the cheese melts. Divide the mac and cheese between serving bowls. Top with chorizo and serve.

Very Rich And Creamy Asparagus Soup

Servings:4
Cooking Time: 5-10 Minutes
Ingredients:
- 1 tablespoon olive oil
- 3 green onions, sliced crosswise into ¼ inch pieces
- 1 pound asparagus, tough ends removed, cut into 1 inch pieces
- 4 cups vegetable stock
- 1 tablespoon unsalted butter
- 1 tablespoon almond flour
- 2 teaspoon salt
- 1 teaspoon white pepper
- ½ cup heavy cream

Directions:
1. Set your Ninja Foodi to "Saute" mode and add oil, let it heat up
2. Add green onions and Saute for a few minutes, add asparagus and stock
3. Lock lid and cook on HIGH pressure for 5 minutes
4. Take a small saucepan and place it over low heat, add butter, flour and stir until the mixture foams and turns into a golden beige, this is your blond roux
5. Remove from heat. Release pressure naturally over 10 minutes
6. Open the lid and add roux, salt, and pepper to the soup
7. Use an immersion blender to puree the soup
8. Taste and season accordingly, swirl in cream and enjoy!

Supreme Cauliflower Soup

Servings:4
Cooking Time: 5 Minutes
Ingredients:
- ½ a small onion, chopped
- 2 tablespoons butter
- 1 large head of cauliflower, leaves and stems removed, coarsely chopped
- 2 cups chicken stock
- 1 teaspoon garlic powder
- 1 teaspoon salt
- 4 ounces cream cheese, cut into cubes
- 1 cup sharp cheddar cheese, cut
- ½ cup cream
- Extra cheddar, sour cream bacon strips, green onion for topping

Directions:
1. Peel the onion and chop up into small pieces
2. Cut the leaves of the cauliflower and steam, making sure to keep the core intact
3. Coarsely chop the cauliflower into pieces
4. Set your Ninja Foodi to Saute mode and add onion, cook for 2-3 minutes
5. Add chopped cauliflower, stock, salt, and garlic powder
6. Lock up the lid and cook on HIGH pressure for 5 minutes. Perform a quick release
7. Prepare the toppings. Use an immersion blender to puree your soup in the Ninja Foodi
8. Serve your soup with a topping of sliced green onions, cheddar, crumbled bacon. Enjoy!

Worthy Caramelized Onion

Servings:6
Cooking Time: 30-35 Minutes
Ingredients:

- 2 tablespoons unsalted butter
- 3 large onions sliced
- 2 tablespoons water
- 1 teaspoon salt

Directions:
1. Set your Ninja Foodi to Sauté mode and add set temperature to medium heat, pre-heat the inner pot for 5 minutes. Add butter and let it melt, add onions, water, and stir
2. Lock lid and cook on HIGH pressure for 30 minutes. Quick release the pressure
3. Remove lid and set the pot to sauté mode, let it sear in Medium-HIGH mode for 15 minutes until all liquid is gone. Serve and enjoy!

A Mishmash Cauliflower Mash

Servings:3
Cooking Time: 5 Minutes
Ingredients:
- 1 tablespoon butter, soft
- ½ cup feta cheese
- Salt and pepper to taste
- 1 large head cauliflower, chopped into large pieces
- 1 garlic cloves, minced
- 2 teaspoons fresh chives, minced

Directions:
1. Add water to your Ninja Foodi and place steamer basket
2. Add cauliflower pieces and lock lid, cook on HIGH pressure for 5 minutes
3. Quick release pressure. Open the lid and use an immersion blender to mash the cauliflower
4. Blend until you have a nice consistency. Enjoy!

Sumptuous Broccoli And Zucchini Tarts

Servings: 4
Cooking Time: 10 Minutes
Ingredients:
- 1 cup (250 mL) water
- 2 cups (500 mL) broccoli florets
- 3 large zucchinis, grated
- 5 eggs, beaten
- 1 onion, diced
- 6 large carrots, grated
- ½ cup (125 mL) all-purpose flour
- ½ cup (125 mL) panko bread crumbs
- ½ teaspoon baking powder
- Salt and black pepper, to taste
- ½ cup (125 mL) grated Cheddar cheese

Directions:
1. Pour the water in the cooking pot. Place a reversible rack in the pot. Grease a springform pan with cooking spray and set aside.
2. In a bowl, mix the broccoli, zucchini, eggs, onion, carrots, flour, panko bread crumbs, baking powder, salt, pepper, and Cheddar cheese. Pour the mixture into the pan, cover with aluminum foil, and place on the reversible rack.
3. Assemble pressure lid, making sure the pressure release valve is in the Seal position. Select Pressure and set to high . Set time to 10 minutes. Press Start to begin.
4. Once cooking is complete, do a quick pressure release. Carefully open the lid and remove the pan. Let cool to firm up.
5. Release the pan, then slice the tart and serve.

Stuffed Manicotti

Servings: 4
Cooking Time: 50 Minutes
Ingredients:
- Nonstick cooking spray
- 8 manicotti shells, cooked & drained
- ½ onion, chopped
- 1 cloves garlic, chopped fine
- 1 cup mushrooms, chopped
- 16 oz. ricotta cheese, fat free
- ½ cup mozzarella cheese, grated
- 1 egg
- 1 cup spinach, chopped
- ¾ tsp Italian seasoning
- ¼ tsp pepper
- 1 cups light spaghetti sauce
- 1 tbsp. parmesan cheese, grated

Directions:
1. Spray the cooking pot and an 8x8-inch baking pan with cooking spray.
2. Set cooker to sauté on med-high heat. Add onion and garlic and cook until tender, about 3-4 minutes.
3. Add mushrooms and cook until browned. Turn off the heat.
4. In a large bowl, combine ricotta and mozzarella cheeses, egg, spinach, Italian seasoning, and pepper, mix well.
5. Add the mushroom mixture to the cheese mixture and stir to combine. Spoon into manicotti shells and lay in the prepared pan.
6. Pour the spaghetti sauce over the top and sprinkle with parmesan cheese. Cover with foil.
7. Place the rack in the cooking pot and add the manicotti. Add the tender-crisp lid and set to bake on 400°F. Bake 30-35 minutes or until heated through. Serve immediately.

Nutrition:
- InfoCalories 367,Total Fat 19g,Total Carbs 27g,Protein 24g,Sodium 308mg.

Creamy Polenta And Mushrooms

Servings: 4
Cooking Time:30 Minutes
Ingredients:
- 4 cups vegetable broth, divided
- 1 cup grits or coarse-ground cornmeal
- 2½ teaspoons sea salt, divided
- 1 cup shiitake mushrooms, sliced
- 1 teaspoon extra-virgin olive oil
- ½ teaspoon freshly ground black pepper
- ¼ cup grated Parmesan cheese
- 2 tablespoons chopped fresh sage, for garnish

Directions:
1. Pour ½ cup of vegetable broth into the pot. Place the grits, 2 teaspoons of salt, and the remaining 3½ cups of broth into the Multi-Purpose Pan or an 8-inch baking pan. Stir to combine.
2. Place the pan onto the Reversible Rack, making sure the rack is in the lower position. Place the rack with the pan in the pot. Assemble the Pressure Lid, making sure the pressure release valve is in the Seal position.
3. Select Pressure and set to High. Set the time to 4 minutes, then select Start/Stop to begin.
4. While the grits are cooking, in a medium mixing bowl, toss the sliced mushrooms with the olive oil, black pepper,

and remaining ½ teaspoon of salt. Coat thoroughly and set aside.
5. When pressure cooking the grits is complete, allow the pressure to naturally release for 10 minutes, then quick release any remaining pressure by moving the pressure release valve to the Vent position. Carefully remove the lid when the pressure has finished releasing.
6. Stir the Parmesan cheese into the grits until completely melted. Lay the mushrooms on top of the grits and close the Crisping Lid. Select Broil and set the time to 8 minutes. Select Start/Stop to begin.
7. When cooking is complete, garnish with the sage and serve.

Peanut Tofu & Noodles

Servings: 4
Cooking Time: 10 Minutes
Ingredients:
- Nonstick cooking spray
- 16 oz. firm tofu, cubed
- ½ lb. linguine
- 2 cups broccoli, chopped
- ¼ cup peanut butter
- ¼ cup soy sauce, low sodium
- 2 tbsp. rice vinegar
- 2 tbsp. peanuts, chopped

Directions:
1. Spray the fryer basket with cooking spray.
2. Place tofu in the basket and add the tender-crisp lid. Set to air fry on 400°F. Cook tofu 10 minutes, turning over halfway through cooking time.
3. Prepare pasta according to package directions. Add the broccoli during the last 5 minutes of cooking time. Drain.
4. In a small bowl, whisk together peanut butter, soy sauce, and vinegar until smooth.
5. Add the tofu and sauce to the pasta and toss until evenly distributed. Ladle onto serving plates and top with peanuts. Serve immediately.

Nutrition:
- InfoCalories 380,Total Fat 19g,Total Carbs 31g,Protein 30g,Sodium 705mg.

Italian Turkey Breast

Servings:4
Cooking Time: 2 Hours
Ingredients:
- 1 and ½ cups Italian dressing
- 2 garlic cloves, minced
- 1 (2 pounds turkey breast, with bone
- 2 tablespoons butter
- Salt and pepper to taste

Directions:
1. Mix in garlic cloves, salt, black pepper and rub turkey breast with mix
2. Grease Ninja Foodi pot and arrange turkey breast. Top with Italian dressing
3. Lock lid and BAKE/ROAST for 2 hours at 230 degrees F. Serve and enjoy!

Veggie Lasagna

Servings: 4
Cooking Time: 35 Minutes
Ingredients:
- Nonstick cooking spray
- 2 Portobello mushrooms, sliced ¼-inch thick
- 1 eggplant, cut lengthwise in 6 slices

- 1 yellow squash, cut lengthwise in 4 slices
- 1 red bell pepper, cut in ½-inch strips
- ½ tsp garlic powder
- ½ tsp salt
- ½ tsp black pepper
- ½ cup ricotta cheese, fat free, divided
- 2 tbsp. fresh basil, chopped, divided
- ¾ cup mozzarella cheese, grated fine, divided
- ¼ cup tomato sauce

Directions:
1. Spray the cooking pot and rack with cooking spray.
2. Place a single layer of vegetables in the cooking pot. Add the rack and place remaining vegetables on it. Season vegetables with garlic powder, salt, and pepper.
3. Add the tender-crisp lid and set to roast on 425°F. Cook vegetables 15-20 minutes until tender, stirring halfway through cooking time. Transfer to a large plate.
4. Spray an 8x8-inch baking pan with cooking spray.
5. Line the bottom of the pan with 3 slices of eggplant. Spread ¼ cup ricotta cheese, 1 tablespoon basil, and ¼ cup mozzarella over eggplant.
6. Layer with remaining vegetables, then remaining ricotta, basil and ¼ cup mozzarella on top. End with 3 slices of eggplant and pour tomato sauce over then sprinkle remaining cheese over the top.
7. Add the rack back to the cooking pot and place the lasagna on it. Add the tender-crisp lid and set to bake on 350°F. Bake 15-20 minutes until cheese is melted and lasagna is heated through, serve.

Nutrition:
- InfoCalories 145,Total Fat 3g,Total Carbs 18g,Protein 14g,Sodium 490mg.

Mushroom Potato Shepherd's Pie

Servings: 6
Cooking Time: 22 Minutes
Ingredients:
- 1 tbsp. extra-virgin olive oil
- 16 ounces (455 g) cremini mushrooms, sliced
- 6 carrots, diced
- 1 onion, diced
- 2 tbsps. tomato paste
- 2 garlic cloves, minced
- 2 cups vegetable broth
- ¼ tsp. dried rosemary
- 1 tsp. dried thyme
- 1 tsp. sea salt
- 2 cups frozen peas
- 2 cups mashed potatoes

Directions:
1. Preheat the pot by selecting Sear/Sauté. Select Start/Stop to begin. Preheat for 5 minutes.
2. Then add the oil, mushrooms, carrots and onion into the preheated pot. Sauté for 5 minutes, until the onion is translucent and the mushrooms have released their liquid. Stir in the tomato paste and garlic, sauté for another 1 minute.
3. Add the vegetable broth and season with the rosemary, thyme, and salt. Assemble the Pressure Lid, set the steamer valve to Seal.
4. Select Pressure, set the time to 3 minutes, then select Start/Stop to begin. After pressure cooking is finish, move the pressure release valve to Vent to quick release the pressure. Remove the lid when the pressure has finished releasing carefully.

5. Add the frozen peas and stir well, then in the bottom of the pot spread with the mixture in an even layer. Evenly spread the mashed potatoes over the mixture. Drag a fork over the potatoes to create a decorative topping, if desired.
6. Close the Crisping Lid. Select Broil and set the time to 5 minutes. Select Start/Stop to begin.
7. After cooking is finish, let the shepherd's pie rest for 10 minutes before serving.

Italian Sausage With Garlic Mash

Servings: 6
Cooking Time: 30 Min
Ingredients:
- 6 Italian sausages
- 4 large potatoes, peeled and cut into 1½-inch chunks
- 2 garlic cloves, smashed
- ⅓ cup butter, melted /44ml
- ¼ cup milk; at room temperature, or more as needed /62.5ml
- 1 ½ cups water /375ml
- 1 tbsp olive oil /15ml
- 1 tbsp chopped chives/15g
- salt and ground black pepper to taste

Directions:
1. Select Sear/Sauté, set to Medium High, and choose Start/Stop to preheat the pot and heat olive oil. Cook for 8-10 minutes, turning periodically until browned. Set aside. Wipe the pot with paper towels. Add in water and set the reversible rack over water. Place potatoes onto the reversible rack.
2. Seal the pressure lid, choose Pressure, set to High, and set the timer to 12 minutes. Press Start.
3. When ready, release the pressure quickly. Remove reversible rack from the pot. Drain water from the pot. Return potatoes to pot. Add in salt, butter, pepper, garlic, and milk and use a hand masher to mash until no large lumps remain.
4. Using an immersion blender, blend potatoes on Low for 1 minute until fluffy and light. Avoid over-blending to ensure the potatoes do not become gluey!
5. Transfer the mash to a serving plate, top with sausages and scatter chopped chives over to serve.

Tahini Sweet Potato Mash

Servings: 4
Cooking Time: 25 Min
Ingredients:
- 2 pounds sweet potatoes, peeled and cubed /900g
- 1 cup water /250ml
- 2 tbsp tahini /30g
- 1 tbsp sugar /15g
- ¼ tsp ground nutmeg /1.25g
- sea salt to taste
- Chopped fresh chives; for garnish

Directions:
1. In the Foodi, add 1 cup or 250ml cold water and set a steamer basket into the pot. Add sweet potato cubes into the steamer basket. Seal the pressure lid, choose Pressure, set to High, and set the timer to 8 minutes. Press Start. When ready, release the pressure quickly.
2. In a large mixing bowl, add cooked sweet potatoes and slightly mash. Using a hand mixer, whip in nutmeg, sugar, and tahini until the sweet potatoes attain the consistency you desire; add salt for seasoning. Top with chives and serve.

Fully Stuffed Whole Chicken

Servings:4
Cooking Time: 8 Hours
Ingredients:
- 1 cup mozzarella cheese
- 4 garlic clove, peeled
- 1 whole chicken, 2 pounds, cleaned and dried
- Salt and pepper to taste
- 2 tablespoons lemon juice

Directions:
1. Stuff chicken cavity with garlic cloves, cheese. Season with salt and pepper
2. Transfer to Ninja Foodi and drizzle lemon juice. Lock lid and SLOW COOK on LOW for 8 hours
3. Transfer to a plate, serve and enjoy!

Veggie Loaded Pasta

Servings:8
Cooking Time: 2 Minutes
Ingredients:
- 1 box dry pasta, such as rigatoni or penne
- 4 cups water
- 2 tablespoons extra-virgin olive oil, divided
- 2 teaspoons kosher salt, divided
- 3 avocados
- Juice of 2 limes
- 2 tablespoons minced cilantro
- 1 red onion, chopped
- 1 cup cherry tomatoes, halved
- 4 heaping cups spinach, half an 11-ounce container
- ¼ cup shredded Parmesan cheese, divided
- Freshly ground black pepper, for serving

Directions:
1. Place the pasta, water, 1 tablespoon of olive oil, and 1 teaspoon of salt in the pot. Stir to incorporate. Assemble pressure lid, making sure the pressure release valve is in the SEAL position.
2. Select PRESSURE and set to LO. Set time to 2 minutes. Select START/STOP to begin.
3. While pasta is cooking, place the avocados in a medium-sized mixing bowl and mash well with a wooden spatula until a thick paste forms. Add all remaining ingredients to the bowl and mix well to combine.
4. When pressure cooking is complete, allow pressure to naturally release for 10 minutes. After 10 minutes, quick release remaining pressure by moving the pressure release valve to the VENT position. Carefully remove lid when unit has finished releasing pressure.
5. If necessary, strain pasta to remove any residual water and return pasta to pot. Add avocado mixture to pot and stir.
6. Garnish pasta with Parmesan cheese and black pepper, as desired, then serve.

Nutrition:
- InfoCalories: 372,Total Fat: 16g,Sodium: 149mg,Carbohydrates: 49g,Protein: 11g.

Turkey Stuffed Potatoes

Servings: 4
Cooking Time: 30 Min
Ingredients:
- 1 pound turkey breasts /450g
- 4 potatoes
- 1 Fresno chili pepper; chopped
- 2 cups vegetable broth /500ml
- 2 tbsp fresh cilantro; chopped /30g
- 1 tsp ground cumin /5g
- ½ tsp onion powder /2.5g
- 1 tsp chili powder /5g
- ½ tsp garlic powder/2.5g

Directions:
1. In the pot, combine chicken broth, cumin, garlic powder, onion powder, and chili powder; toss in turkey to coat.
2. Place a reversible rack over the turkey. Use a fork to pierce the potatoes and set them into the reversible rack.
3. Seal the pressure lid, choose Pressure, set to High, and set the timer to 20 minutes. Press Start. When ready, release the pressure quickly. Remove reversible rack from the cooker. Place the potatoes on a plate.
4. Place turkey in a mixing bowl and use two forks to shred. Half each potato lengthwise. Stuff with shredded turkey; top with cilantro, onion, and fresno pepper and serve.

Green Lasagna Soup

Servings: 4
Cooking Time: 30 Min
Ingredients:
- ½ pound broccoli; chopped /225g
- 3 lasagna noodles
- 1 carrot; chopped
- 2 garlic cloves minced
- 1 cup tomato paste /250ml
- 1 cup tomatoes; chopped /130g
- ¼ cup dried green lentils /32.5g
- 2 cups vegetable broth /500ml
- 1 cup leeks; chopped /130g
- 1 tsp olive oil /5ml
- 2 tsp Italian seasoning /10g
- salt to taste

Directions:
1. Warm oil on Sear/Sauté. Add garlic and leeks and cook for 2 minutes until soft; add tomato paste, carrot, Italian seasoning, broccoli, tomatoes, lentils, and salt. Stir in vegetable broth and lasagna pieces.
2. Seal the pressure lid, choose Pressure, set to High, and set the timer to 3 minutes. Press Start.
3. Release pressure naturally for 10 minutes, then release the remaining pressure quickly. Divide soup into serving bowls and serve.

Saucy Kale

Servings: 4
Cooking Time: 15 Minutes
Ingredients:
- 1-pound kale, torn
- 2 leeks, sliced
- 2 tablespoons balsamic vinegar
- 1 tablespoon parsley, chopped
- Black pepper and salt to the taste
- 2 shallots, chopped
- ½ cup tomato sauce

Directions:
1. In your Ninja Foodi, combine the kale with the leeks and the other ingredients.
2. Put the Ninja Foodi's lid on and cook on High for 15 minutes.

3. Release the pressure quickly for 5 minutes, divide the mix between plates and serve.
Nutrition:
- InfoCalories: 100; Fat: 2g; Carbohydrates: 3.4g; Protein: 4g

Quick Indian-style Curry
Servings:8
Cooking Time: 35 Minutes
Ingredients:
- 1 tablespoon vegetable oil
- 1 small onion, diced
- 1 small bell pepper, diced
- 1 large potato, cut into 1-inch cubes
- 1 teaspoon ground turmeric
- 1 teaspoon cumin seeds
- 1 teaspoon ground cumin
- 1 teaspoon garam masala (optional)
- 1 teaspoon curry powder
- 1 jar curry sauce, plus 1 jar water
- 1 can diced tomatoes
- 1 cup dried red lentils
- 8 ounces paneer, cubed (optional)
- 1 cup fresh cilantro, roughly chopped (optional)
- Salt
- Freshly ground black pepper

Directions:
1. Select SEAR/SAUTÉ and set temperature to HI. Select START/STOP to begin and allow to preheat for 5 minutes.
2. Add the oil to the pot and allow to heat for 1 minute. Add the onion and bell pepper and sauté for 3 to 4 minutes.
3. Add the potato, turmeric, cumin seeds, cumin, garam masala, and curry powder. Stir and cook for 5 minutes.
4. Stir in the curry sauce, water, tomatoes, and lentils.
5. Assemble the pressure lid, making sure the pressure release valve is in the SEAL position.
6. Select PRESSURE and set to HI. Set the time to 15 minutes. Select START/STOP to begin.
7. When pressure cooking is complete, allow the pressure to naturally release for 10 minutes. After 10 minutes, quick release any remaining pressure by moving the pressure release valve to the VENT position. Carefully remove the lid when the unit has finished releasing pressure.
8. Stir in the paneer (if using) and cilantro. Taste and season with salt and pepper, as needed.

Nutrition:
- InfoCalories: 217,Total Fat: 6g,Sodium: 27mg,Carbohydrates: 33g,Protein: 8g.

Healthy Rosemary And Celery Dish
Servings: 4

Cooking Time: 5 Minutes
Ingredients:
- 1 pound celery, cubed
- 1 cup of water
- 2 garlic cloves, minced
- Salt and pepper
- ¼ teaspoon dry rosemary
- 1 tablespoon olive oil

Directions:
1. Add water to your Ninja Foodi and place steamer basket
2. Add celery cubs to basket and lock lid, cook on HIGH pressure for 4 minutes
3. Quick release pressure. Take a bowl and add mix in oil, garlic, and rosemary. Whisk well
4. Add steamed celery to the bowl and toss well, spread on a lined baking sheet
5. Broil for 3 minutes using the Air Crisping lid at 250 degrees F. Serve and enjoy!

Beet Thoran Keralite Sadhya
Servings: 4
Cooking Time: 20 Minutes
Ingredients:
- 1 cup (250 mL) water
- ½ pound (227 g) small beets
- 2 tablespoons olive oil
- ½ chili pepper, chopped
- 1 garlic clove, minced
- ½ cup (125 mL) shallots, chopped
- 5 curry leaves
- ⅓ teaspoon turmeric powder
- Sea salt and ground black pepper, to taste

Directions:
1. Pour the water in the cooking pot and place the reversible rack in pot. Put the beets on the rack.
2. Assemble pressure lid, making sure the pressure release valve is in the Seal position. Select Steam and set to high . Set time to 15 minutes. Press Start to begin.
3. Once cooking is complete, perform a quick pressure release. Carefully open the lid. Allow the beets to cool for a few minutes.
4. Once the beets are cool enough to touch, transfer them to a cutting board, then peel and chop them into small pieces.
5. Press the Sauté button and heat the olive oil until shimmering.
6. Add and sauté the chili pepper, garlic, shallots, and curry leaves for about 4 minutes or until softened.
7. Sprinkle with the turmeric, salt, and black pepper. Fold in the cooked beets. Serve warm.

Chapter 7: Fish & Seafood

Italian Flounder

Servings: 4
Cooking Time: 70 Min
Ingredients:
- 4 flounder fillets
- 3 slices prosciutto; chopped
- 2 bags baby kale /180g
- ½ small red onion; chopped
- ½ cup whipping cream /125ml
- 1 cup panko breadcrumbs /130g
- 2 tbsps chopped fresh parsley /30g
- 3 tbsps unsalted butter, melted and divided /45g
- ¼ tsp fresh ground black pepper /1.25g
- ½ tsp salt; divided /2.5g

Directions:
1. On the Foodi, choose Sear/Sauté and adjust to Medium. Press Start to preheat the inner pot. Add the prosciutto and cook until crispy, about 6 minutes. Stir in the red onions and cook for about 2 minutes or until the onions start to soften. Sprinkle with half of the salt.
2. Fetch the kale into the pot and cook, stirring frequently until wilted and most of the liquid has evaporated, about 4-5 minutes. Mix in the whipping cream.
3. Lay the flounder fillets over the kale in a single layer. Brush 1 tbsp or 15ml of the melted butter over the fillets and sprinkle with the remaining salt and black pepper.
4. Close the crisping lid and choose Bake/Roast. Adjust the temperature to 300°F or 149°C and the cook time to 3 minutes. Press Start.
5. Combine the remaining butter, the parsley and breadcrumbs in a bowl.
6. When done cooking, open the crisping lid. Spoon the breadcrumbs mixture on the fillets.
7. Close the crisping lid and Choose Bake/Roast. Adjust the temperature to 400°F or 205°C and the cook time to 6 minutes. Press Start.
8. After about 4 minutes, open the lid and check the fish. The breadcrumbs should be golden brown and crisp. If not, close the lid and continue to cook for an additional two minutes.

Shrimp Egg Rolls

Servings: 10
Cooking Time: 10 Minutes
Ingredients:
- Nonstick cooking spray
- ¼ cup soy sauce, low sodium
- 2 tbsp. brown sugar
- 1 tsp ginger, grated
- 1 tsp garlic powder
- 5 cups coleslaw mix
- 2 green onions, sliced thin
- 3 tbsp. cilantro, chopped
- 1 cup small shrimp, chopped
- 10 egg roll wrappers

Directions:
1. Spray the fryer basket with cooking spray.
2. In a small bowl, whisk together, soy sauce, brown sugar, ginger, and garlic powder until combined.
3. In a large bowl, combine coleslaw, green onions, cilantro, and shrimp and mix well.
4. Pour the soy sauce over the coleslaw and toss well to coat. Let sit 15 minutes. After 15 minutes, place in a colander and squeeze to remove as much liquid as possible.
5. Place egg roll wrappers on a work surface. Spoon about 1/3 cup of shrimp mixture in the center of each wrapper. Fold opposite sides over filling, then one corner and roll up egg roll fashion. Place seam side down in fryer basket and spray lightly with cooking spray.
6. Add the tender-crisp lid and set to air fry on 425°F. Cook 8-10 minutes until golden brown and crisp, turning over halfway through cooking time.

Nutrition:
- InfoCalories 138, Total Fat 1g, Total Carbs 24g, Protein 7g, Sodium 532mg.

Garlicky Shrimp With Broccoli

Servings: 4
Cooking Time: 5 Minutes
Ingredients:
- 2 tablespoons unsalted butter
- 1 shallot, minced
- 3 garlic cloves, minced
- ¼ cup white wine
- ½ cup chicken stock
- Juice of ½ lemon
- ½ teaspoon sea salt
- ½ teaspoon freshly ground black pepper
- 1½ pounds (680 g) frozen shrimp, thawed
- 1 large head broccoli, cut into florets

Directions:
1. Add the butter. Select SEAR/SAUTÉ and set to MED. Select START/STOP to begin.
2. Once the butter is melted, add the shallots and cook for 3 minutes. Add the garlic and cook for 1 minute.
3. Deglaze the pot by adding the wine and using a wooden spoon to scrape the bits of garlic and shallot off the bottom of the pot. Stir in the chicken stock, lemon juice, salt, pepper, and shrimp.

4. Place the broccoli florets on top of the shrimp mixture. Assemble pressure lid, making sure the pressure release valve is in the SEAL position.
5. Select PRESSURE and set to HI. Set time to 0 minutes. Select START/STOP to begin.
6. When pressure cooking is complete, quick release the pressure by moving the pressure release valve to the VENT position. Carefully remove lid when the unit has finished releasing pressure. Serve immediately.

Seafood Pasta With Arrabbiata Sauce
Servings: 4
Cooking Time: 23 Minutes
Ingredients:
- 1 tbsp. extra-virgin olive oil
- 1 onion, diced
- 4 garlic cloves, minced
- 16 ounces (455 g) linguine
- 3 cups chicken broth, divided
- 1 (24-ounce, 672 g) jar Arrabbiata sauce
- ½ tsp. freshly ground black pepper
- ½ tsp. sea salt
- 8 ounces (227 g) scallops
- 8 ounces (227 g) shrimp, peeled and deveined
- 12 mussels, cleaned and debearded

Directions:
1. Preheat the pot by selecting Sear/Sauté. Select Start/Stop to begin. Preheat for 5 minutes.
2. In the preheated pot, add the oil and onion, cook for 5 minutes, stirring occasionally. Stir in the garlic and cook for 1 minute, until fragrant.
3. Break the linguine in half and add to the pot along with 2 cups of broth amd the Arrabbiata sauce. Season with the pepper and salt, stir to combine.
4. Assemble the Pressure Lid, set the pressure release valve to Seal. Select Pressure. Set the time to 2 minutes, then select Start/Stop to begin.
5. After pressure cooking is finish, move the pressure release valve to the Vent position to quick release the pressure. Remove the lid when the pressure has finished releasing carefully.
6. Select Sear/Sauté. Select Start/Stop to begin. Add the remaining 1 cup of broth, the scallops, shrimp, and mussels to the pot. Stir until all of the seafood is covered by the sauce evenly.
7. Assemble the Pressure Lid, set the pressure release valve to Vent. Cover and cook for 5 minutes, until the shrimp and scallops are opaque and cooked through and the mussels have opened. Discard any unopened mussels. Serve immediately.

Salmon, Cashew & Kale Bowl
Servings: 6
Cooking Time: 15 Minutes
Ingredients:
- 12 oz. salmon filets, skin off
- 2 tbsp. olive oil, divided
- ½ tsp salt
- ¼ tsp pepper
- 2 cloves garlic, chopped fine
- 4 cups kale, stems removed & chopped
- ½ cup carrot, grated
- 2 cups quinoa, cooked according to package directions
- ¼ cup cashews, chopped

Directions:
1. Place the rack in the cooking pot and set to bake on 400°F. Place a sheet of parchment paper on the rack.
2. Brush the salmon with 1 tablespoon of oil and season with salt and pepper. Place the fish on the parchment paper.
3. Add the tender-crisp lid and cook 15 minutes or until salmon reaches desired doneness. Transfer the fish to a plate and keep warm.
4. Set the cooker to sauté on medium heat and add the remaining oil. Once the oil is hot, add garlic, kale, and carrot and cook, stirring frequently, until kale is wilted and soft, about 2-3 minutes.
5. Add the quinoa and cashews and cook just until heated through. Spoon mixture evenly into bowl and top with a piece of salmon. Serve immediately.
Nutrition:
- InfoCalories 294,Total Fat 17g,Total Carbs 18g,Protein 17g,Sodium 243mg.

Kung Pao Shrimp
Servings: 4
Cooking Time: 15 Minutes
Ingredients:
- 1 tbsp. olive oil
- 1 red bell pepper, seeded & chopped
- 1 green bell pepper, seeded & chopped
- 3 cloves garlic, chopped fine
- 1 lb. large shrimp, peeled & deveined
- ¼ cup soy sauce
- 1 tsp sesame oil
- 1 tsp brown sugar
- 1 tsp Sriracha
- 1/8 tsp red pepper flakes
- 1 tsp cornstarch
- 1 tbsp. water
- ¼ cup peanuts
- ¼ cup green onions, sliced thin

Directions:
1. Add oil to the cooking pot and set to sauté on med-high heat.
2. Add the bell peppers and garlic and cook, 3-5 minutes, until pepper is almost tender.
3. Add the shrimp and cook until they turn pink, 2-3 minutes.
4. In a small bowl, whisk together soy sauce, sesame oil, brown sugar, Sriracha, and pepper flakes until combined.
5. In a separate small bowl, whisk together cornstarch and water until smooth. Whisk into sauce and pour over shrimp mixture. Add the peanuts.
6. Cook, stirring, until the sauce has thickened, about 2-3 minutes. Serve garnished with green onions.
Nutrition:
- InfoCalories 212,Total Fat 11g,Total Carbs 10g,Protein 20g,Sodium 1729mg.

New England Lobster Rolls
Servings:4
Cooking Time: 20 Minutes
Ingredients:
- 4 lobster tails
- ¼ cup mayonnaise
- 1 celery stalk, minced
- Zest of 1 lemon
- Juice of 1 lemon

- ¼ teaspoon celery seed
- Kosher salt
- Freshly ground black pepper
- 4 split-top hot dog buns
- 4 tablespoons unsalted butter, at room temperature
- 4 leaves butter lettuce

Directions:
1. Insert Cook & Crisp Basket into the pot and close the crisping lid. Select AIR CRISP, set temperature to 375°F, and set time to 15 minutes. Select START/STOP to begin. Let preheat for 5 minutes.
2. Once unit has preheated, open lid and add the lobster tails to the basket. Close the lid and cook for 10 minutes.
3. In a medium bowl, mix together the mayonnaise, celery, lemon zest and juice, and celery seed, and add salt and pepper.
4. Fill a large bowl with a tray of ice cubes and enough water to cover the ice.
5. When cooking is complete, open lid. Transfer the lobster into the ice bath for 5 minutes. Close lid to keep unit warm.
6. Spread butter on the hot dog buns. Open lid and place the buns in the basket. Close crisping lid.
7. Select AIR CRISP, set temperature to 375°F, and set time to 4 minutes. Select START/STOP to begin.
8. Remove the lobster meat from the shells and roughly chop. Place in the bowl with the mayonnaise mixture and stir.
9. When cooking is complete, open lid and remove the buns. Place lettuce in each bun, then fill with the lobster salad.

Nutrition:
- InfoCalories: 408,Total Fat: 24g,Sodium: 798mg,Carbohydrates: 22g,Protein: 26g.

Salmon Chowder

Servings: 8
Cooking Time: 30 Minutes
Ingredients:
- 3 tbsp. butter
- ½ cup celery, chopped
- ½ cup onion, chopped
- ½ cup green bell pepper, chopped
- 1 clove garlic, chopped fine
- 14 ½ oz. chicken broth, low sodium
- 1 cup potatoes, peeled & cubed
- 1 cup carrots, chopped
- 1 tsp salt
- ½ tsp pepper
- 1 tsp fresh dill, chopped
- 1 can cream-style corn
- 2 cups half and half
- 2 cups salmon, cut in 1-inch pieces

Directions:
1. Add the butter to the cooking pot and set to sauté on med-high heat.
2. Add the celery, onion, green pepper, and garlic and cook, stirring frequently, until vegetables start to soften.
3. Add the broth, potatoes, carrots, salt, pepper and dill and stir to mix.
4. Add the lid and set to pressure cook on high. Set the timer for 10 minutes. When the timer goes off, release the pressure with quick release.

5. Set back to sauté on medium and add the corn, cream, and salmon. Bring to a simmer and cook 15 minutes, or until salmon is cooked through. Serve.

Nutrition:
- InfoCalories 244,Total Fat 10g,Total Carbs 21g,Protein 18g,Sodium 905mg.

Fish And Shrimp Stew With Tomatoes

Servings: 6
Cooking Time: 46 Minutes
Ingredients:
- 2 (14.5-ounce (411 g)) cans fire-roasted tomatoes
- 1 pound (455 g) medium (21-30 count) shrimp, peeled and deveined
- 1 pound (455 g) raw white fish (cod or haddock), cubed
- 1 cup dry white wine
- 2 cups chicken stock
- 1 yellow onion, diced
- 1 fennel bulb, tops removed and bulb diced
- 3 garlic cloves, minced
- 2 tbsps. extra-virgin olive oil
- Freshly ground black pepper
- Salt
- Fresh basil, torn

Directions:
1. Select the Saute mode, to preheat for 3 minutes.
2. Put the olive oil, onions, fennel, and garlic in the pot. Cook until translucent.
3. Add the white wine and deglaze, and scrape any stuck bits from the bottom of the pot with a silicone spatula. Put roasted tomatoes and chicken stock in the pot. Cook for 25 to 30 minutes and then add the shrimp and white fish.
4. Select SEAR/SAUTÉ. Select START/STOP to begin.
5. Cook 10 minutes and stir frequently. Season with salt and pepper.
6. Ladle into a bowl. Top with torn basil.

Spiced Up Cajun Style Tilapia

Servings:4
Cooking Time: 5 Minutes
Ingredients:
- 4 tilapia fillets, 6 ounces each
- 1 cup ghee
- 2 teaspoons cayenne pepper
- 2 tablespoons smoked paprika
- 2 teaspoons garlic powder
- 2 teaspoons onion powder
- Pinch of salt
- 1 teaspoon dried oregano
- 1 teaspoon dried thyme
- 1 cup of water

Directions:
1. Take a small bowl and add cayenne pepper, smoked paprika, garlic powder, onion powder, salt, pepper, dried oregano, dried thyme and ghee
2. Dip the fillets into the seasoned ghee mix. Add 1 cup of water to your Ninja Foodi
3. Place steamer rack and place the fillets on the rack
4. Lock lid and cook on HIGH pressure for 5 minutes. Release naturally over 10 minutes
5. Transfer to serving platter and garnish with parsley. Serve and enjoy!

Coconut Shrimp

Servings: 2
Cooking Time: 30 Min
Ingredients:
- 8 large shrimp
- ½ cup orange jam /65g
- ½ cup shredded coconut /65g
- ½ cup breadcrumbs /65g
- 8 oz. coconut milk /240ml
- 1 tbsp honey /15ml
- ½ tsp cayenne pepper/2.5g
- ¼ tsp hot sauce /1.25ml
- 1 tsp mustard /5g
- ¼ tsp salt /1.25g
- ¼ tsp pepper /1.25g

Directions:
1. Combine the breadcrumbs, cayenne pepper, shredded coconut, salt, and pepper in a small bowl. Dip the shrimp in the coconut milk, first, and then in the coconut crumbs.
2. Arrange in the lined Ninja Foodi basket, close the crisping lid and cook for 20 minutes on Air Crisp mode at 350 °F or 177°C.
3. Meanwhile whisk the jam, honey, hot sauce, and mustard. Serve the shrimp with the sauce.

The Rich Guy Lobster And Butter

Servings: 4
Cooking Time: 20 Minutes
Ingredients:
- 6 Lobster Tails
- 4 garlic cloves,
- ¼ cup butter

Directions:
1. Preheat the Ninja Foodi to 400 degrees F at first
2. Open the lobster tails gently by using kitchen scissors
3. Remove the lobster meat gently from the shells but keep it inside the shells
4. Take a plate and place it
5. Add some butter in a pan and allow it melt
6. Put some garlic cloves in it and heat it over medium-low heat
7. Pour the garlic butter mixture all over the lobster tail meat
8. Let the fryer to broil the lobster at 130 degrees F
9. Remove the lobster meat from Ninja Foodi and set aside
10. Use a fork to pull out the lobster meat from the shells entirely
11. Pour some garlic butter over it if needed. Serve and enjoy!

Crab Cakes With Spicy Dipping Sauce

Servings: 4
Cooking Time: 20 Minutes
Ingredients:
- Nonstick cooking spray
- 1/3 cup + ¼ cup mayonnaise, divided
- 1 tbsp. + 2 tsp spicy brown mustard, divided
- 1 tsp hot sauce
- ¼ cup + 1 tbsp. celery, chopped fine, divided
- ¼ cup + 1 tbsp. red bell pepper, chopped fine, divided
- 4 tsp Cajun seasoning, divided
- 2 tbsp. fresh parsley, chopped, divided
- 8 oz. jumbo lump crab meat
- ¼ cup green bell pepper, chopped fine
- 2 tbsp. green onions, chopped fine
- ¼ cup bread crumbs

Directions:
1. Spray the fryer basket with cooking spray.
2. In a small bowl, combine 1/3 cup mayonnaise, 2 teaspoons mustard, hot sauce, 1 tablespoon celery, 1 tablespoon red bell pepper, 2 teaspoons Cajun seasoning, and 1 tablespoon parsley, mix well. Cover and refrigerate until ready to use.
3. In a large bowl, combine all remaining ingredients with the crab, green bell pepper, onions, and bread crumbs, mix well. Form into 8 patties.
4. Place the patties in the fryer basket and add the tender-crisp lid. Set to air fry on 400 °F. Cook 20 minutes, or until golden brown, turning over halfway through cooking time.
5. Serve with prepared sauce for dipping.
Nutrition:
- InfoCalories 166,Total Fat 8g,Total Carbs 11g,Protein 11g,Sodium 723mg.

Simple Crab Legs

Servings: 5
Cooking Time: 3 Minutes
Ingredients:
- 1 cup (250 mL) water
- 2 pounds (907 g) crab legs, thawed

Directions:
1. Pour the water in the cooking pot and add a reversible rack. Put the crab legs on the reversible rack.
2. Assemble pressure lid, making sure the pressure release valve is in the Seal position. Select Pressure and set to high . Set time to 3 minutes. Press Start to begin.
3. Once cooking is complete, do a quick pressure release. Carefully open the lid.
4. Transfer the crab legs to a plate and serve.

Delightful Salmon Fillets

Servings:4
Cooking Time: 5 Minutes
Ingredients:
- 2 salmon fillets
- ¼ cup onion, chopped
- 2 stalks green onion stalks, chopped
- 1 whole egg
- Almond meal as needed
- Salt and pepper to taste
- 2 tablespoons olive oil

Directions:
1. Add a cup of water to your Ninja Foodi and place a steamer rack on top
2. Place the fish. Season the fish with salt and pepper and lock up the lid
3. Cook on HIGH pressure for 3 minutes. Once done, quick release the pressure
4. Remove the fish and allow it to cool
5. Break the fillets into a bowl and add egg, yellow and green onions
6. Add ½ a cup of almond meal and mix with your hand. Divide the mixture into patties
7. Take a large skillet and place it over medium heat. Add oil and cook the patties.Enjoy!

Adventurous Sweet And Sour Fish

Servings: 4
Cooking Time: 6 Minutes
Ingredients:
- 2 drops liquid stevia
- ¼ cup butter
- 1 pound fish chunks
- 1 tablespoon vinegar
- Salt and pepper to taste

Directions:
1. Set your Ninja Foodi to Saute mode and add butter, let it melt
2. Add fish chunks and Saute for 3 minutes. Add stevia, salt, and pepper, stir
3. Lock Crisping Lid and cook on "Air Crisp" mode for 3 minutes at 360 degrees F
4. Serve once done and enjoy!

Cajun Salmon With Lemon

Servings: 1
Cooking Time: 10 Min
Ingredients:
- 1 salmon fillet
- Juice of ½ lemon
- 2 lemon wedges
- 1 tbsp Cajun seasoning /15g
- 1 tbsp chopped parsley; for garnishing /15g
- ¼ tsp brown sugar /1.25g

Directions:
1. Meanwhile, combine the sugar and lemon and coat the salmon with this mixture thoroughly. Coat the salmon with the Cajun seasoning as well.
2. Place a parchment paper into the Ninja Foodi, close the crisping lid and cook the salmon for 7 minutes on Air Crisp mode at 350 °F or 177°C. If you use a thicker fillet, cook no more than 6 minutes. Serve with lemon wedges and chopped parsley.

Seafood Minestrone

Servings: 14
Cooking Time: 20 Minutes
Ingredients:
- 3 14 oz. cans beef broth, low sodium
- 28 oz. tomatoes, crushed
- 19 oz. garbanzo beans, undrained
- 15 ¼ oz. red kidney beans, undrained
- 16 oz. pkg. frozen mixed vegetables, thawed
- 16 oz. frozen spinach, thawed, chopped & drained
- 1 onion, chopped
- 1 tsp garlic powder
- ½ tsp pepper
- ½ cup elbow macaroni, uncooked
- 1 lb. cod, cut in 1-inch pieces
- 1 lb. shrimp, peeled & deveined

Directions:
1. Set cooker to sauté on med-high. Add the broth, tomatoes, garbanzo beans, kidney beans, vegetables, spinach, onion, and seasonings to the cooking pot, stir to mix. Bring to a boil.
2. Stir in the macaroni and cook until tender, about 8 minutes.
3. Reduce the heat to med-low and add the fish and shrimp. Cook 5-7 minutes until shrimp turn pink and fish flakes easily. Serve immediately.

Nutrition:
- InfoCalories 292,Total Fat 3g,Total Carbs 42g,Protein 25g,Sodium 645mg.

Alaskan Cod Divine

Servings: 4
Cooking Time: 5-10 Minutes
Ingredients:
- 1 large fillet, Alaskan Cod (Frozen)
- 1 cup cherry tomatoes
- Salt and pepper to taste
- Seasoning as you need
- 2 tablespoons butter
- Olive oil as needed

Directions:
1. Take an ovenproof dish small enough to fit inside your pot
2. Add tomatoes to the dish, cut large fish fillet into 2-3 serving pieces and lay them on top of tomatoes. Season with salt, pepper, and your seasoning
3. Top each fillet with 1 tablespoon butter and drizzle olive oil
4. Add 1 cup of water to the pot.Place trivet to the Ninja Foodi and place dish on the trivet
5. Lock lid and cook on HIGH pressure for 9 minutes.Release pressure naturally over 10 minutes
6. Serve and enjoy!

Shrimp And Tomato Delight

Servings:4
Cooking Time: 5 Minutes
Ingredients:
- 3 tablespoons unsalted butter
- 1 tablespoon garlic
- ½ teaspoon red pepper flakes
- 1 and ½ cup onion, chopped
- 1 can (14 and ½ ounces tomatoes, diced
- 1 teaspoon dried oregano
- 1 teaspoon salt
- 1 pound frozen shrimp, peeled
- 1 cup crumbled feta cheese
- ½ cup black olives, sliced
- ½ cup parsley, chopped

Directions:
1. Pre-heat your Ninja Foodi by setting in in the Saute mode on HIGH settings, add butter and let it melt. Add garlic, pepper flakes, cook for 1 minute
2. Add onion, tomato, oregano, salt and stir well. Add frozen shrimp
3. Lock lid and cook on HIGH pressure for 1 minute. Quick release pressure
4. Mix shrimp with tomato broth, let it cool and serve with a sprinkle of feta, olives, and parsley
5. Enjoy!

Almond Crusted Haddock

Servings: 4
Cooking Time: 30 Minutes
Ingredients:
- 1 tbsp. sugar
- ¾ tsp cinnamon
- ¼ tsp red pepper
- ½ tsp salt
- 1 ½ lbs. haddock filets

- 1 egg white, beaten
- 2 cups almonds, sliced
- 2 tbsp. butter
- ½ cup Amaretto liqueur

Directions:

1. In a small bowl, combine sugar, cinnamon, red pepper, and salt until combined. Use 1 teaspoon of the mixture to season the fish.
2. Spray the fryer basket with cooking spray and place it in the cooking pot.
3. In a shallow dish, beat the egg white.
4. In a separate shallow dish, place the almonds. Dip each filet in the egg white then coat with almonds. Place them in the fryer basket and spray them lightly with cooking spray.
5. Add the tender-crisp lid and set to air fry on 350°F. Cook the fish 5 minutes, then turn over and spray with cooking spray again. Cook another 2-3 minutes until golden brown. Transfer to serving plate and keep warm.
6. In a small saucepan over medium heat, melt the butter. Add the remaining sugar mixture and Amaretto to the pan. Reduce heat to low, and cook, stirring, 1-2 minutes until sauce has thickened. Pour over fish and serve immediately.

Nutrition:
- InfoCalories 576,Total Fat 30g,Total Carbs 26g,Protein 38g,Sodium 715mg.

Salmon Pudding

Servings: 4
Cooking Time: 40 Minutes
Ingredients:
- 1 pound (455 g) Yukon gold potatoes (3 or 4 medium potatoes), peeled and cut into ¼-inch slices
- ¾ tsp. kosher salt (or a scant ½ tsp. fine salt), divided
- ⅔ cup whole milk
- 3 large eggs
- ½ cup heavy (whipping) cream
- ¼ tsp. freshly ground black pepper, plus more for finishing
- 3 tbsps. melted unsalted butter, divided
- 6 ounces (170 g) smoked salmon, cut into chunks
- 3 tbsps. chopped fresh dill, divided

Directions:

1. In the Foodi inner pot, add 1 cup of water. Put the potato slices on the Reversible Rack, or in a steaming basket, and place the rack in the pot in the lower position.
2. Lock the Pressure Lid into place, set the valve to Seal. Select Pressure, adjust the cook time to 3 minutes. Press Start.
3. After cooking, quick release the pressure. Open and remove the Pressure Lid carefully. Take the rack out, sprinkle ¼ teaspoon of kosher salt over the potatoes, and allow them to cool. Empty the water out of the pot.
4. While the potatoes cook and cool, whisk the milk, eggs, remaining ½ teaspoon of kosher salt , heavy cream and the pepper in a large bowl.
5. Use 2 teaspoons or so of melted butter to grease a 1-quart, high-sided, round dish. Lay one-third of the potatoes on the base of the dish, spread with half the salmon, and sprinkle with 1 tablespoon of dill. Place another third of the potatoes over, and cover with the remaining salmon spread, 1 tablespoon of dill followed by the remaining third of the potatoes. Pour over with the custard, it should come up just to the top layer of potatoes but not cover them.

6. In the inner pot, add 1 cup of water. Put the Reversible Rack in the pot in the lower position and put the baking dish on top.
7. Lock the Pressure Lid into place, set the valve to Seal. Select Pressure, adjust the cook time to 15 minutes. Press Start.
8. When the cooking is complete, naturally release the pressure for 10 minutes, then quick release any remaining pressure. Open and remove the Pressure Lid carefully.
9. Take the baking dish and rack out from the inner pot and pour the water out of the pot. Place the inner pot back to the base and place the rack back in the pot. Close the Crisping Lid and select Broil. Adjust the time to 2 minutes to preheat. Press Start.
10. Meanwhile, drizzle over the top of the potatoes with the remaining melted butter. Open the Crisping Lid and place the dish on the rack. Close the lid, select Broil, and set the cook time to 5 minutes. Press Start.
11. After broiling, open the lid and carefully remove the pudding. Allow to cool for a few minutes. Sprinkle with the remaining 1 tablespoon of dill and season with additional pepper as desired.

Shrimp Etouffee

Servings: 6
Cooking Time: 30 Minutes
Ingredients:
- ¼ cup olive oil
- ¼ cup flour
- 1 stalk celery, chopped
- 1 green bell pepper, chopped
- 2 jalapeno peppers, chopped
- ½ onion, chopped
- 4 cloves garlic, chopped
- 2 cups clam juice
- 1 tbsp. Cajun seasoning
- ½ tsp celery seed
- 1 tbsp. paprika
- 2 pounds shrimp, shell on, deveined
- 3 green onions, chopped
- Hot sauce to taste

Directions:

1. Add the oil to the cooking pot and set to sauté on medium heat. Whisk in the flour until smooth. Cook until a deep brown, whisking frequently, about 10 minutes.
2. Add celery, bell pepper, jalapeno, and onion and cook 4 minutes, stirring occasionally. Add the garlic and cook 2 minutes more.
3. Slowly stir in clam juice, a little at a time, until combined. The sauce should resemble syrup, add more juice if needed.
4. Add Cajun seasoning, celery seed, and paprika and mix well. Add the shrimp. Cover, reduce heat to low and cook 10 minutes.
5. Stir in green onions and hot sauce. Serve over rice.

Nutrition:
- InfoCalories 83,Total Fat 3g,Total Carbs 6g,Protein 7g,Sodium 395mg.

Mediterranean Cod

Servings: 4
Cooking Time: 20 Min
Ingredients:
- 4 fillets cod
- 1 bunch fresh thyme sprigs
- 1 pound cherry tomatoes, halved /450g
- 1 clove garlic, pressed
- 1 cup white rice /130g
- 2 cups water /500ml
- 1 cup Kalamata olives /130g
- 2 tbsp pickled capers /30g
- 1 tbsp olive oil; divided /15ml
- 1 tsp olive oil /15ml
- 1 pinch ground black pepper
- 3 pinches salt

Directions:
1. Line a parchment paper to the steamer basket of your Foodi. Place about half the tomatoes in a single layer on the paper. Sprinkle with thyme, reserving some for garnish. Arrange cod fillets on the top of tomatoes. Sprinkle with a little bit of olive oil.
2. Spread the garlic, pepper, salt, and remaining tomatoes over the fish. In the pot, mix rice and water. Lay a trivet over the rice and water. Lower steamer basket onto the trivet.
3. Seal the pressure lid, choose Pressure, set to High, and set the timer to 7 minutes. Press Start. When ready, release the pressure quickly.
4. Remove the steamer basket and trivet from the pot. Use a fork to fluff rice. Plate the fish fillets and apply a garnish of olives, reserved thyme, pepper, remaining olive oil, and capers. Serve with rice.

Panko Crusted Cod

Servings: 4
Cooking Time: 15 Minutes
Ingredients:
- 2 uncooked cod fillets
- 3 teaspoons kosher salt
- ¾ cup panko bread crumbs
- 2 tablespoons butter, melted
- 1/4 cup fresh parsley, minced
- 1 lemon. Zested and juiced

Directions:
1. Pre-heat your Ninja Foodi at 390 °F and place the Air Crisper basket inside.
2. Season cod and salt.
3. Take a suitable and stir in bread crumbs, parsley, lemon juice, zest, butter, and mix well.
4. Coat fillets with the bread crumbs mixture and place fillets in your Air Crisping basket.
5. Lock Air Crisping lid and cook on Air Crisp mode for 15 minutes at 360 °F.
6. Serve and enjoy.

Nutrition:
- InfoCalories: 554; Fat: 24g; Carbohydrates: 5g; Protein: 37g

Roasted Bbq Shrimp

Servings: 2
Cooking Time: 7 Minutes
Ingredients:
- 3 tablespoons chipotle in adobo sauce, minced

- 1/4 teaspoon salt
- 1/4 cup BBQ sauce
- 1/2 orange, juiced
- 1/2-pound large shrimps

Directions:
1. Toss shrimp with chipotles and rest of the ingredients in a suitable bowl.
2. Preheat Ninja Foodi by pressing the "Bake/Roast" mode and setting it to "400 °F" and timer to 7 minutes.
3. Let it preheat until you hear a beep.
4. Set shrimps over Grill Grate and lock lid, cook until the timer runs out.
5. Serve and enjoy.

Nutrition:
- InfoCalories: 173; Fat: 2g; Carbohydrates: 21g; Protein: 17g

Glazed Salmon

Servings: 4
Cooking Time: 25 Minutes
Ingredients:
- 1-2 Coho salmon filets
- 1 cup of water
- 1/4 cup of soy sauce
- 1/4 cup brown erythritol
- 1 tablespoon choc zero maple syrup
- 1 and 1/2 tablespoons ginger roots, minced
- 1/2 teaspoon white pepper
- 2 tablespoons cornstarch
- 1/4 cup of cold water

Directions:
1. Preheat Ninja Foodi by pressing the "GRILL" option and setting it to "HIGH" for 15 minutes.
2. Take a medium saucepan over medium heat, combine sauce ingredients. except for salmon, cornstarch and cold water and bring to a low boil.
3. Then add cornstarch and water in another bowl, whisk cornstarch mixture slowly into sauce until it thickens.
4. Stir in one chunk of pecan wood to the hot coal of your grill.
5. Brush sauce onto the salmon filet.
6. Place on the grill grate, then close the hood.
7. Cook for 15 minutes.
8. Brush the salmon with another coat of sauce.
9. Serve and enjoy.

Nutrition:
- InfoCalories: 163; Fat: 0g; Carbohydrates: 15g; Protein: 0g

Pepper Smothered Cod

Servings: 4
Cooking Time: 20 Minutes
Ingredients:
- ¼ cup olive oil
- ½ cup red onion, chopped
- 2 tsp garlic, chopped
- ½ cup red bell pepper, chopped
- ½ cup green bell pepper, chopped
- Salt and pepper, to taste
- 4 tbsp. flour
- 2 cups chicken broth, low sodium
- ½ cup tomato, seeded & chopped
- 2 tsp fresh thyme, chopped
- 4 cod filets

Directions:
1. Set to sauté on med-high heat and add oil to the cooking pot.
2. Add the onion and garlic and cook, stirring, 1 minute.
3. Add the peppers, salt, and pepper and cook, stirring frequently about 2-3 minutes, or until peppers start to get tender.
4. Stir in the flour and cook until it turns a light brown.
5. Pour in the broth and cook, stirring, until smooth and the sauce starts to thicken. Stir in tomato and thyme.
6. Season the fish with salt and pepper. Place in the pot and add the lid. Cook 3-4 minutes, then turn the fish over and cook another 3-4 minute or until fish flakes easily with a fork. Transfer the fish to serving plates and top with sauce. Serve immediately.

Nutrition:
- InfoCalories 249,Total Fat 14g,Total Carbs 11g,Protein 19g,Sodium 1107mg.

Lovely Carb Soup

Servings: 4
Cooking Time: 6-7 Hours
Ingredients:
- 1 cup crab meat, cubed
- 1 tablespoon garlic, minced
- Salt as needed
- Red chili flakes as needed
- 3 cups vegetable broth
- 1 teaspoon salt

Directions:
1. Coat the crab cubes in lime juice and let them sit for a while
2. Add the all to your Ninja Foodi and lock lid
3. Cook on SLOW COOK MODE for 3 hours
4. Let it sit for a while
5. Unlock lid and set to Saute mode, simmer the soup for 5 minutes more on LOW
6. Stir and check to season. Enjoy!

Shrimp Fried Rice

Servings: 6
Cooking Time: 15 Minutes
Ingredients:
- 2 tbsp. sesame oil
- 2 tbsp. olive oil
- 1 lb. medium shrimp, peeled & deveined
- 1 cup frozen peas & carrots
- 1/2 cup corn
- 3 cloves garlic, chopped fine
- ½ tsp ginger
- 3 eggs, lightly beaten
- 4 cups brown rice, cooked
- 3 green onions, sliced
- 3 tbsp. tamari
- ½ tsp salt
- ½ tsp pepper

Directions:
1. Add the sesame and olive oils to the cooking pot and set to sauté on med-high heat.
2. Add the shrimp and cook 3 minutes, or until they turn pink, turning shrimp over halfway through. Use a slotted spoon to transfer shrimp to a plate.

3. Add the peas, carrots, and corn to the pot and cook 2 minutes until vegetables start to soften, stirring occasionally. Add the garlic and ginger and cook 1 minute more.
4. Push the vegetables to one side and add the eggs, cook to scramble, stirring frequently. Add the shrimp, rice, and onions and stir to mix all ingredients together.
5. Drizzle with tamari and season with salt and pepper, stir to combine. Cook 2 minutes or until everything is heated through. Serve immediately.

Nutrition:
- InfoCalories 361,Total Fat 13g,Total Carbs 38g,Protein 24g,Sodium 1013mg.

Baked Cod Casserole

Servings: 6
Cooking Time: 20 Minutes
Ingredients:
- Nonstick cooking spray
- 1 lb. mushrooms, chopped
- 1 onion, chopped
- ½ cup fresh parsley, chopped
- ½ tsp salt, divided
- ½ tsp pepper, divided
- 6 cod fillets
- ¾ cup dry white wine
- ¾ cup plain bread crumbs
- 2 tbsp. butter, melted
- 1 cup Swiss cheese, grated

Directions:
1. Spray the cooking pot with cooking spray.
2. In a medium bowl, combine mushrooms, onion, parsley, ¼ teaspoon salt, and ¼ teaspoon pepper and mix well. Spread evenly on the bottom of the cooking pot.
3. Place the fish on top of the mushroom mixture and pour the wine over them.
4. In a separate medium bowl, combine remaining ingredients and mix well. Sprinkle over the fish.
5. Add the tender-crisp lid and set to bake on 450°F. Bake 15-20 minutes or until golden brown and fish flakes easily with a fork. Serve immediately.

Nutrition:
- InfoCalories 284,Total Fat 10g,Total Carbs 16g,Protein 27g,Sodium 693mg.

Caribbean Catfish With Mango Salsa

Servings: 4
Cooking Time: 10 Minutes
Ingredients:
- 1 red pepper, roasted & chopped
- 1 mango, peeled & chopped
- 1 orange, peeled & chopped
- ¼ cup cilantro, chopped fine
- ¼ cup green onion, chopped fine
- 1 tsp jalapeno, chopped
- 1 tbsp. olive oil
- 1 tsp salt, divided
- ½ tsp pepper, divided
- ½ cup panko bread crumbs
- ½ cup coconut, shredded
- 4 catfish fillets
- Nonstick cooking spray

Directions:

1. In a medium bowl, combine red pepper, mango, orange, cilantro, green onion, jalapeno, olive oil, ¼ tsp salt, and ¼ tsp pepper. Cover and let sit until ready to use.
2. In a shallow dish, stir together bread crumbs and coconut until combined.
3. Season catfish with salt and pepper. Dredge in bread crumbs coating both sides thoroughly.
4. Spray the fryer basket with cooking spray. Lay the catfish in the basket in a single layer. Add the tender-crisp lid and set to air fry on 375°F. Cook fish 8-10 minutes per side until golden brown and fish flakes easily with a fork.
5. Transfer fish to serving plates and top with mango salsa. Serve immediately.

Nutrition:
- InfoCalories 357,Total Fat 12g,Total Carbs 34g,Protein 30g,Sodium 534mg.

Fish And Chips

Servings: 4
Cooking Time:39 Minutes
Ingredients:
- 2 eggs
- 8 ounces ale beer
- 1 cup cornstarch
- 1 cup all-purpose flour
- ½ tablespoon chili powder
- 1 tablespoon ground cumin
- 1 teaspoon sea salt, plus more for seasoning
- 1 teaspoon freshly ground black pepper, plus more for seasoning
- 4 (5- to 6-ounce) cod fillets
- Nonstick cooking spray
- 2 russet potatoes, cut into ¼- to ½-inch matchsticks
- 2 tablespoons vegetable oil

Directions:
1. Place the Cook & Crisp Basket in the pot and close the Crisping Lid. Preheat the unit by selecting Air Crisp, setting the temperature to 375°F, and setting the time to 5 minutes.
2. Meanwhile, in a shallow mixing bowl, whisk together the eggs and beer. In a separate medium bowl whisk together the cornstarch, flour, chili powder, cumin, salt, and pepper.
3. Coat each cod fillet in the egg mixture, then dredge in the flour mixture, coating on all sides.
4. Spray the preheated Cook & Crisp Basket with nonstick cooking spray. Place the fish fillets in the basket and coat them with cooking spray.
5. Close the Crisping Lid. Select Air Crisp, set the temperature to 375°F, and set the time to 15 minutes. Press Start/Stop to begin.
6. Meanwhile, toss the potatoes with the oil and season with salt and pepper.
7. After 15 minutes, check the fish for your desired crispiness. Remove the fish from the basket.
8. Place the potatoes in the Cook & Crisp™ Basket. Close the Crisping Lid. Select Air Crisp, set the temperature to 400°F, and set the time to 24 minutes. Press Start/Stop to begin.
9. After 12 minutes, open the lid, then lift the basket and shake the fries. Lower the basket back into the pot and close the lid to resume cooking until they reach your desired crispiness.

Chorizo And Shrimp Veg Potpie

Servings:6
Cooking Time: 23 Minutes
Ingredients:
- ¼ cup unsalted butter
- ½ large onion, diced
- 1 celery stalk, diced
- 1 carrot, peeled and diced
- 8 ounces (227 g) chorizo, fully cooked, cut into ½-inch wheels
- ¼ cup all-purpose flour
- 16 ounces (454 g) frozen tail-off shrimp, cleaned and deveined
- ¾ cup chicken stock
- 1 tablespoon Cajun spice mix
- ½ cup heavy (whipping) cream
- Sea salt
- Freshly ground black pepper
- 1 refrigerated store-bought pie crust, at room temperature

Directions:
1. Select SEAR/SAUTÉ and set to MD:HI. Select START/STOP to begin. Let preheat for 5 minutes.
2. Add the butter. Once melted, add the onion, celery, carrot, and sausage, and cook until softened, about 3 minutes. Stir in the flour and cook 2 minutes, stirring occasionally.
3. Add the shrimp, stock, Cajun spice mix, and cream and season with salt and pepper. Stir until sauce thickens and bubbles, about 3 minutes.
4. Lay the pie crust evenly on top of the filling, folding over the edges if necessary. Make a small cut in center of pie crust so that steam can escape during baking. Close crisping lid.
5. Select BROIL and set time to 10 minutes. Select START/STOP to begin.
6. When cooking is complete, open lid and remove pot from unit. Let rest 10 to 15 minutes before serving.

Spicy Shrimp Pasta With Vodka Sauce

Servings:6
Cooking Time: 11 Minutes
Ingredients:
- 2 tablespoons extra-virgin olive oil
- 2 tablespoons minced garlic
- 1 teaspoon crushed red pepper flakes
- 1 small red onion, diced
- Kosher salt
- Freshly ground black pepper
- ¼ cup vodka
- 2¾ cups vegetable stock
- 1 can crushed tomatoes
- 1 box penne pasta
- 1 pound frozen shrimp, peeled and deveined
- 1 package cream cheese, cubed
- 4 cups shredded mozzarella cheese

Directions:
1. Select SEAR/SAUTÉ and set to MD:HI. Select START/STOP to begin. Let preheat for 5 minutes.
2. Add the olive oil, garlic, and crushed red pepper flakes. Cook until garlic is golden brown, about 1 minute. Add the onions and season with salt and pepper and cook until translucent, about 2 minutes.
3. Stir in the vodka, vegetable stock, crushed tomatoes, penne pasta, and frozen shrimp. Assemble pressure lid,

making sure the pressure release valve is in the SEAL position.

4. Select PRESSURE and set temperature to HI. Set time to 6 minutes. Select START/STOP to begin.

5. When pressure cooking is complete, quick release the pressure by turning the pressure release valve to the VENT position. Carefully remove lid when unit has finished releasing pressure.

6. Stir in the cream cheese until it has melted. Layer the mozzarella on top of the pasta. Close crisping lid.

7. Select AIR CRISP, set temperature to 400°F, and set time to 5 minutes. Select START/STOP to begin.

8. When cooking is complete, open lid and serve.

Nutrition:

• InfoCalories: 789,Total Fat: 35g,Sodium: 1302mg,Carbohydrates: 63g,Protein: 47g.

Pistachio Crusted Salmon

Servings: 1
Cooking Time: 15 Min
Ingredients:

• 1 salmon fillet
• 3 tbsp pistachios /45g
• 1 tsp grated Parmesan cheese /5g
• 1 tsp lemon juice /5ml
• 1 tsp mustard /5g
• 1 tsp olive oil /5ml
• Pinch of sea salt
• Pinch of garlic powder
• Pinch of black pepper

Directions:

1. Whisk the mustard and lemon juice together. Season the salmon with salt, pepper, and garlic powder. Brush the olive oil on all sides.

2. Brush the mustard-lemon mixture on top of the salmon. Chop the pistachios finely, and combine them with the Parmesan cheese.

3. Sprinkle them on top of the salmon. Place the salmon in the Ninja Foodi basket with the skin side down.

4. Close the crisping lid and cook for 10 minutes on Air Crisp mode at 350 °F or 177°C.

Asian Salmon And Veggie Meal

Servings:4
Cooking Time: 2 Hours
Ingredients:

• For Fish
• 2 medium salmon fillets
• 1 garlic cloves, diced
• 2 teaspoons ginger, grated
• ¼ a long red chili, diced
• Salt as needed
• 2 tablespoons coconut aminos
• 1 teaspoon agave nectar
• For Veggies
• ½ pound mixed green veggies
• 1 large carrot, sliced
• 1 garlic clove, diced
• ½ lime, juice
• 1 tablespoon tamari sauce
• 1 tablespoon olive oil
• ½ teaspoon sesame oil

Directions:

1. Add 1 cup of water to your Ninja Foodi and place a trivet inside

2. Place fish fillets inside a heatproof tin and sprinkle diced garlic, chili, and ginger on top. Season with salt and pepper

3. Take a small bowl and create a mixture of tamari and agave nectar

4. Pour the mixture over the fillets. Place tin with salmon on top of the trivet

5. Lock up the lid and cook on HIGH pressure for 3 minutes and perform a quick release

6. Cut the vegetables and place the veggies in a steam basket. Sprinkle garlic

7. Place the steamer basket with veggies on top of the salmon tin and drizzle lime juice, olive oil, tamari, sesame oil. Season with salt and pepper

8. Lock up the lid and cook on HIGH pressure for 0 minutes . Quick release the remove the and basket and tin

9. Transfer the salmon to a plate alongside veggies and pour any remaining sauce over the salmon, enjoy!

Haddock With Sanfaina

Servings: 4
Cooking Time: 40 Min
Ingredients:

• 4 haddock fillets
• 1 can diced tomatoes, drained /435g
• ½ small onion; sliced
• 1 small jalapeño pepper, seeded and minced
• 2 large garlic cloves, minced
• 1 eggplant; cubed
• 1 bell pepper; chopped
• 1 bay leaf
• ⅓ cup sliced green olives /44g
• ¼ cup chopped fresh chervil; divided /32.5g
• 3 tbsps olive oil /45ml
• 3 tbsps capers; divided/45g
• ½ tsp dried basil /2.5g
• ¼ tsp salt /1.25g

Directions:

1. Season the fish on both sides with salt, place in the refrigerator, and make the sauce. Press Sear/Sauté and set to Medium. Press Start. Melt the butter until no longer foaming. Add onion, eggplant, bell pepper, jalapeño, and garlic; sauté for 5 minutes.

2. Stir in the tomatoes, bay leaf, basil, olives, half of the chervil, and half of the capers. Remove the fish from the refrigerator and lay on the vegetables in the pot.

3. Seal the pressure lid, choose Pressure; adjust the pressure to Low and the cook time to 3 minutes; press Start. After cooking, do a quick pressure release and carefully open the lid. Remove and discard the bay leaf.

4. Transfer the fish to a serving platter and spoon the sauce over. Sprinkle with the remaining chervil and capers. Serve.

Crabs With Coconut Milk

Servings: 2 To 4
Cooking Time: 9 Minutes
Ingredients:

• 1 tablespoon olive oil
• 1 onion, chopped
• 3 cloves garlic, minced
• 1 pound (454 g) crabs, halved

- 1 can coconut milk
- 1 lemongrass stalk
- 1 thumb-size ginger, sliced
- Salt and ground black pepper, to taste

Directions:
1. Press the Sauté button and heat the oil.
2. Add the onion and sauté for 2 minutes until tender.
3. Mix in the garlic and sauté for another 1 minute until fragrant.
4. Add the crabs, coconut milk, lemongrass stalk, ginger, salt, and pepper.
5. Assemble pressure lid, making sure the pressure release valve is in the Seal position. Select Pressure and set to high . Set time to 6 minutes. Press Start to begin.
6. Once the timer beeps, do a quick pressure release. Carefully remove the lid.
7. Transfer to a serving plate and serve immediately.

Shrimp And Sausage Boil

Servings: 2
Cooking Time: 4 Minutes
Ingredients:
- ½ pound (227 g) red potatoes, halved
- 1 cup (250 mL) water
- 2 ears of corn, shucked and broken in half
- 1 medium sweet onion, chopped
- ½ pound (227 g) fully cooked kielbasa sausage, cut into 2-inch slices
- 2 tablespoons crab boil seasoning (optional)
- 2 tablespoons Old Bay seasoning, plus more for seasoning
- ½ teaspoon kosher salt
- 1 pound (454 g) peel-on large raw shrimp, deveined

Directions:
1. Mix together the potatoes, water, corn, onion, kielbasa, the crab boil seasoning , 2 tablespoons of Old Bay, and salt in your cooking pot.
2. Assemble pressure lid, making sure the pressure release valve is in the Seal position. Select Pressure and set to high . Set time to 4 minutes. Press Start to begin.
3. Once cooking is complete, do a quick pressure release. Carefully open the lid.
4. Mix in the shrimp and stir well. Replace the lid loosely and let stand for 3 to 4 minutes. Sprinkle with the salt and Old Bay. Transfer the shrimp to a large colander and drain.
5. Serve.

Salmon With Balsamic-glazed Brussels Sprouts

Servings:2
Cooking Time: 57 Minutes
Ingredients:
- 2 cups brown rice
- 2½ cups water
- 2 salmon fillets
- 4 tablespoons everything bagel seasoning, divided
- 1 pound Brussels sprouts, ends trimmed, cut in half
- 1 tablespoon olive oil
- 2 tablespoons balsamic glaze

Directions:
1. Place the rice and water in the cooking pot. Assemble the pressure lid, making sure the pressure release valve is in the SEAL position.

2. Select PRESSURE and set to HI. Set the time to 30 minutes. Select START/STOP to begin.
3. Meanwhile, season both sides of the salmon fillets with the everything bagel seasoning, using one tablespoon per fillet. Set aside.
4. When pressure cooking is complete, allow the pressure to release naturally for 10 minutes. After 10 minutes, quick release any remaining pressure by moving the pressure release valve to the VENT position. Carefully remove the lid when the unit has finished releasing pressure.
5. Season both sides of each salmon fillet with one tablespoon of the everything bagel seasoning.
6. In a medium bowl, combine the Brussels sprouts and olive oil. Toss to coat, and then sprinkle with one tablespoon of the everything bagel seasoning. Toss again to ensure Brussels sprouts are coated.
7. Place the Cook & Crisp Basket into the cooking pot. Close the crisping lid. Select AIR CRISP, set the temperature to 390°F, and set the time to 16 minutes. Select START/STOP to begin. Allow to preheat for 5 minutes, then add the sprouts to the Cook & Crisp Basket. Close the crisping lid to begin cooking.
8. After 8 minutes, open the crisping lid, lift the basket, and shake the sprouts. Lower the basket back into the pot and close the lid to resume cooking another 8 minutes or until the Brussels sprouts reach your desired crispiness.
9. Once timer is complete, transfer the sprouts to a bowl and toss with remaining tablespoon of seasoning and the balsamic glaze.
10. Close the crisping lid. Select AIR CRISP, set the temperature to 390°F, and set the time to 11 minutes. Select START/STOP to begin. Allow to preheat for 5 minutes, then add the salmon fillets to the Cook & Crisp basket. Close the lid to begin cooking.
11. Once timer is complete, remove fillets from basket and serve alongside sprouts and rice.

Nutrition:
- InfoCalories: 1028,Total Fat: 30g,Sodium: 1440mg,Carbohydrates: 154g,Protein: 55g.

Simple Salmon & Asparagus

Servings: 4
Cooking Time: 15 Minutes
Ingredients:
- 4 salmon filets
- 1 tsp rosemary
- ½ tsp pepper, divided
- 14 oz. vegetable broth, low sodium
- 1 tbsp. lemon juice
- ½ lb. asparagus, trimmed & cut in 2-inch pieces

Directions:
1. Season the fish with rosemary and ¼ teaspoon pepper and add to cooking pot.
2. In a small bowl, whisk together broth, lemon juice, and remaining pepper until smooth. Pour over fish.
3. Add the lid and set to sauté on medium heat. Once mixture reaches a boil, reduce heat to low and simmer 5 minutes.
4. Add the asparagus around the salmon, recover, and cook another 5 minutes until asparagus is fork-tender and fish flakes easily. Serve immediately..

Nutrition:
- InfoCalories 163,Total Fat 5g,Total Carbs 3g,Protein 25g,Sodium 454mg.

Fresh Steamed Salmon

Servings:4
Cooking Time: 5 Minutes
Ingredients:
- 2 salmon fillets
- ¼ cup onion, chopped
- 2 stalks green onion stalks, chopped
- 1 whole egg
- Almond meal
- Salt and pepper to taste
- 2 tablespoons olive oil

Directions:
1. Add a cup of water to your Ninja Foodi and place a steamer rack on top
2. Place the fish. Season the fish with salt and pepper and lock up the lid
3. Cook on HIGH pressure for 3 minutes. Once done, quick release the pressure
4. Remove the fish and allow it to cool
5. Break the fillets into a bowl and add egg, yellow and green onions
6. Add ½ a cup of almond meal and mix with your hand. Divide the mixture into patties
7. Take a large skillet and place it over medium heat. Add oil and cook the patties.Enjoy!

Easy Clam Chowder

Servings: 6
Cooking Time: 3 Hours
Ingredients:
- 5 slices bacon, chopped
- 2 cloves garlic, chopped fine
- ½ onion, chopped
- ½ tsp thyme
- 1 cup chicken broth, low sodium
- 4 oz. cream cheese
- 18 oz. clams, chopped & drained
- 1 bay leaf
- 3 cups cauliflower, separated in florets
- 1 cup almond milk, unsweetened
- 1 cup heavy cream
- 2 tbsp. fresh parsley, chopped

Directions:
1. Add the bacon to the cooking pot and set to sauté on med-high heat. Cook until crisp, transfer to a paper-towel lined plate. Pour out all but 3 tablespoons of the fat.
2. Add the onion and garlic and cook 2-3 minutes until onion is translucent. Add the thyme and cook 1 minute more.
3. Add the broth, cream cheese, clams, bay leaf, and cauliflower, mix until combined. Add the lid and set to slow cook on low. Cook 2-3 hours until cauliflower is tender. Stir in the milk and cream and cook until heated through.
4. Ladle into bowls and top with bacon and parsley. Serve warm.

Nutrition:
- InfoCalories 377,Total Fat 24g,Total Carbs 13g,Protein 27g,Sodium 468mg.

Curried Salmon & Sweet Potatoes

Servings: 4
Cooking Time: 20 Minutes
Ingredients:
- Nonstick cooking spray
- 2 sweet potatoes, peeled & cubed
- 1 tbsp. + 1 tsp olive oil, divided
- ½ tsp salt
- 1 tsp thyme
- 1 tsp curry powder
- 1 tsp honey
- ½ tsp lime zest
- 1/8 tsp crushed red pepper flakes
- 4 salmon filets

Directions:
1. Spray the cooking pot with cooking spray.
2. In a large bowl, combine potatoes, 1 tablespoon oil, salt, and thyme and toss to coat the potatoes. Place in the cooking pot.
3. Add the tender-crisp lid and set to roast on 400°F. Cook potatoes 10 minutes.
4. In a small bowl, whisk together remaining oil, curry powder, honey, zest, and pepper flakes. Lay the salmon on a sheet of foil and brush the curry mixture over the top.
5. Open the lid and stir the potatoes. Add the rack to the cooking pot and place the salmon, with the foil, on the rack. Close the lid and continue to cook another 10-15 minutes until potatoes are tender and fish flakes easily with a fork. Serve.

Nutrition:
- InfoCalories 239,Total Fat 8g,Total Carbs 15g,Protein 25g,Sodium 347mg.

Clam & Corn Chowder

Servings: 4
Cooking Time: 5 Hours
Ingredients:
- 1 cup chicken broth, fat free
- 2 cups potatoes, peeled & cubed
- 1 cup corn
- 1 onion, peeled & chopped
- 1 bay leaf
- ½ tsp marjoram
- ½ tsp salt
- ¼ tsp pepper
- 1 cup skim milk
- 10½ oz. minced clams, undrained
- 2 tsp cornstarch

Directions:
1. Add the chicken broth, potatoes, corn, onion, bay leaf, marjoram, salt and pepper to the cooking pot, stir to mix.
2. Add the lid and set to slow cooking on high. Cook 4-5 hours or until potatoes are tender. Discard the bay leaf.
3. Transfer the mixture to a food processor and pulse until smooth. Return to the cooking pot.
4. Stir in ¾ cup milk and clams. Cover and cook another 15 minutes.
5. In a glass measuring cup, whisk together remaining milk and cornstarch until smooth. Stir into chowder and cook, stirring 2-3 minutes or until thickened. Serve.

Nutrition:
- InfoCalories 267,Total Fat 4g,Total Carbs 34g,Protein 23g,Sodium 348mg.

Cod With Ginger And Scallion Sauce

Servings:4
Cooking Time: 10 Minutes
Ingredients:
- 2 tablespoons rice vinegar
- 2 tablespoons soy sauce
- 1 tablespoon chicken stock
- 1 tablespoon grated fresh ginger
- 4 skinless cod fillets
- Sea salt
- Freshly ground black pepper
- Greens of 6 scallions, thinly sliced

Directions:
1. In a small bowl, mix together the rice vinegar, soy sauce, chicken stock, and ginger.
2. Season the cod fillets on both sides with salt and pepper. Place them in the pot and cover with the vinegar mixture.
3. Select SEAR/SAUTÉ and set to MED. Bring the liquid to a low boil.
4. Once boiling, turn the heat to LO and cover with the pressure lid. Cook for 8 minutes.
5. Remove lid and add the scallion greens to the top of the fish. Cover with the pressure lid and cook for 2 minutes more. Serve.

Nutrition:
- InfoCalories: 149,Total Fat: 2g,Sodium: 642mg,Carbohydrates: 2g,Protein: 30g.

Shrimp Scampi With Tomatoes

Servings: 2 To 4
Cooking Time: 3 Minutes
Ingredients:
- 2 tablespoons olive oil
- 1 clove garlic, minced
- 1 pound (454 g) shrimp, peeled and deveined
- 10 ounces (284 g) canned tomatoes, chopped
- ⅓ cup (83 mL) tomato paste
- ⅓ cup (83 mL) water
- 1 tablespoon parsley, finely chopped
- ¼ teaspoon dried oregano
- ½ teaspoon kosher salt
- ½ teaspoon ground black pepper, to taste
- 1 cup (250 mL) grated Parmesan Cheese

Directions:
1. Press the Sauté button and heat the oil.
2. Add the garlic and sauté for 1 minute until fragrant.
3. Stir in the shrimp, tomatoes, tomato paste, water, parsley, oregano, salt and pepper.
4. Assemble pressure lid, making sure the pressure release valve is in the Seal position. Select Pressure and set to high . Set time to 3 minutes. Press Start to begin.
5. When the timer beeps, do a quick pressure release. Carefully remove the lid.
6. Serve scattered with the Parmesan Cheese.

Sesame Tuna Steaks

Servings: 4
Cooking Time: 10 Minutes
Ingredients:
- Nonstick cooking spray
- 2 tsp sesame oil
- 1 clove garlic, chopped fine
- 4 tuna steaks
- 1/8 tsp salt
- ½ tsp pepper
- ½ cup sesame seeds

Directions:
1. Place the rack in the cooking pot and spray it with cooking spray.
2. In a small bowl combine the oil and garlic. Rub it on both sides of the fish. Season with salt and pepper.
3. Place the sesame seeds in a shallow dish. Press the fish in the sesame seeds to coat completely. Place them on the rack.
4. Add the tender-crisp lid and set to roast on 350°F. Cook 8-10 minutes, turning over halfway through cooking time, until fish flakes with a fork. Serve immediately.

Nutrition:
- InfoCalories 263,Total Fat 14g,Total Carbs 3g,Protein 32g,Sodium 60mg.

Corn Chowder With Spicy Shrimp

Servings: 4
Cooking Time:35 Minutes
Ingredients:
- 4 slices bacon, chopped
- 1 onion, diced
- 4 tablespoons minced garlic, divided
- 2 Yukon Gold potatoes, chopped
- 16 ounces frozen corn
- 2 cups vegetable broth
- 1 teaspoon dried thyme
- 1 teaspoon sea salt, divided
- 1 teaspoon freshly ground black pepper, divided
- 16 jumbo shrimp, fresh or defrosted from frozen, peeled and deveined
- 1 tablespoon extra-virgin olive oil
- ½ teaspoon red pepper flakes
- ¾ cup heavy (whipping) cream

Directions:
1. Select Sear/Sauté and set to Medium High. Select Start/Stop to begin. Allow the pot to preheat for 5 minutes.
2. Combine the bacon, onion, and 2 tablespoons of garlic in the preheated pot. Cook, stirring occasionally, for 5 minutes. Reserve some of the bacon for garnish.
3. Add the potatoes, corn, vegetable broth, thyme, ½ teaspoon of salt, and ½ teaspoon of black pepper to the pot. Assemble the Pressure Lid, making sure the pressure release valve is in the Seal position.
4. Select Pressure and set to High. Set the time to 10 minutes, then select Start/Stop to begin.
5. While the chowder is cooking, in a medium mixing bowl, toss the shrimp in the remaining 2 tablespoons of garlic, ½ teaspoon of salt, ½ teaspoon of black pepper, the olive oil, and the red pepper flakes.
6. When pressure cooking the chowder is complete, quick release the pressure by moving the pressure release valve to the Vent position. Carefully remove the lid when the pressure has finished releasing.
7. Stir the cream into the chowder. Place the Reversible Rack inside the pot over the chowder, making sure the rack is in the higher position. Place the shrimp on the rack.
8. Close the Crisping Lid. Select Broil and set the time to 8 minutes. Select Start/Stop to begin.
9. When cooking is complete, remove the rack from the pot. Ladle the corn chowder into bowls and top with the shrimp and reserved bacon. Serve immediately.

Cheesy Potato And Clam Cracker Chowder

Servings: 4
Cooking Time: 30 Minutes
Ingredients:
- 2 cups oyster crackers
- 2 tbsps. melted unsalted butter
- ½ tsp. granulated garlic
- ¼ cup finely grated Parmesan or similar cheese
- 1 tsp. kosher salt (or ½ tsp. fine salt), divided
- 2 thick bacon slices, cut into thirds
- 2 celery stalks, chopped (about ⅔ cup)
- 1 medium onion, chopped (about ¾ cup)
- 1 tbsp. all-purpose flour
- ¼ cup white wine
- 1 pound (455 g) Yukon Gold potatoes, peeled and cut into 1-inch chunks
- 1 cup clam juice
- 3 (6-ounce, 170 g) cans chopped clams, drained, liquid reserved
- 1 tsp. dried thyme leaves
- 1 bay leaf
- 2 tbsps. chopped fresh parsley or chives
- 1½ cups half-and-half

Directions:
1. Lock the Crisping Lid and select Air Crisp, adjust the temperature to 375°F and set the time to 2 minutes to preheat. Press Start.
2. Meanwhile, in a medium bowl, add the oyster crackers. Drizzle with the melted butter and sprinkle with the granulated garlic, Parmesan, and ½ teaspoon of kosher salt . Toss to coat the crackers. Then place them into the Crisp Basket.
3. After the pot is heated, open the Foodi's lid and insert the basket. Close the lid and select Air Crisp, adjust the temperature to 375°F and the cook time to 6 minutes. Press Start. After 3 minutes, open the lid and stir the crackers. Close the lid and continue cooking until crisp and lightly browned. Take the basket out and set aside to cool.
4. On the Foodi, preheat the pot by selecting Sear/Sauté. Press Start. Preheat for 5 minutes. In the pot, add the bacon, cook for about 5 minutes, until the bacon is crisp and the fat is rendered, turning once or twice. Transfer the bacon to a paper towel-lined plate to drain with tongs or a slotted spoon, and set aside. Leave the fat in the pot.
5. Add the celery and onion to the pot. Cook and stir for about 1 minute, until the vegetables begin to soften. Add the flour and stir to coat the vegetables. Add the wine and bring to a simmer. Cook for about 1 minute or until reduced by about one-third. Add the potatoes, clam juice, the reserved clam liquid , thyme, remaining ½ teaspoon of kosher salt , and bay leaf.
6. Lock the Pressure Lid into place, set the valve to Seal. Select Pressure, adjust the cook time to 4 minutes. Press Start.
7. When cooking is complete, naturally release the pressure for 5 minutes, then quick release any remaining pressure. Unlock and remove the Pressure Lid carefully.
8. Stir in half-and-half and the clams. Select Sear/Sauté. Press Start. Bring the soup to a simmer to heat the clams through. Remove the bay leaf. Ladle the soup into bowls and over the top crumble with the bacon. Garnish with a handful of crackers and the parsley, serving the remaining crackers on the side.

Basil Lemon Shrimp & Asparagus

Servings: 4
Cooking Time: 10 Minutes
Ingredients:
- 3 tbsp. water, divided
- 2 cloves garlic, chopped fine
- 2 tbsp. onion, chopped fine
- ½ tsp fresh ginger, grated
- ½ tsp salt
- ¼ tsp pepper
- ¼ tsp red pepper flakes
- 1 tbsp. fresh lemon juice
- 1 lb. asparagus, trimmed & cut in 1-inch pieces
- 1 lb. medium shrimp, peeled, deveined, tails removed
- 1 tsp lemon zest
- 3 tbsp. fresh basil, chopped

Directions:
1. Add 2 tablespoons water, garlic, and onion to the cooking pot and set to sauté on medium heat. Cook 1 minute, stirring.
2. Add remaining water, ginger, salt, pepper, red pepper flakes, lemon juice, and asparagus, stir to combine. Add the lid and cook 2-3 minutes until asparagus starts to turn bright green.
3. Add the shrimp and stir. Recover and cook another 3-5 minutes or until shrimp are pink and asparagus is fork-tender.
4. Stir in the lemon zest and basil and serve.

Nutrition:
- InfoCalories 110,Total Fat 1g,Total Carbs 7g,Protein 18g,Sodium 645mg.

Stuffed Cod

Servings: 4
Cooking Time: 40 Minutes
Ingredients:
- ½ cup bread crumbs
- 2 ½ tsp garlic powder, divided
- 1 ½ tsp onion powder, divided
- 1 tbsp. parsley
- ¼ cup parmesan cheese
- ½ tsp salt
- ½ lb. scallops, rinsed & dried
- 7 tbsp. butter, divided
- ½ lb. shrimp, peeled & deveined
- 1 tbsp. flour
- ¾ cup chicken broth, low sodium
- ½ tsp dill
- ½ cup sour cream
- ½ tbsp. lemon juice
- 4 cod filets, patted dry

Directions:
1. Set cooker to bake on 400°F. Place the rack in the cooking pot.
2. In a small bowl, combine bread crumbs, 2 teaspoons garlic powder, 1 teaspoon onion powder, parsley, parmesan cheese, and salt, mix well.
3. Place the scallops in a baking pan and pour 3 tablespoons melted butter over top. Add the bread crumb mixture, and with a spatula mix together so scallops are coated on all sides.
4. Cover with foil and place in the cooking pot. Add the tender-crisp lid and bake 10 minutes.

5. Uncover and add the shrimp and 3 tablespoons butter to the scallops, use the spatula again to coat the shrimp. Recover the dish and bake another 10 minutes. Remove from cooking pot and uncover to cool.

6. In a small saucepan over medium heat, melt the remaining tablespoon of butter. Add the flour and cook, whisking, for 1 minute.

7. Whisk in broth, remaining garlic and onion powder, and dill until combined. Bring mixture just to boil, whisking constantly, and cook until thickened, about 5 minutes. Remove from heat let cool 5 minutes before stirring in sour cream and lemon juice.

8. Pour the scallop mixture onto a cutting board and chop. Add it back to the baking dish.

9. Spoon stuffing mixture onto the wide end of the fish filets and fold in half. Secure with a toothpick. Place on a small baking sheet.

10. Spoon a small amount of the sauce over fish and place on the rack in the cooking pot. Set to bake on 375°F. Add the tender-crisp lid and cook 20 minutes. Transfer to serving plates and top with more sauce. Serve immediately.

Nutrition:
- InfoCalories 483,Total Fat 27g,Total Carbs 19g,Protein 41g,Sodium 1459mg.

Pistachio Crusted Mahi Mahi

Servings: 6
Cooking Time: 20 Minutes
Ingredients:
- Nonstick cooking spray
- 6 fresh Mahi Mahi filets
- 2 tbsp. fresh lemon juice
- ½ tsp nutmeg
- ¼ tsp pepper
- ¼ tsp salt
- ½ cup pistachio nuts, chopped
- 2 tbsp. butter, melted

Directions:
1. Place the rack in the cooking pot. Lightly spray a small baking sheet with cooking spray.
2. Place the fish on the prepared pan. Season with lemon juice and spices. Top with pistachios and drizzle melted butter over the tops.
3. Place the pan on the rack and add the tender-crisp lid. Set to bake on 350°F. Cook fish 15-20 minutes or until it flakes easily with a fork. Serve immediately.

Nutrition:
- InfoCalories 464,Total Fat 14g,Total Carbs 3g,Protein 77g,Sodium 405mg.

Cod Cornflakes Nuggets

Servings: 4
Cooking Time: 25 Min
Ingredients:
- 1 ¼ lb. cod fillets, cut into chunks /662.5g
- 1 egg
- 1 cup cornflakes /130g
- ½ cup flour /65g
- 1 tbsp olive oil/15ml
- 1 tbsp water /15ml
- Salt and pepper, to taste

Directions:
1. Add the oil and cornflakes in a food processor, and process until crumbed. Season the fish chunks with salt and pepper.
2. Beat the egg along with 1 tbsp or 15ml water. Dredge the chunks in flour first, then dip in the egg, and coat with cornflakes. Arrange on a lined sheet. Close the crisping lid and cook at 350 °F or 177°C for 15 minutes on Air Crisp mode.

Chapter 8: Poultry

Buttermilk-breaded Crispy Chicken

Servings:4
Cooking Time: 30 Minutes
Ingredients:
- 1½ pounds (680 g) boneless, skinless chicken breasts
- 1 to 2 cups buttermilk
- 2 large eggs
- ¾ cup all-purpose flour
- ¾ cup potato starch
- ½ teaspoon granulated garlic, divided
- 1 teaspoon salt, divided
- 2 teaspoons freshly ground black pepper, divided
- 1 cup bread crumbs
- ½ cup panko bread crumbs
- Olive oil or cooking spray

Directions:
1. In a large bowl, combine the chicken breasts and buttermilk, turning the chicken to coat. Cover the bowl with plastic wrap and refrigerate the chicken to soak at least 4 hours or overnight.
2. In a medium shallow bowl, whisk the eggs. In a second shallow bowl, stir together the flour, potato starch, ¼ teaspoon of granulated garlic, ½ teaspoon of salt, and 1 teaspoon of pepper. In a third shallow bowl, stir together the bread crumbs, panko, remaining ¼ teaspoon of granulated garlic, remaining ½ teaspoon of salt, and remaining 1 teaspoon of pepper.
3. Working one piece at a time, remove the chicken from the buttermilk, letting the excess drip into the bowl. Dredge the chicken in the flour mixture, coating well on both sides. Then dip the chicken in the eggs, coating both sides. Finally, dip the chicken in the bread crumb mixture, coating both sides and pressing the crumbs onto the chicken. Spritz both sides of the coated chicken pieces with olive oil.
4. Place the Cook & Crisp Basket into the unit.
5. Select AIR CRISP, set the temperature to 400ºF , and set the time to 30 minutes. Select START/STOP to begin and allow to preheat for 5 minutes.
6. Spritz both sides of the coated chicken pieces with olive oil. Working in batches as needed, place the chicken breasts in the Cook & Crisp Basket, ensuring the chicken pieces do not touch each other.
7. After 12 minutes, turn the chicken with a spatula so you don't tear the breading. Close the crisping lid and continue to cook, checking the chicken for an internal temperature of 165ºF .
8. When cooking is complete, transfer the chicken to a wire rack to cool.

Hearty Chicken Yum

Servings:4
Cooking Time: 40 Minutes
Ingredients:
- 2 tablespoons fresh boneless chicken thigh
- 3 tablespoons homemade ketchup
- 1 and ½ teaspoon salt
- 2 teaspoons garlic powder
- ¼ cup ghee
- ½ teaspoon ground black pepper
- 3 tablespoons organic tamari
- ¼ cup stevia

Directions:
1. Add the listed to your Ninja Foodi and give it a nice stir
2. Lock up the lid and cook for about 18 minutes under HIGH pressure
3. Quick release the pressure. Open the lid and transfer the chicken to a bowl
4. Shred it u using a fork
5. Set your pot to Saute mode and allow the liquid to be reduced for 5 minutes
6. Pour the sauce over your chicken Yum and serve with vegetables. Enjoy!

Your's Truly Lime Chicken Chili

Servings:6
Cooking Time: 23 Minutes
Ingredients:
- ¼ cup cooking wine (Keto-Friendly)
- ½ cup organic chicken broth
- 1 onion, diced
- 1 teaspoon salt
- ½ teaspoon paprika
- 5 garlic cloves, minced
- 1 tablespoon lime juice
- ¼ cup butter
- 2 pounds chicken thighs
- 1 teaspoon dried parsley
- 3 green chilies, chopped

Directions:
1. Set your Ninja-Foodi to Sauté mode and add onion and garlic
2. Sauté for 3 minutes, add remaining
3. Lock lid and cook on Medium-HIGH pressure for 20 minutes
4. Release pressure naturally over 10 minutes. Serve and enjoy!

Hassel Back Chicken

Servings: 4
Cooking Time: 60 Minutes
Ingredients:
- 4 tablespoons butter
- Black pepper and salt to taste
- 2 cups fresh mozzarella cheese, sliced
- 8 large chicken breasts
- 4 large Roma tomatoes, sliced

Directions:
1. Make few deep slits in chicken breasts, season with black pepper and salt.
2. Stuff mozzarella cheese slices and tomatoes in chicken slits.
3. Grease Ninja Foodi pot with butter and set stuffed chicken breasts.
4. Lock and secure the Ninja Foodi's lid and "Bake/Roast" for 1 hour at 365 °F.
5. Serve and enjoy.

Nutrition:
- InfoCalories: 278; Fat: 15g; Carbohydrates: 3.8g; Protein: 15g

Thyme Turkey Nuggets

Servings: 2
Cooking Time: 20 Min
Ingredients:
- 8 oz. turkey breast, boneless and skinless /240g
- 1 cup breadcrumbs /130g
- 1 egg, beaten
- 1 tbsp dried thyme /15g
- ½ tsp dried parsley /2.5g
- Salt and pepper, to taste

Directions:
1. Mince the turkey in a food processor. Transfer to a bowl. Stir in the thyme and parsley, and season with salt and pepper.
2. Take a nugget-sized piece of the turkey mixture and shape it into a ball, or another form. Dip it in the breadcrumbs, then egg, then in the breadcrumbs again. Place the nuggets onto a prepared baking dish. Close the crisping lid and cook for 10 minutes on Air Crisp mode at 350 °F or 177°C

Chicken Puttanesca

Servings:6
Cooking Time: 50 Minutes
Ingredients:
- 6 chicken thigh, skin on
- 2 tablespoons extra virgin olive oil
- 2 garlic cloves, crushed
- Salt and pepper to taste
- ½ teaspoon red chili flakes
- 14 and ½ ounces tomatoes, chopped
- 6 ounces black olives, pitted
- 1 tablespoon capers
- 1 tablespoon fresh basil, chopped
- ¾ cup of water

Directions:
1. Set your Ninja Foodi to Saute mode and add oil, allow the oil to heat up
2. Add chicken pieces and Saute for 5 minutes until browned, transfer the browned chicken to a platter
3. Add chopped tomatoes, olives, water, capers, garlic, chopped basil, salt, pepper, red chili flakes and stir well,

bring the mix to a simmer. Add the chicken pieces to your pot
4. Lock up the lid and cook on HIGH pressure for 12 minutes
5. Release the pressure naturally. Serve with a side of veggies if wanted, enjoy!

Spicy Chicken Tortilla Soup

Servings: 8
Cooking Time: 20 Minutes
Ingredients:
- 1 pound (455 g) boneless, skinless chicken breasts
- 1 (15-ounce (425 g)) can black beans, rinsed and drained
- 2 cups frozen corn
- 6 cups chicken broth
- 1 tbsp. extra-virgin olive oil
- 1 onion, chopped
- 1 (12-ounce (340 g)) jar salsa
- 4 ounces (113 g) tomato paste
- 1 tbsp. chili powder
- 2 tsps. cumin
- ½ tsp. freshly ground black pepper
- 1 pinch of cayenne pepper
- ½ tsp. sea salt
- Tortilla strips, for garnish

Directions:
1. Select the Saute mode to preheat for 5 minutes.
2. Combine the olive oil and onions in the pot. Cook 5 minutes, stirring occasionally.
3. Add chicken breast, chicken broth, salsa, tomato paste, chili powder, cumin, salt, pepper, and cayenne pepper to the pot. Assemble pressure lid, set the steamer valve to Seal.
4. Select Pressure, set time 10 minutes.
5. After cooking is complete, move pressure release valve to VENT to quickly release the pressure. Carefully remove lid.
6. Take chicken breasts out from pot and use two forks to shred them.
7. Add the black beans and corn. Select SEAR/SAUTÉ. Cook 5 minutes.
8. Add shredded chicken back to the pot. Decorate with tortilla strips before serving.

Honey Chicken & Veggies

Servings: 6
Cooking Time: 6 Hours
Ingredients:
- ½ cup honey
- 1/3 cup balsamic vinegar
- 3 tbsp. tomato paste
- ½ tsp salt
- ½ tsp pepper
- 3 cloves garlic, chopped fine
- 1 tsp ginger
- ¼ tsp red pepper flakes
- 6 chicken thighs
- 2 cups baby carrots
- 2 cups baby red potatoes, quartered
- 1 tbsp. fresh parsley, chopped

Directions:
1. In a small bowl, whisk together honey, vinegar, tomato paste, salt, pepper, garlic, ginger, and pepper flakes until combined.
2. Add chicken, carrots, and potatoes to the cooking pot.

3. Pour honey mixture over the top, reserving ½ cup. Toss gently to mix.
4. Add the lid and set to slow cook on low. Cook 6-8 hours until vegetables are tender and chicken is cooked through.
5. Pour remaining glaze over chicken and vegetables and serve garnished with parsley.

Nutrition:
- InfoCalories 299,Total Fat 13g,Total Carbs 34g,Protein 14g,Sodium 320mg.

Asian Chicken

Servings: 4
Cooking Time: 35 Min
Ingredients:
- 1 lb. chicken; cut in stripes /450g
- 1 large onion
- 3 green peppers; cut in stripes
- 2 tomatoes; cubed
- 1 pinch fresh and chopped coriander
- 1 pinch ginger
- 1 tbsp mustard /15g
- 1 tbsp cumin powder /15g
- 2 tbsp oil /30ml
- Salt and black pepper

Directions:
1. Heat the oil in a deep pan. Add in the mustard, onion, ginger, cumin and green chili peppers. Sauté the mixture for 2-3 minutes. Then, add the tomatoes, coriander, and salt and keep stirring.
2. Coat the chicken with oil, salt, and pepper and cook for 25 minutes on Air Crisp mode at 380 °F or 194°C. Remove from the Foodi and pour the sauce over and around.

Buttermilk Fried Chicken

Servings:4
Cooking Time: 30 Minutes
Ingredients:
- 1½ pounds boneless, skinless chicken breasts
- 1 to 2 cups buttermilk
- 2 large eggs
- ¾ cup all-purpose flour
- ¾ cup potato starch
- ½ teaspoon granulated garlic, divided
- 1 teaspoon salt, divided
- 2 teaspoons freshly ground black pepper, divided
- 1 cup bread crumbs
- ½ cup panko bread crumbs
- Olive oil or cooking spray

Directions:
1. In a large bowl, combine the chicken breasts and buttermilk, turning the chicken to coat. Cover the bowl with plastic wrap and refrigerate the chicken to soak at least 4 hours or overnight.
2. In a medium shallow bowl, whisk the eggs. In a second shallow bowl, stir together the flour, potato starch, ¼ teaspoon of granulated garlic, ½ teaspoon of salt, and 1 teaspoon of pepper. In a third shallow bowl, stir together the bread crumbs, panko, remaining ¼ teaspoon of granulated garlic, remaining ½ teaspoon of salt, and remaining 1 teaspoon of pepper.
3. Working one piece at a time, remove the chicken from the buttermilk, letting the excess drip into the bowl. Dredge the chicken in the flour mixture, coating well on both sides. Then dip the chicken in the eggs, coating both sides. Finally, dip the chicken in the bread crumb mixture, coating both sides and pressing the crumbs onto the chicken. Spritz both sides of the coated chicken pieces with olive oil.
4. Place the Cook & Crisp Basket into the unit.
5. Select AIR CRISP, set the temperature to 400°F, and set the time to 30 minutes. Select START/STOP to begin and allow to preheat for 5 minutes.
6. Spritz both sides of the coated chicken pieces with olive oil. Working in batches as needed, place the chicken breasts in the Cook & Crisp Basket, ensuring the chicken pieces do not touch each other.
7. After 12 minutes, turn the chicken with a spatula so you don't tear the breading. Close the crisping lid and continue to cook, checking the chicken for an internal temperature of 165°F.
8. When cooking is complete, transfer the chicken to a wire rack to cool.

Nutrition:
- InfoCalories: 574,Total Fat: 7g,Sodium: 995mg,Carbohydrates: 67g,Protein: 51g.

Bruschetta Chicken Meal

Servings: 4
Cooking Time: 9 Minutes
Ingredients:
- 2 tablespoons balsamic vinegar
- 1/3 cup olive oil
- 2 teaspoons garlic cloves, minced
- 1 teaspoon black pepper
- ½ teaspoon salt
- ½ cup sun-dried tomatoes, in olive oil
- 2 pounds chicken breasts, quartered, boneless
- 2 tablespoons fresh basil, chopped

Directions:
1. Take a bowl and whisk in vinegar, oil, garlic, pepper, salt
2. Fold in tomatoes, basil and add breast, mix well. Transfer to fridge and let it sit for 30 minutes
3. Add everything to Ninja Foodi and lock lid, cook on High Pressure for 9 minutes
4. Quick release pressure. Serve and enjoy!

Stuffed Whole Chicken

Servings: 6
Cooking Time: 8 Hours
Ingredients:
- 1 cup mozzarella cheese
- 4 whole garlic cloves, peeled
- 1 whole chicken 2 pounds, cleaned and pat dried
- Black pepper and salt, to taste
- 2 tablespoons fresh lemon juice

Directions:
1. Stuff the chicken cavity with garlic cloves and mozzarella cheese.
2. Season chicken generously with black pepper and salt.
3. Transfer chicken to your Ninja Foodi and drizzle lemon juice.
4. Lock and secure the Ninja Foodi's lid and set to "Slow Cooker" mode, let it cook on LOW for 8 hours.
5. Once done, serve and enjoy.

Nutrition:
- InfoCalories: 309; Fat: 12g; Carbohydrates: 1.6g; Protein: 45g

Baked Ranch Chicken And Bacon

Servings:6
Cooking Time: 30 Minutes
Ingredients:
- 1 pound (454 g) chicken breast, cut in 1-inch cubes
- 2 tablespoons extra-virgin olive oil
- 3 tablespoons ranch seasoning mix, divided
- 4 strips bacon, chopped
- 1 small onion, chopped
- 2 garlic cloves, minced
- 1 cup long-grain white rice
- 2 cups chicken broth
- ½ cup half-and-half
- 2 cups shredded Cheddar cheese, divided
- 2 tablespoons chopped fresh parsley

Directions:
1. Select SEAR/SAUTÉ and set to HI. Select START/STOP to begin. Let preheat for 5 minutes.
2. In a large bowl, toss the chicken with the olive oil and 2 tablespoons of ranch seasoning mix.
3. Add the bacon to the pot and cook, stirring frequently, for about 6 minutes, or until crispy. Using a slotted spoon, transfer the bacon to a paper towel-lined plate to drain.
4. Add the onion and cook for about 5 minutes. Add the garlic and cook for 1 minute more. Add the chicken and stir, cooking until chicken is cooked through, about 3 minutes.
5. Add the rice, chicken broth, and remaining ranch mix. Assemble pressure lid, making sure the pressure release valve is in the SEAL position.
6. Select PRESSURE and set to HI. Set time to 7 minutes. Select START/STOP to begin.
7. When complete, quick release the pressure by turning the valve to the VENT position. Carefully remove lid when unit has finished releasing pressure.
8. Stir in half-and-half and 1 cup of Cheddar cheese. Top with the remaining 1 cup of cheese. Close crisping lid.
9. Select BROIL and set time to 8 minutes. Select START/STOP to begin. When cooking is complete, serve garnished with fresh parsley.

Paprika Chicken

Servings: 4
Cooking Time: 5 Minutes
Ingredients:
- 4 chicken breasts, skin on
- Black pepper and salt, to taste
- 1 tablespoon olive oil
- ½ cup sweet onion, chopped
- ½ cup heavy whip cream
- 2 teaspoons smoked paprika
- ½ cup sour cream
- 2 tablespoons fresh parsley, chopped

Directions:
1. Season the four chicken breasts with black pepper and salt.
2. Select "Sauté" mode on your Ninja Foodi and add oil; let the oil heat up.
3. Add chicken and sear both sides until properly browned, should take about 15 minutes.
4. Remove chicken and transfer them to a plate.
5. Take a suitable skillet and place it over medium heat; stir in onion.
6. Sauté for 4 minutes until tender.
7. Stir in cream, paprika and bring the liquid to a simmer.
8. Return chicken to the skillet and alongside any juices.

9. Transfer the whole mixture to your Ninja Foodi and lock lid, cook on "HIGH" pressure for 5 minutes.
10. Release pressure naturally over 10 minutes.
11. Stir in sour cream, serve and enjoy.
Nutrition:
- InfoCalories: 389; Fat: 30g; Carbohydrates: 4g; Protein: 25g

Chicken With Sun Dried Pesto

Servings: 4
Cooking Time: 20 Minutes
Ingredients:
- 4 chicken breasts, boneless & skinless
- 5 sun-dried tomatoes
- ¼ cup fresh basil
- 2 tbsp. walnuts
- 1 ½ tbsp. olive oil
- 1 clove garlic
- 1/8 tsp salt
- 1/8 tsp pepper
- 1 tbsp. parmesan cheese

Directions:
1. Place the rack in the cooking pot. Spray a small baking sheet with cooking spray.
2. Place remaining ingredients, except parmesan, in a food processor or blender and pulse until thoroughly mixed.
3. Place chicken on prepared pan and spread pesto evenly over the top. Place on the rack and add the tender-crisp lid. Set to roast on 350°F. Cook chicken 20-25 minutes until cooked through. Sprinkle with parmesan cheese and serve.
Nutrition:
- InfoCalories 235,Total Fat 12g,Total Carbs 2g,Protein 30g,Sodium 352mg.

Creamy Turkey And Mushroom Ragu

Servings:4
Cooking Time: 40 Minutes
Ingredients:
- 2 tablespoons unsalted butter
- 1 pound ground turkey
- 8 ounces cremini mushrooms, sliced
- 1 can condensed cream of celery soup
- 4 cups chicken stock
- 1 package egg noodles
- 16 ounces frozen peas
- 1 cup sour cream
- ¾ cup grated Parmesan cheese
- Kosher salt
- Freshly ground black pepper

Directions:
1. Select SEAR/SAUTÉ and set to MED. Press START/STOP to begin. Let preheat for 3 minutes.
2. Add the butter, ground turkey, and mushrooms. Using a silicone-tipped utensil, break up the turkey as it browns, about 10 minutes.
3. Add the condensed soup and stock. Whisk well to combine. Bring to a simmer for 15 minutes.
4. Add the egg noodles and peas and stir well. Cook until the noodles are tender and cooked through, 8 to 10 minutes.
5. Select START/STOP to stop cooking. Stir in sour cream and Parmesan cheese until melted and incorporated. Season with salt and pepper. Serve immediately.
Nutrition:
- InfoCalories: 854,Total Fat: 39g,Sodium: 1714mg,Carbohydrates: 79g,Protein: 48g.

Bacon & Cranberry Stuffed Turkey Breast

Servings: 4
Cooking Time: 1 Hour
Ingredients:
- ¼ oz. porcini mushrooms, dried
- 1 slice bacon, thick cut, chopped
- ¼ cup shallot, chopped fine
- 2 tbsp. cranberries, dried, chopped
- 1 tsp fresh sage, chopped fine
- ½ cup bread crumbs
- 1 tbsp. fresh parsley, chopped
- 3 tbsp. chicken broth, low sodium
- 2 lb. turkey breast, boneless
- 2 tbsp. butter, soft
- ½ tsp salt

Directions:
1. In a small bowl, add the mushrooms and enough hot water to cover them. Let sit 15 minutes, then drain and chop them.
2. Set the cooker to sauté on medium heat. Add the bacon and cook until crisp. Transfer to a paper-towel lined plate.
3. Add the shallots and cook until they start to brown, about 3-5 minutes. Add the cranberries, sage, and mushrooms and cook, stirring frequently, 2-3 minutes.
4. Stir in bread crumbs, parsley, bacon, and broth and mix well. Transfer to a bowl to cool.
5. Remove the skin from the turkey, in one piece, do not discard. Butterfly the turkey breast and place between 2 sheets of plastic wrap. Pound out to ¼-inch thick.
6. Spread the stuffing over the turkey, leaving a ¾-inch border. Start with a short end and roll up the turkey. Wrap the skin back around the roll.
7. Use butcher string to tie the turkey. Place in the cooking pot and rub with butter. Sprinkle with salt.
8. Add the tender-crisp lid and set to roast on 400°F. Cook 20 minutes, then decrease the heat to 325°F. Cook another 10-15 minutes or until juices run clear. Let rest 10 minutes before slicing and serving.

Nutrition:
- InfoCalories 159,Total Fat 7g,Total Carbs 3g,Protein 19g,Sodium 120mg.

Blackened Turkey Cutlets

Servings: 4
Cooking Time: 5 Minutes
Ingredients:
- Nonstick cooking spray
- 2 tsp paprika
- 1 tsp thyme
- ½ tsp sugar
- ½ tsp onion powder
- ½ tsp garlic powder
- ½ tsp salt
- ½ tsp pepper
- ¼ tsp cayenne pepper
- 4 turkey breast cutlets, boneless & skinless

Directions:
1. Spray the fryer basket with cooking spray.
2. In a small bowl, combine everything but the turkey and mix well. Rub both sides of the cutlets with the seasoning mixture and place in the basket.

3. Add the tender-crisp lid and set to air fry on 350°F. Cook 4-5 minutes per side or until turkey is cooked through. Serve immediately.

Nutrition:
- InfoCalories 134,Total Fat 2g,Total Carbs 1g,Protein 27g,Sodium 419mg.

Turkey & Cabbage Enchiladas

Servings: 4
Cooking Time: 30 Minutes
Ingredients:
- Nonstick cooking spray
- 8 large cabbage leaves
- 1 tbsp. olive oil
- ½ cup onion, chopped
- ½ red bell pepper, chopped
- 3 cloves garlic, chopped fine
- 2 tsp cumin
- 1 tbsp. chili powder
- 1 tsp salt
- ¼ tsp crushed red pepper flakes
- 2 cups turkey, cooked & shredded
- 1 cup enchilada sauce, sugar free
- ½ cup cheddar cheese, fat free, grated

Directions:
1. Spray a small baking dish with cooking spray.
2. Bring a large pot of water to boil. Add cabbage leaves and cook 30 seconds. Transfer leaves to paper towel lined surface and pat dry.
3. Add the oil to the cooking pot and set to sauté on medium heat.
4. Add the onion, bell pepper, and garlic and cook, stirring occasionally, until onions are translucent, about 5 minutes.
5. Stir in cumin, chili powder, salt, red pepper flakes, and turkey. Cook just until heat through. Transfer mixture to a bowl.
6. Add the rack to the cooking pot.
7. Lay cabbage leaves on work surface. Divide turkey mixture evenly between leaves. Fold in the sides and roll up. Place in the prepared dish, seam side down. Pour the enchilada sauce over the top and sprinkle with cheese.
8. Place dish on the rack and add the tender-crisp lid. Set to bake on 400°F. Cook enchiladas 15-20 minutes until cheese is melted and bubbly. Let rest 5 minutes before serving.

Nutrition:
- InfoCalories 289,Total Fat 12g,Total Carbs 4g,Protein 32g,Sodium 735mg.

Keto-friendly Chicken Tortilla

Servings:4
Cooking Time: 15 Minutes
Ingredients:
- 1 tablespoon avocado oil
- 1 pound pastured organic boneless chicken breasts
- ½ cup of orange juice
- 2 teaspoons gluten-free Worcestershire sauce
- 1 teaspoon garlic powder
- 1 teaspoon salt
- ½ teaspoon chili powder
- ½ teaspoon paprika

Directions:

1. Set your Ninja Foodi to Sauté mode and add oil, let the oil heat up
2. Add chicken on top, take a bowl and add remaining mix well
3. Pour the mixture over chicken. Lock lid and cook on HIGH pressure for 15 minutes
4. Release pressure naturally over 10 minutes
5. Shred the chicken and serve over salad green shells such as cabbage or lettuce. Enjoy!

The Original Mexican Chicken Cacciatore

Servings:4
Cooking Time: 33 Minutes
Ingredients:
- Extra virgin olive oil'
- 3 shallots, chopped
- 4 garlic cloves, crushed
- 1 green bell pepper, sliced
- ½ cup organic chicken broth
- 10 ounces mushrooms, sliced
- 5-6 skinless chicken breasts
- 2 cans (14.5 ounces organic crushed tomatoes
- 2 tablespoons organic tomato paste
- 1 can (14.5 ounces black olives, pitted
- Fresh parsley
- Salt and pepper to taste

Directions:
1. Add oil to your pot and set the Ninja Foodi to Saute mode
2. Add shallots, bell pepper and cook for 2 minutes
3. Add broth and bring to a boil for 23 minutes. Add garlic and mushrooms
4. Gently place the chicken on the top of the whole mixture
5. Cover the chicken with tomato paste and crushed tomatoes
6. Lock up the lid and cook on HIGH pressure for 8 minutes
7. Release the pressure naturally over 10 minutes and stir in parsley, olive oil, pepper, salt, and red pepper flakes. Serve!

Turkey Meatballs

Servings: 4
Cooking Time: 4 Minutes
Ingredients:
- 1-pound ground turkey
- 1 cup onion, shredded
- 1/4 cup heavy whip cream
- 2 teaspoon salt
- 1 cup carrots, shredded
- 1/2 teaspoon ground caraway seeds
- 1 and 1/2 teaspoons black pepper
- 1/4 teaspoon ground allspice
- 1 cup almond meal
- 1/2 cup almond milk
- 2 tablespoons unsalted butter

Directions:
1. Transfer meat to a suitable.
2. Add cream, almond meal, onion, carrot, 1 teaspoon salt, caraway, 1/2 teaspoon pepper, allspice, and mix well.
3. Refrigerate the mixture for 30 minutes.

4. Once the mixture is cooled, use your hands to scoop the mixture into meatballs.
5. Place the turkey balls in your Ninja Foodi pot.
6. Add milk, pats of butter and sprinkle 1 teaspoon salt, 1 teaspoon black pepper.
7. Lock and secure the Ninja Foodi's lid, then cook on "HIGH" pressure for 4 minutes.
8. Quick-release pressure.
9. Unlock and secure the Ninja Foodi's lid and serve.
10. Enjoy.
Nutrition:
- InfoCalories: 338; Fat: 23g; Carbohydrates: 7g; Protein: 23g

Chicken And Broccoli Platter

Servings:4
Cooking Time: 15 Minutes
Ingredients:
- 1 tablespoon olive oil
- 1 tablespoon butter
- 2 large chicken breasts, boneless
- ½ cup onion, chopped
- 14 ounces chicken broth
- ½ teaspoon salt
- ½ teaspoon pepper
- 1/8 teaspoon red pepper flakes
- 1 tablespoon parsley
- 1 tablespoon arrowroot
- 2 tablespoons water
- 4 ounces light cream cheese, cubed
- 1 cup cheddar cheese, shredded
- 3 cups steamed broccoli, chopped

Directions:
1. Season the chicken breast with pepper and salt
2. Set your Ninja Foodi to Saute mode and add butter and vegetable oil
3. Allow it to melt and transfer the seasoned chicken to the pot. Allow it to brown
4. Remove the chicken and add the onions to the pot, Saute them for 5 minutes
5. Add chicken broth, pepper, red pepper and salt, parsley. Add the browned breast
6. Lock up the lid and cook for about 5 minutes at high pressure
7. Once done, quick release the pressure. Remove the chicken and shred it up into small portions
8. Take a bowl and add 2 tablespoons of water and dissolve cornstarch |
9. Select the simmer mode and add the mixture to the Ninja Foodi
10. Toss in the cubed and shredded cheese. Stir completely until everything is melted
11. Toss in the diced chicken again and the steamed broccoli and cook for 5 minutes
12. Once done, sever with white rice and shredded cheese as garnish

Hot And Spicy Paprika Chicken

Servings: 4
Cooking Time: 20-25 Minutes
Ingredients:
- 4 piece (4 ounces each) chicken breast, skin on
- Salt and pepper to taste
- ½ cup sweet onion, chopped

- ½ cup heavy whip cream
- 2 teaspoons smoked paprika
- ½ cup sour cream
- 2 tablespoons fresh parsley, chopped

Directions:
1. Season chicken with salt and pepper
2. Set your Foodi to Saute mode and add oil, let it heat up
3. Add chicken and sear both sides until nicely browned. Should take around 15 minutes
4. Remove chicken and transfer to a plate
5. Take a skillet and place it over medium heat, add onion and Sauté for 4 minutes
6. Stir in cream, paprika, bring the liquid to simmer. Return chicken to skillet and warm
7. Transfer the whole mixture to your Foodi and lock lid, cook on HIGH pressure for 5 minutes
8. Release pressure naturally over 10 minutes. Stir in cream, serve and enjoy!

Chicken Breasts

Servings: 4
Cooking Time: 15 Min
Ingredients:
- 4 boneless; skinless chicken breasts
- 1/4 cup dry white wine /62.5ml
- 1 cup water /250ml
- ½ tsp marjoram /2.5g
- ½ tsp sage /2.5g
- ½ tsp rosemary /2.5g
- ½ tsp mint /2.5g
- ½ tsp salt /2.5g

Directions:
1. Sprinkle salt over the chicken and set in the pot of the Foodi. Mix in mint, rosemary, marjoram, and sage. Pour wine and water around the chicken.
2. Seal the pressure lid, choose Pressure, set to High, and set the timer to 6 minutes. Press Start. Release the pressure naturally for 10 minutes.

Pesto Stuffed Chicken With Green Beans.

Servings: 4
Cooking Time: 20 Min
Ingredients:
- 4 chicken breasts
- ¼ cup dry white wine /62.5ml
- 1 cup green beans, trimmed and cut into 1-inch pieces /130g
- ¾ cup chicken stock /188ml
- 1 tbsp butter /15g
- 1 tbsp olive oil /15ml
- 1 tsp salt /5g
- For pesto:
- ¼ cup Parmesan cheese /32.5g
- ¼ cup extra virgin olive oil /62.5ml
- 1 cup fresh basil /130g
- 1 garlic clove, smashed
- 2 tbsp pine nuts /30g

Directions:
1. First make the pesto: in a bowl, mix fresh basil, pine nuts, garlic, salt, pepper and Parmesan and place in food processor. Add in oil and process until the desired consistency is attained. Adjust seasoning.
2. Apply a thin layer of pesto to one side of each chicken breast; tightly roll into a cylinder and fasten closed with small skewers. Press Sear/Sauté. Add oil and butter. Cook chicken rolls for 1 to 2 minutes per side until browned.
3. Add in wine cook until the wine has evaporated, about 3-4 minutes. Add stock and salt into the pot. Top the chicken with green beans.
4. Seal the pressure lid, choose Pressure, set to High, and set the timer to 5 minutes. Press Start. When ready, release the pressure quickly. Serve chicken rolls with cooking liquid and green beans.

The Great Hainanese Chicken

Servings: 4
Cooking Time: 4 Hours
Ingredients:
- 1 ounces ginger, peeled
- 6 garlic cloves, crushed
- 6 bundles cilantro/basil leaves
- 1 teaspoon salt
- 1 tablespoon sesame oil
- 3 (1 and ½ pounds each) chicken meat, ready to cook
- For Dip
- 2 tablespoons ginger, minced
- 1 teaspoon garlic, minced
- 1 tablespoon chicken stock
- 1 teaspoon sesame oil
- ½ teaspoon sugar
- Salt to taste

Directions:
1. Add chicken, garlic, ginger, leaves, and salt in your Ninja Food
2. Add enough water to fully submerge chicken, lock lid cook on SLOW COOK mode on LOW for 4 hours. Release pressure naturally
3. Take chicken out of pot and chill for 10 minutes
4. Take a bowl and add all the dipping and blend well in a food processor
5. Take chicken out of ice bath and drain, chop into serving pieces. Arrange onto a serving platter
6. Brush chicken with sesame oil. Serve with ginger dip. Enjoy!

Hungry Man's Indian Chicken Keema

Servings:6
Cooking Time: 10 Minutes
Ingredients:
- 1 tablespoon coconut oil
- 1 teaspoon cumin seeds
- ½ teaspoon turmeric
- 1 tablespoon garlic, grated
- 1 tablespoon ginger, grated
- 1 large onion, diced
- 2 tomatoes, diced
- 2 teaspoons mild red chili powder
- 1 teaspoon Garam masala
- 1 teaspoon salt
- 2 tablespoons coriander powder
- 1 pound ground chicken
- ½ cup cilantro

Directions:
1. Set your Ninja Foodi to Saute mode and add cumin seeds
2. Toast for 30 seconds. Add turmeric powder and give it a nice mix

3.   Add garlic, ginger and mix well again. Add onion and Saute for 2 minutes
4.   Add tomatoes, Garam Masala, red chili powder, coriander, salt and mix well
5.   Add ground chicken and keep Sautéing it while breaking it up with a spatula
6.   Add ½ a cup of water . Lock up the lid and cook on HIGH pressure for 4 minutes
7.   Release the pressure naturally over 10 minutes
8.   Garnish with a bit of cilantro and serve . Enjoy!

Chicken And Peas Casserole With Cheese

Servings: 4
Cooking Time: 30 Minutes
Ingredients:
- 2 pounds (907 g) chicken breast, skinless, boneless and cubed
- 1 cup (250 mL) veggie stock
- 1 cup (250 mL) peas
- 1 tablespoon Italian seasoning
- 1 tablespoon sweet paprika
- A pinch of salt and black pepper
- 1 cup (250 mL) coconut cream
- 1 cup (250 mL) shredded Cheddar cheese

Directions:
1.   Stir together the chicken cubes, veggie stock, peas, Italian seasoning, paprika, salt, and pepper in the cooking pot. Pour the coconut cream over top.
2.   Assemble pressure lid, making sure the pressure release valve is in the Seal position. Select Pressure and set to high . Set time to 20 minutes. Press Start to begin.
3.   Once cooking is complete, do a quick pressure release. Remove the lid.
4.   Scatter the shredded cheese all over. Put the lid back on and cook on High Pressure for an additional 10 minutes.
5.   Once cooking is complete, do a quick pressure release. Carefully open the lid.
6.   Serve warm.

Shredded Chicken Salsa

Servings: 4
Cooking Time: 20 Minutes
Ingredients:
- 1-pound chicken breast, boneless
- ¾ teaspoon cumin
- ½ teaspoon salt
- Pinch of oregano
- Pepper to taste
- 1 cup chunky salsa

Directions:
1.   Season chicken with spices and add to Ninja Foodi.
2.   Cover with salsa and lock lid, cook on "HIGH" pressure for 20 minutes.
3.   Quick-release pressure.
4.   Add chicken to a platter and shred the chicken.
5.   Serve and enjoy.
Nutrition:
- InfoCalories: 125; Fat: 3g; Carbohydrates: 2g; Protein: 22g

Heartfelt Chicken Curry Soup

Servings:4
Cooking Time: 10 Minutes
Ingredients:

- 1 teaspoon Garam Masala
- ½ teaspoon cayenne
- ½ teaspoon ground turmeric
- 1 teaspoon salt
- 4 ounces baby spinach
- 1 cup mushrooms, sliced
- 1 (2-inch piece) ginger, finely chopped
- 3-4 garlic cloves, crushed
- ½ onion, diced
- 1 and ½ cups unsweetened coconut milk
- 1 pound boneless, skinless chicken thighs
- ¼ cup chopped fresh cilantro

Directions:
1.   Add chicken, coconut milk, onion, garlic, ginger, mushrooms, spinach, salt, turmeric, cayenne, garam masala and cilantro to the inner pot of your Ninja Foodi
2.   Lock lid and cook on HIGH pressure for 10 minutes
3.   Release pressure naturally over 10 minutes. Use tongs to transfer chicken to a plate, shred it
4.   Stir chicken back to the soup and stir. Enjoy!

Skinny Chicken & Dumplings

Servings: 6
Cooking Time: 4 Hours 30 Minutes
Ingredients:
- 6 cups chicken broth, low sodium
- 2 chicken breast, boneless & skinless
- ½ cup peas, frozen
- ½ cup carrots, chopped fine
- 1 onion, chopped fine
- ½ cup celery, chopped fine
- 3 cloves garlic, chopped fine
- 2 tsp thyme
- 2 tsp basil
- 1 tsp sage
- 1 cup whole wheat flour
- 1 tsp baking powder
- ½ tsp garlic powder
- ½ tsp onion powder
- 3 tbsp. butter, cubed
- 1/3 cup skim milk

Directions:
1.   Add the broth, chicken, peas, carrots, onion, celery, garlic, thyme, basil, and sage in the cooking pot, stir to mix.
2.   Add the lid and set to slow cook on high. Cook 4 hours, stirring occasionally.
3.   In a large bowl, flour, baking powder, garlic powder, and onion powder. Cut in butter with a pastry blender until mixture resembles fine crumbs.
4.   Slowly add the milk until a thick, sticky batter forms.
5.   Transfer the chicken to a cutting board and shred. Return it to the pot. Drop the dumpling batter by tablespoons into the pot. Recover and cook 20-30 minutes or until dumplings are cooked. Serve immediately.
Nutrition:
- InfoCalories 297,Total Fat 10g,Total Carbs 23g,Protein 20g,Sodium 194mg.

Chicken With Rice And Peas

Servings: 4
Cooking Time: 30 Min
Ingredients:
- 4 boneless; skinless chicken breasts; sliced

- 1 onion; chopped
- 1 celery stalk; diced
- 1 garlic clove; minced
- 2 cups chicken broth; divided /500ml
- 1 cup long grain rice /130g
- 1 cup frozen green peas /130g
- 1 tbsp oil olive /15ml
- 1 tbsp tomato puree /15ml
- ½ tsp paprika /2.5g
- ¼ tsp dried oregano/1.25g
- ¼ tsp dried thyme /1.25g
- ⅛ tsp cayenne pepper /0.625g
- ⅛ tsp ground white pepper /0.625g
- Salt to taste

Directions:

1. Season chicken with garlic powder, oregano, white pepper, thyme, paprika, cayenne pepper, and salt. Warm the oil on Sear/Sauté. Add in onion and cook for 4 minutes until fragrant. Mix in tomato puree to coat.
2. Add ¼ cup or 65ml chicken stock into the Foodi to deglaze the pan, scrape the pan's bottom to get rid of browned bits of food. Mix in celery, rice, and the seasoned chicken. Add in the remaining broth to the chicken mixture.
3. Seal the pressure lid, choose Pressure, set to High, and set the timer to 8 minutes. Press Start. Once ready, do a quick release. Mix in green peas, cover with the lid and let sit for 5 minutes. Serve warm.

Garlic Turkey Breasts

Servings: 4
Cooking Time: 17 Minutes
Ingredients:

- ½ teaspoon garlic powder
- 4 tablespoons butter
- ¼ teaspoon dried oregano
- 1-pound turkey breasts, boneless
- 1 teaspoon pepper
- ½ teaspoon salt
- ¼ teaspoon dried basil

Directions:

1. Season turkey on both sides generously with garlic, dried oregano, dried basil, black pepper and salt.
2. Select "Sauté" mode on your Ninja Foodi and stir in butter; let the butter melt.
3. Add turkey breasts and sauté for 2 minutes on each side.
4. Lock the lid and select the "Bake/Roast" setting; bake for 15 minutes at 355 °F.
5. Serve and enjoy once done.

Nutrition:

- InfoCalories: 223; Fat: 13g; Carbohydrates: 5g; Protein: 19g

Chinese Flavor Spicy Chicken With Cashew

Servings:4
Cooking Time: 13 Minutes
Ingredients:

- 1 pound (454 g) chicken breast, cut into ½-inch pieces
- 4 tablespoons stir-fry sauce, divided
- 3 tablespoons canola oil
- 12 arbol chiles
- 1 teaspoon Sichuan peppercorns
- 2 teaspoons grated fresh ginger

- 2 garlic cloves, minced
- ¾ cup cashews
- 6 scallions, cut into 1-inch pieces
- 2 teaspoons dark soy sauce
- ½ teaspoon sesame oil

Directions:

1. Place the chicken in a zip-top bag and add 2 tablespoons of stir-fry sauce. Let marinate for 4 hours, or overnight.
2. Select SEAR/SAUTÉ and set to HI. Select START/STOP to begin. Let preheat for 5 minutes.
3. Add the oil, chiles, peppercorns, ginger, and garlic and cook for 1 minute.
4. Add half the chicken and cook for 2 minutes, stirring occasionally. Transfer the chicken to a plate and set aside. Add the remaining chicken and cook for 2 minutes, stirring occasionally. Return the first batch of chicken to the pot and add the cashews. Cook for 2 minutes, stirring occasionally.
5. Add the scallions, soy sauce, sesame oil, and remaining 2 tablespoons of stir-fry sauce to pot and cook for 1 minute, stirring frequently.
6. When cooking is complete, serve immediately over steamed rice, if desired.

Easy Chicken Coq Au Vin

Servings: 4
Cooking Time: 50 Minutes
Ingredients:

- 4 chicken leg quarters, skin on
- 1½ tsps. kosher salt (or ¾ tsp. fine salt), divided
- 2 bacon slices, cut into thirds
- ¼ cup sliced onion
- 1¼ cups dry red wine, divided
- 1½ tsps. tomato paste
- ⅓ cup Chicken Stock, or store-bought low-sodium chicken broth
- ½ tsp. brown sugar
- Freshly ground black pepper
- ¾ cup frozen pearl onions, thawed and drained
- ½ cup Sautéed Mushrooms

Directions:

1. Sprinkle on both sides of the chicken quarters with 1 teaspoon of kosher salt and set aside on a wire rack.
2. On your Foodi, preheat the inner pot by selecting Sear/Sauté. Press Start. Preheat for 5 minutes. Place the bacon in the pot in a single layer and cook it for 3 to 4 minutes or until browned on the first side. Turn and brown the other side. Transfer the bacon to a paper towel-lined plate with tongs, and drain well, leaving the fat in the pot.
3. Place the chicken quarters to the pot, skin-side down. Cook for 5 minutes or until the skin is golden brown and some of the fat under the skin has rendered out, undisturbed. Turn the quarters to the other side and cook for about 2 minutes or until that side is a light golden brown. Transfer the chicken to a plate.
4. Carefully pour off almost all the fat, leaving just enough to cover the bottom of the pot with a thick coat . Stir in the sliced onion to the pot. Cook until the onion begins to brown, about 3 minutes, stirring. Add ½ cup of wine and scrape the bottom of the pan to release any browned bits. Boil the mixture for 2 minutes, until the wine reduces by about one-third in volume. Add the remaining ¾ cup of wine, the tomato paste, chicken stock, brown sugar, and a few grinds of pepper. Bring the sauce to a boil and

cook for about 1 minute, stirring to make sure the tomato paste is incorporated. Add the chicken pieces, skin-side up, to the pot.
5.   Lock the Pressure Lid into place, set the steamer valve to Seal. Select Pressure, adjust the cook time to 12 minutes. Press Start.
6.   When the cooking is complete, naturally release the pressure for 8 minutes, then quick release any remaining pressure. Open and remove the Pressure Lid carefully.
7.   Take the chicken pieces out from the pot. Strain the sauce into a fat separator and allow the sauce to sit for 5 minutes, until the fat rises to the surface.
8.   Return the sauce into the pot and stir in the pearl onions and mushrooms. On top of the sauce, place with the chicken, skin-side up.
9.   Close the Crisping Lid and select Broil. Adjust the cook time to 7 minutes. Press Start.
10.   After cooking, open the lid and transfer the chicken to a serving platter. Spoon the sauce around the chicken along with the pearl onions and mushrooms, and top with the reserved bacon crumbled and serve.

Jerk Chicken With Sweet Mash
Servings:6
Cooking Time: 20 Minutes
Ingredients:
- 4 boneless, skin-on chicken thighs
- ½ cup spicy jerk marinade
- 3 large sweet potatoes, peeled and cut into 1-inch cubes
- ½ cup unsweetened full-fat coconut milk
- Kosher salt
- Freshly ground black pepper
- 2 bananas, peeled and quartered
- 2 tablespoons agave nectar

Directions:
1.   Place the chicken thighs and jerk marinade in a container, rubbing the marinade all over the chicken. Cover the container with plastic wrap and marinate 15 minutes.
2.   Place the sweet potatoes, coconut milk, salt, and pepper in the pot. Place Reversible Rack in pot, making sure it is in the higher position. Place the chicken skin-side up on the rack, leaving space between the pieces. Assemble pressure lid, making sure the pressure release valve is in the SEAL position.
3.   Select PRESSURE and set to HI. Set time to 4 minutes. Select START/STOP to begin.
4.   When pressure cooking is complete, quick release the pressure by turning the pressure release valve to the VENT position. Carefully remove lid when unit has finished releasing pressure.
5.   Place the bananas in the spaces between chicken thighs. Close crisping lid.
6.   Select BROIL and set time to 15 minutes. Select START/STOP to begin.
7.   After 10 minutes, remove the bananas and set aside. Turn over the chicken thighs. Close lid and continue cooking.
8.   When cooking is complete, remove rack and chicken and let rest 5 to 10 minutes. Add the roasted bananas and agave nectar and mash them along with the sweet potatoes. Once rested, serve the chicken and sweet potato and banana mash.

Taiwanese Chicken Delight
Servings: 4

Cooking Time: 10 Minutes
Ingredients:
- 6 dried red chilis
- ¼ cup sesame oil
- 2 tablespoons ginger
- ¼ cup garlic, minced
- ¼ cup red wine vinegar
- ¼ cup coconut aminos
- Salt as needed
- 1.2 teaspoon xanthan gum (for the finish)
- ¼ cup Thai basil, chopped

Directions:
1.   Set your Ninja Foodi to Saute mode and add ginger, chilis, garlic and Saute for 2 minutes
2.   Add remaining . Lock lid and cook on HIGH pressure for 10 minutes
3.   Quick release pressure. Serve and enjoy!

Bacon Lime Chicken
Servings: 4
Cooking Time: 30 Minutes
Ingredients:
- 8 chicken thighs, boneless & skinless
- 1 tsp salt
- 2 tsp honey
- 1 tsp granulated garlic
- 1 tsp granulated onion
- ½ tsp pepper
- 2 tsp lime juice
- ¼ tsp cayenne pepper
- 8 slices bacon

Directions:
1.   Place the chicken and seasonings in a large bowl. Use your hands to mix and rub the seasonings into the meat until chicken is evenly coated.
2.   Roll the chicken along the long side and wrap each with a slice of bacon.
3.   Place chicken in the fryer basket, with bacon ends on the bottom. Add the tender-crisp lid and set to air fry on 400°F. Cook chicken 25-30 minutes, turning over halfway through cooking time. Serve hot.

Nutrition:
- InfoCalories 371,Total Fat 23g,Total Carbs 6g,Protein 32g,Sodium 878mg.

Moringa Chicken Soup
Servings: 8
Cooking Time: 18 Minutes
Ingredients:
- 1½ pounds (680 g) chicken breasts
- 5 cups (1.25 L) water
- 1 cup (250 mL) chopped tomatoes
- 2 cloves garlic, minced
- 1 onion, chopped
- 1 thumb-size ginger
- Salt and pepper, to taste
- 2 cups (500 mL) moringa leaves or kale leaves

Directions:
1.   Combine all the ingredients except the moringa leaves in the cooking pot.
2.   Assemble pressure lid, making sure the pressure release valve is in the Seal position. Select Pressure and set to high . Set time to 15 minutes. Press Start to begin.

3. Once cooking is complete, do a natural pressure release for 10 minutes, then release any remaining pressure. Carefully open the lid.
4. Press the Sauté button and stir in the moringa leaves. Allow to simmer for 3 minutes until softened.
5. Divide into bowls and serve warm.

Cheesy Chipotle Chicken
Servings: 6
Cooking Time: 35 Minutes
Ingredients:
- 15 oz. fire roasted tomatoes
- ¼ cup red onion, chopped
- 1 clove garlic
- ½ cup cilantro, chopped, packed
- 2 chipotle chili peppers in adobo sauce
- 1 tsp adobo sauce
- 1 tsp fresh lime juice
- 1 tsp salt
- 1 ½ lbs. chicken, cut in 3-inch pieces
- 1 cup Monterey Jack cheese, grated

Directions:
1. Add the tomatoes, onion, garlic, cilantro, chipotle peppers, lime juice, and salt to a food processor or blender. Pulse until vegetables are chopped but not until the salsa is smooth.
2. Place the chicken in the cooking pot. Pour the salsa over the tops. Turn the chicken to coat with salsa on all sides.
3. Add the tender-crisp lid and set to bake on 350°F. Bake 25 minutes. Remove the lid and sprinkle the cheese over the top.
4. Recover and bake another 10 minutes or until chicken is cooked through and cheese is melted and starting to brown. Serve.

Nutrition:
- InfoCalories 92,Total Fat 4g,Total Carbs 2g,Protein 12g,Sodium 342mg.

Chicken And Sweet Potato Corn Chowder
Servings: 8
Cooking Time: 40 Min
Ingredients:
- 4 boneless; skinless chicken breast; diced
- 19 ounces corn kernels, frozen /570g
- 1 sweet potato, peeled and cubed
- 4 ounces canned diced green chiles, drained /120g
- 3 garlic cloves; minced
- 2 cups cheddar cheese, shredded /260g
- 2 cups creme fraiche /500ml
- 1 cup chicken stock /250ml
- Cilantro leaves; chopped
- 2 tsp chili powder /10g
- 1 tsp ground cumin /5g
- Salt and black pepper to taste

Directions:
1. Mix chicken, corn, chili powder, cumin, chicken stock, sweet potato, green chiles, and garlic in the pot of the Foodi. Seal the pressure lid, choose Pressure, set to High, and set the timer to 10 minutes. Press Start.
2. When ready, release the pressure quickly. Set the chicken to a cutting board and use two forks to shred it. Return to pot and stir well into the liquid.

3. Stir in cheese and creme fraiche; season with pepper and salt. Cook for 2 to 3 minutes until cheese is melted. Place chowder into plates and top with cilantro.

Complex Garlic And Lemon Chicken
Servings:6
Cooking Time: 30 Minutes
Ingredients:
- 1-2 pounds chicken breast
- 1 teaspoon salt
- 1 onion, diced
- 1 tablespoon ghee
- 5 garlic cloves, minced
- ½ cup organic chicken broth
- 1 teaspoon dried parsley
- 1 large lemon juice
- 3-4 teaspoon arrowroot flour

Directions:
1. Set your Ninja Foodi to Saute mode. Add diced up onion and cooking fat
2. Allow the onions to cook for 5 -10 minutes
3. Add the rest of the except arrowroot flour
4. Lock up the lid and set the pot to poultry mode. Cook until the timer runs out
5. Allow the pressure to release naturally
6. Once done, remove ¼ cup of the sauce from the pot and add arrowroot to make a slurry
7. Add the slurry to the pot to make the gravy thick. Keep stirring well. Serve!

Herb Roasted Drumsticks
Servings: 3
Cooking Time: 40 Minutes
Ingredients:
- Nonstick cooking spray
- 1 tsp paprika
- ¼ tsp salt
- ½ tsp garlic powder
- ¼ tsp onion powder
- ¼ tsp dried thyme
- ¼ tsp pepper
- 6 chicken drumsticks, skin removed, rinsed & patted dry
- ½ tbsp. butter, melted

Directions:
1. Place the rack in the cooking pot and spray it with cooking spray.
2. In a small bowl, combine spices, mix well.
3. Place chicken on the rack and sprinkle evenly over chicken. Drizzle with melted butter.
4. Add the tender-crisp lid and set to roast on 375°F. Bake 35-40 minutes until juices run clear. Serve.

Nutrition:
- InfoCalories 319,Total Fat 12g,Total Carbs 0g,Protein 50g,Sodium 505mg.

Cheesy Chicken And Broccoli Casserole
Servings:6
Cooking Time: 30 Minutes
Ingredients:
- 4 boneless, skinless chicken breasts
- 2 cups chicken stock
- 1 cup whole milk
- 1 cans condensed Cheddar cheese soup
- 1 teaspoon paprika

- 2 cups shredded Cheddar cheese
- Kosher salt
- Freshly ground black pepper
- 2 cups crushed buttered crackers

Directions:
1. Place the chicken and stock in the pot. Assemble pressure lid, making sure the pressure release valve is in the SEAL position.
2. Select PRESSURE and set to HI. Set timer to 20 minutes. Select START/STOP to begin.
3. When pressure cooking is complete, quick release the pressure by turning the pressure release valve to the VENT position. Carefully remove lid when unit has finished releasing pressure.
4. Using silicone-tipped utensils, shred the chicken inside the pot.
5. Add the milk, condensed soup, paprika, and cheese. Stir to combine with the chicken. Season with salt and pepper. Top with the crushed crackers. Close crisping lid.
6. Select AIR CRISP, set temperature to 360°F, and set time to 10 minutes. Select START/STOP to begin.
7. When cooking is complete, open lid and let cool before serving.

Nutrition:
- InfoCalories: 449,Total Fat: 23g,Sodium: 925mg,Carbohydrates: 18g,Protein: 42g.

Cheesy Chicken Chili

Servings: 6
Cooking Time: 4 Hours
Ingredients:
- 2 chicken breasts, boneless & skinless
- 15 oz. corn, drained
- 15 oz. black beans, drained & rinsed
- 10 oz. tomatoes and green chilies, undrained
- 2 cups chicken broth, low sodium
- 1 cup bacon, cooked & crumbled
- 1 pkt. ranch dressing mix
- 1 tsp cumin
- 1 tbsp. chili powder
- 1 tsp onion powder
- 8 oz. cream cheese, cubed
- 1 cup cheddar cheese, grated

Directions:
1. Add the chicken, corn, beans, tomatoes with chilies, broth, cumin, chili powder, onion powder, ranch seasoning, and bacon to the cooking pot. Top with cream cheese.
2. Add the lid and set to slow cook on low. Cook 6-8 hours, stirring occasionally.
3. Transfer chicken to a cutting board and shred with a fork, Return to the pot.
4. Add the cheese and stir until melted. Ladle into bowls and serve hot.

Nutrition:
- InfoCalories 815,Total Fat 62g,Total Carbs 32g,Protein 34g,Sodium 994mg.

Creamy Chicken Curry

Servings: 4
Cooking Time: 10 Hours
Ingredients:
- 10 bone-in chicken thighs, skinless
- 1 cup sour cream
- 2 tablespoons. Curry powder
- 1 onion, chopped

- 1 jar (16 ounces chunky salsa sauce

Directions:
1. Add chicken thigh to your Ninja Foodi
2. Add onions, salsa, curry powder over chicken, stir and place the lid
3. Cook SLOW COOK MODE for 10 hours. Open lid and transfer chicken to a serving platter
4. Pour sour cream into the sauce in the Ninja Foodi
5. Stir well and pour the sauce over chicken. Serve!

Lemon And Artichoke Medley

Servings: 6
Cooking Time: 8 Hours
Ingredients:
- 1 pound boneless and skinless chicken breast
- 1 pound boneless and skinless chicken thigh
- 14 ounces (can) artichoke hearts, packed in water and drained
- 1 onion, diced
- 2 carrots, diced
- 3 garlic cloves, minced
- 1 bay leaf
- ½ teaspoon pepper
- 3 cups turnips, peeled and cubed
- 6 cups chicken broth
- 14 cup fresh lemon juice
- ¼ cup parsley, chopped

Directions:
1. Add the above mentioned to your Ninja Foodi except for lemon juice and parsley
2. Cook on Slow Cooker for 8 hours. Remove the chicken and shred it up
3. Return it back to the Ninja Foodi. Season with some pepper and salt!
4. Stir in parsley and lemon juice and serve!

Easy Tandoori Chicken

Servings: 4
Cooking Time: 18 To 23 Minutes
Ingredients:
- ⅔ cup (167 mL) plain low-fat yogurt
- 2 tablespoons freshly squeezed lemon juice
- 2 teaspoons curry powder
- ½ teaspoon ground cinnamon
- 2 garlic cloves, minced
- 2 teaspoons olive oil
- 4 (5-ounce / 142-g) low-sodium boneless, skinless chicken breasts

Directions:
1. In a medium bowl, whisk the yogurt, lemon juice, curry powder, cinnamon, garlic, and olive oil.
2. With a sharp knife, cut thin slashes into the chicken. Add it to the yogurt mixture and turn to coat. Let stand for 10 minutes at room temperature. You can also prepare this ahead of time and marinate the chicken in the refrigerator for up to 24 hours.
3. Preheat the Ninja Foodi Deluxe Pressure Cooker to 360°F .
4. Remove the chicken from the marinade and shake off any excess liquid. Discard any remaining marinade and transfer to cooking pot.
5. Close crisping lid. Select Roast and set time to 18 to 21 minutes. Press Start to begin. After 10 minutes, with tongs, carefully turn each piece and roast for 8 to 13 minutes more,

or until the chicken reaches an internal temperature of 165ºF on a meat thermometer. Serve immediately.

Garlic Chicken And Bacon Pasta

Servings:4
Cooking Time: 10 Minutes
Ingredients:
- 3 strips bacon, chopped
- ½ pound boneless, skinless chicken breast, cut into ½-pieces
- 1 teaspoon dried basil
- 1 teaspoon dried oregano
- ¼ teaspoon sea salt
- 1 tablespoon unsalted butter
- 3 garlic cloves, minced
- 1 cup chicken stock
- 1½ cups water
- 8 ounces dry penne pasta
- ½ cup half-and-half
- ½ cup grated Parmesan cheese, plus more for serving

Directions:
1. Select SEAR/SAUTÉ and set to HI. Select START/STOP to begin. Let preheat for 5 minutes.
2. Add the bacon and cook, stirring frequently, for about 5 minutes or until crispy. Using a slotted spoon, transfer the bacon to a paper towel-lined plate to drain.
3. Season the chicken with the basil, oregano, and salt, coating all the pieces.
4. Add the butter, chicken, and garlic and sauté for 2 minutes, until the chicken begins to brown and the garlic is fragrant.
5. Add the chicken stock, water, and penne pasta. Assemble pressure lid, making sure the pressure release valve is in the SEAL position.
6. Select PRESSURE and set to HI. Set time to 3 minutes. Select START/STOP to begin.
7. When pressure cooking is complete, allow pressure to naturally release for 2 minutes. After 2 minutes, quick release remaining pressure by moving the pressure release valve to the VENT position. Carefully remove lid when unit has finished releasing pressure.
8. Add the half-and-half, cheese, and bacon, and stir constantly to thicken the sauce and melt the cheese. Serve immediately, with additional Parmesan cheese to garnish.

Nutrition:
- InfoCalories: 458,Total Fat: 18g,Sodium: 809mg,Carbohydrates: 45g,Protein: 30g.

Spicy Chicken Wings.

Servings: 2
Cooking Time: 25 Min
Ingredients:
- 10 chicken wings
- ½ tbsp honey /15ml
- 2 tbsp hot chili sauce /30ml
- ½ tbsp lime juice /7.5ml
- ½ tsp kosher salt /2.5g
- ½ tsp black pepper /2.5g

Directions:
1. Mix the lime juice, honey, and chili sauce. Toss the mixture over the chicken wings.
2. Put the wings in the fryer's basket, close the crisping lid and cook for 25 minutes on Air Crisp mode at 350 °F or 177°C. Shake the basket every 5 minutes.

Butter Chicken

Servings: 6
Cooking Time: 30 Min
Ingredients:
- 2 pounds boneless; skinless chicken legs /900g
- 3 Roma tomatoes, pureed in a blender
- 1 can coconut milk, refrigerated overnight /435ml
- 1 large onion; minced
- ½ cup chopped fresh cilantro; divided /65g
- 2 tbsp Indian curry paste /30ml
- 2 tbsp dried fenugreek /30g
- 1 tbsp Kashmiri red chili powder /15g
- 2 tbsp butter /30g
- 1 tbsp grated fresh ginger /15g
- 1 tbsp minced fresh garlic /15g
- 1 tsp salt /5g
- 2 tsp sugar /10g
- ½ tsp ground turmeric /2.5g
- 1 tsp garam masala /5g
- Salt to taste

Directions:
1. Set your Foodi to Sear/Sauté, set to Medium High, and choose Start/Stop to preheat the pot and melt butter. Add in 1 tsp salt and onion. Cook for 2 to 3 minutes until fragrant. Stir in ginger, turmeric, garlic, and red chili powder to coat; cook for 2 more minutes.
2. Place water and coconut cream into separate bowls. Stir the water from the coconut milk can, pureed tomatoes, and chicken with the onion mixture. Seal the pressure lid, choose Pressure, set to High, and set the timer to 8 minutes. Press Start. When ready, release the pressure quickly.
3. Stir sugar, coconut cream, fenugreek, curry paste, half the cilantro, and garam masala through the chicken mixture; apply salt for seasoning. Simmer the mixture and cook for 10 minutes until the sauce thickens, on Sear/Sauté. Garnish with the rest of the cilantro before serving.

Cheesy Chicken & Artichokes

Servings: 4
Cooking Time: 30 Minutes
Ingredients:
- Nonstick cooking spray
- 2 cups baby spinach, chopped & packed
- 1 cup plain yogurt
- 1 cup marinated artichoke hearts, drained & chopped
- ½ tsp garlic powder
- 1 tsp Dijon mustard
- 4 chicken breasts, boneless & skinless
- 8 slices mozzarella cheese

Directions:
1. Spray the cooking pot with cooking spray.
2. In a large bowl, combine spinach, yogurt, artichokes, garlic powder, and mustard, mix well.
3. Place chicken between 2 sheets of plastic wrap and pound out slightly. Place in the cooking pot.
4. Top chicken with spinach mixture. Lay 2 slices of cheese on top of each piece of chicken.
5. Add the tender-crisp lid and set to bake on 400°F. Bake 30 minutes or until chicken is cooked through. Let rest 5 minutes before serving.

Nutrition:
- InfoCalories 602,Total Fat 33g,Total Carbs 7g,Protein 66g,Sodium 348mg.

Moo Shu Chicken

Servings: 4
Cooking Time: 20 Minutes
Ingredients:
- 1 tbsp. sesame oil
- 1 cup mushrooms, sliced
- 2 cups cabbage, shredded
- ½ cup green onion, sliced thin
- 3 cups chicken, cooked & shredded
- 2 eggs, lightly beaten
- ¼ cup hoisin sauce
- 2 tbsp. tamari
- 2 tsp sriracha sauce

Directions:
1. Add the oil to the cooking pot and set to sauté on med-high heat.
2. Add the mushrooms and cook 5-6 minutes, stirring frequently, until mushrooms have browned and liquid has evaporated.
3. Add cabbage and green onion, cook, stirring, 2 minutes.
4. Stir in chicken and cook 3-5 minutes until heated through.
5. Add the eggs and cook, stirring to scramble, until eggs are cooked.
6. Stir in remaining ingredients. Reduce heat and simmer until heated through. Serve immediately.

Nutrition:
- InfoCalories 378,Total Fat 25g,Total Carbs 15g,Protein 23g,Sodium 1067mg.

Awesome Ligurian Chicken

Servings:4
Cooking Time: 15 Minutes
Ingredients:
- 2 garlic cloves, chopped
- 3 sprigs fresh rosemary
- 2 sprigs fresh sage
- ½ bunch parsley
- 3 lemon, juiced
- 4 tablespoons extra virgin olive oil
- 1 teaspoon salt
- ¼ teaspoon pepper
- 1 and ½ cup of water
- 1 whole chicken, cut into parts
- 3 and ½ ounces black gourmet salt-cured olives
- 1 fresh lemon

Directions:
1. Take a bowl and add chopped up garlic, parsley, sage, and rosemary
2. Pour lemon juice, olive oil to a bowl and season with salt and pepper
3. Remove the chicken skin and from the chicken pieces and carefully transfer them to a dish
4. Pour the marinade on top of the chicken pieces and allow them to chill for 2-4 hours
5. Set your Ninja Foodi to Saute mode and add olive oil, allow it to heat up. Add chicken and browned on all sides
6. Measure out the marinade and add to the pot . Lock up the lid and cook on HIGH pressure for 10 minutes
7. Release the pressure naturally. The chicken out and transfer to a platter
8. Cover with a foil and allow them to coolSet your pot in Saute mode and reduce the liquid to ¼
9. Add the chicken pieces again to the pot and allow them to warm
10. Sprinkle a bit of olive, lemon slices, and rosemary. Enjoy!

Chapter 9: Beef, Pork & Lamb

Speedy Pork Stir Fry

Servings: 4
Cooking Time: 5 Minutes
Ingredients:
* 2 tbsp. soy sauce, low sodium
* 1 tsp sugar
* 1 tsp cornstarch
* 1 lb. pork loin, cut in ¼-inch strips
* 4 tbsp. peanut oil
* 5 cloves garlic, sliced thin
* 1 tsp. red pepper flakes
* 10 green onions, sliced
* ½ tsp sesame oil

Directions:
1. In a large bowl, whisk together soy sauce, sugar, and cornstarch until smooth.
2. Add the pork to the bowl and toss to coat. Let sit for 10 minutes.
3. Add the oil to the cooking pot and set to sauté on med-high heat.
4. Add the garlic and pepper flakes and cook, stirring, about 30 seconds or until garlic starts to brown.
5. Add the pork mixture and cook until meat is no longer pink, stirring constantly.
6. Add the green onions and cook 1 minute more. Turn off the heat and stir in the sesame oil. Serve as is or over hot, cooked rice.

Nutrition:
* InfoCalories 182,Total Fat 12g,Total Carbs 3g,Protein 15g,Sodium 279mg.

Hearty Korean Meatloaf

Servings:4
Cooking Time: 30 Minutes
Ingredients:
* 1 pound (454 g) beef, pork, and veal meatloaf mix
* 1 large egg
* 1 cup panko bread crumbs
* ½ cup whole milk
* ⅓ cup minced onion
* ¼ cup chopped cilantro
* 1 garlic clove, grated
* 1 tablespoon grated fresh ginger
* ½ tablespoon fish sauce
* 1½ teaspoons sesame oil
* 1 tablespoon, plus 1 teaspoon soy sauce
* ¼ cup, plus 1 tablespoon gochujang
* 1 cup water
* 1 tablespoon honey

Directions:
1. In a large bowl, stir together the beef, egg, bread crumbs, milk, onion, cilantro, garlic, ginger, fish sauce, sesame oil, 1 teaspoon of soy sauce, and 1 tablespoon of gochujang.
2. Place the meat mixture in the Ninja Loaf Pan or an 8½-inch loaf pan and cover tightly with aluminum foil.
3. Pour the water into the pot. Place the loaf pan on the Reversible Rack, making sure the rack is in the lower position. Place the rack with pan in the pot. Assemble pressure lid, making sure the pressure release valve is in the SEAL position.
4. Select PRESSURE and set to HI. Set time to 15 minutes. Select START/STOP to begin.
5. When pressure cooking is complete, quick release the pressure by moving the pressure release valve to the VENT position. Carefully remove lid when unit has finished releasing pressure.
6. Carefully remove the foil from the pan. Close crisping lid.
7. Select BAKE/ROAST, set temperature to 360ºF , and set time to 15 minutes. Select START/STOP to begin.
8. In a small bowl stir together the remaining ¼ cup of gochujang, 1 tablespoon of soy sauce, and honey.
9. After 7 minutes, open lid and top the meatloaf with the gochujang barbecue mixture. Close lid and continue cooking.
10. When cooking is complete, open lid and remove meatloaf from the pot. Let cool for 10 minutes before serving.

All-buttered Up Beef

Servings:6
Cooking Time: 60 Minutes
Ingredients:
* 3 pounds beef roast
* 1 tablespoon olive oil
* 2 tablespoons Keto-Friendly ranch dressing
* 1 jar pepper rings, with juices
* 8 tablespoons butter
* 1 cup of water

Directions:
1. Set your Ninja Foodi to Saute mode and add 1 tablespoon of oil
2. Once the oil is hot, add roast and sear both sides
3. Set the Saute off and add water, seasoning mix, reserved juice, and pepper rings on top of your beef. Lock up the lid and cook on HIGH pressure for 60 minutes
4. Release the pressure naturally over 10 minutes. Cut the beef with salad sheers and serve with pureed cauliflower. Enjoy!

Beef And Cherry Tagine

Servings: 4
Cooking Time: 1 Hr 20 Min
Ingredients:
- 1 ½ pounds stewing beef, trimmed /675g
- 1 onion; chopped
- 1-star anise
- ¼ cup toasted almonds, slivered /32.5g
- 1 cup dried cherries, halved /130g
- 1 cup water /250ml
- 1 tbsp honey /15ml
- 2 tbsp olive oil /30ml
- ¼ tsp ground allspice /1.25g
- 1 tsp ground cinnamon /5g
- ½ tsp paprika /2.5g
- ½ tsp turmeric /2.5g
- ½ tsp salt /2.5g
- ¼ tsp ground ginger /1.25g

Directions:
1. Set your Foodi to Sear/Sauté, set to Medium High, and choose Start/Stop to preheat the pot. Warm olive oil. Add in onions and cook for 3 minutes until fragrant. Mix in beef and cook for 2 minutes each side until browned.
2. Stir in anise, cinnamon, turmeric, allspice, salt, paprika, and ginger; cook for 2 minutes until aromatic.
3. Add in honey and water. Seal the pressure lid, choose Pressure, set to High, and set the timer to 50 minutes. Press Start.
4. Meanwhile, in a bowl, soak dried cherries in hot water until softened. Once ready, release pressure naturally for 15 minutes. Drain cherries and stir into the tagine. Top with toasted almonds before serving.

Ground Beef Stuffed Empanadas

Servings: 2
Cooking Time: 60 Min
Ingredients:
- ¼ pound ground beef /112.5g
- 2 small tomatoes; chopped
- 8 square gyoza wrappers
- 1 egg, beaten
- 1 garlic clove; minced
- ½ white onion; chopped
- 6 green olives, pitted and chopped
- 1 tbsp olive oil /15ml
- ¼ tsp cumin powder /1.25g
- ¼ tsp paprika /1.25g
- ⅛ tsp cinnamon powder /0.625g

Directions:
1. Choose Sear/Sauté on the pot and set to Medium High. Choose Start/Stop to preheat the pot. Put the oil, garlic, onion, and beef in the preheated pot and cook for 5 minutes, stirring occasionally, until the fragrant and the beef is no longer pink.
2. Stir in the olives, cumin, paprika, and cinnamon and cook for an additional 3 minutes. Add the tomatoes and cook for 1 more minute.
3. Spoon the beef mixture into a plate and allow cooling for a few minutes.
4. Meanwhile, put the Crisping Basket in the pot. Close the crisping lid; choose Air Crisp, set the temperature to 400°F or 205°C, and the time to 5 minutes. Press Start.

5. Lay the gyoza wrappers on a flat surface. Place 1 to 2 tbsps of the beef mixture in the middle of each wrapper. Brush the edges of the wrapper with egg and fold in half to form a triangle. Pinch the edges together to seal.
6. Place 4 empanadas in a single layer in the preheated Basket. Close the crisping lid. Choose Air Crisp, set the temperature to 400°F or 205°C, and set the time to 7 minutes. Choose Start/Stop to begin frying.
7. Once the timer is done, remove the empanadas from the basket and transfer to a plate. Repeat with the remaining empanadas.

African Pork Stew

Servings: 6
Cooking Time: 8 Hours
Ingredients:
- 14½ oz. yellow hominy, drained
- 3 cups red beans, drained & rinsed
- 1 onion, chopped
- 2 tbsp. garlic, chopped fine
- 2 bay leaves
- 1 tsp Adobo powder
- 2 lbs. pork loin, cubed
- 2 potatoes, peeled & cubed
- 1 lb. smoked sausage, sliced
- 1 can diced tomatoes
- 2 tbsp. olive oil
- 3 slices bacon, chopped

Directions:
1. Add all the ingredients to the cooking pot and stir to combine.
2. Add the lid and set to slow cook on low. Cook 6-8 hours or until meat and vegetables are tender.
3. Discard the bay leaves, stir well and serve.

Nutrition:
- InfoCalories 784,Total Fat 37g,Total Carbs 55g,Protein 55g,Sodium 1185mg.

Beer Braised Bacon & Cabbage

Servings: 4
Cooking Time: 15 Minutes
Ingredients:
- 1 tbsp. butter
- 1 onion, sliced in strips
- 3 ½ oz. bacon, chopped
- 1 savoy cabbage, sliced in strips
- 1 cup blonde beer

Directions:
1. Add the butter to the cooking pot and set to sauté on medium heat.
2. Once butter has melted, add onion and bacon and cook, stirring occasionally, until onions is soft, about 5 minutes.
3. Add the cabbage and beer, stir to mix.
4. Add the lid and set to pressure cook on high. Set the timer for 3 minutes. When the timer goes off, use manual release to remove the pressure.
5. Stir and serve immediately.

Nutrition:
- InfoCalories 267,Total Fat 18g,Total Carbs 15g,Protein 9g,Sodium 257mg.

Meat Dredged Loaf

Servings:6
Cooking Time: 1 Hour 10 Minutes
Ingredients:
- ½ cup onion, chopped
- 2 garlic cloves, minced
- ¼ cup sugar-free ketchup
- 1 pound grass fed lean ground beef
- ½ cup green bell pepper, seeded and chopped
- 1 cup cheddar cheese, grated
- 2 organic eggs, beaten
- 1 teaspoon dried thyme, crushed
- 3 cups fresh spinach, chopped
- 6 cups mozzarella cheese, freshly grated
- Black pepper to taste

Directions:
1. Take a bowl and add all of the listed except cheese and spinach
2. Place a wax paper on a smooth surface and arrange the meat over it
3. Top with spinach, cheese and roll the paper around the paper to form a nice meatloaf
4. Remove wax paper and transfer loaf to your Ninja Foodi
5. Lock lid and select "Bake/Roast" mode, setting the timer to 70 minutes and temperature to 380 degrees F. Let it bake and take the dish out once done. Serve and enjoy!

Sassy Evergreen Pork Chops

Servings:4
Cooking Time: 4 Hours
Ingredients:
- 6-8 boneless pork chops
- ¼ cup arrowroot flour
- 2 teaspoons dry mustard
- 1 teaspoon garlic powder
- 1 and ½ cups beef stock
- Cooking fat
- Salt and pepper to taste

Directions:
1. Take a bowl and add flour, garlic powder, black pepper, dry mustard and salt
2. Coat the pork chop with the mixture and keep any extra flour on the side
3. Take a skillet and place it over medium-high heat. Add cooking fat and allow the fat to melt
4. Brown the chops for 1-2 minutes per side and transfer to your Ninja Foodi
5. Add beef stock to the flour mixture and mix well
6. Pour the beef stock mix to the chops and place lid
7. Cook on SLOW COOK MODE for 3 hours. Enjoy!

Pork, Green Beans, And Corn

Servings: 4
Cooking Time: 35 Minutes
Ingredients:
- 2 pounds (907 g) pork shoulder, boneless and cubed
- 1 cup (250 mL) green beans, trimmed and halved
- 1 cup (250 mL) corn
- 1 cup (250 mL) beef stock
- 2 garlic cloves, minced
- 1 teaspoon ground cumin
- A pinch of salt and black pepper

Directions:

1. Combine all the ingredients in the cooking pot.
2. Assemble pressure lid, making sure the pressure release valve is in the Seal position. Select Pressure and set to high . Set time to 35 minutes. Press Start to begin.
3. Once cooking is complete, do a natural pressure release for 10 minutes, then release any remaining pressure. Carefully open the lid.
4. Divide the mix among four plates and serve.

Italian Beef Steak

Servings: 8
Cooking Time: 4 Hours
Ingredients:
- Nonstick cooking spray
- 2 lbs. round steak, cut in 1-inch pieces
- ½ tsp salt
- ¼ tsp pepper
- 1 onion, sliced thin
- 1 tsp oregano
- 1 tsp basil
- 1 tsp rosemary
- ½ tsp thyme
- 4 cloves garlic, chopped fine
- ½ cup balsamic vinegar
- 28 oz. tomatoes, diced & undrained

Directions:
1. Spray the cooking pot with cooking spray.
2. Season the beef with salt and pepper and add it to the cooking pot.
3. Top the beef with onion and herbs to cover it evenly. Sprinkle the garlic overall then add the vinegar and tomatoes, do not stir.
4. Add the lid and set to slow cook on high. Cook 4 hours or until beef is tender. Stir to mix and serve over pasta or rice.

Nutrition:
- InfoCalories 200,Total Fat 9g,Total Carbs 9g,Protein 26g,Sodium 218mg.

Beef Rice Noodles

Servings: 4
Cooking Time: 16 Minutes
Ingredients:
- 6 cups (1.5 L) boiled water
- 8 ounces (227 g) rice noodles
- 1 tablespoon sesame oil
- 1 pound (454 g) ground beef
- 2 cups (500 mL) sliced shitake mushrooms
- ½ cup (125 mL) julienned carrots
- 1 yellow onion, sliced
- 1 cup (250 mL) shredded green cabbage
- ¼ cup (63 mL) sliced scallions, for garnish
- Sesame seeds, for garnish
- Sauce:
- ¼ cup (63 mL) tamarind sauce
- 1 tablespoon hoisin sauce
- 1 teaspoon grated ginger
- 1 teaspoon maple syrup

Directions:
1. In a medium bowl, whisk together the ingredients for the sauce. Set aside.
2. Pour boiling water into a bowl and add rice noodles. Cover the bowl and allow the noodles to soften for 5 minutes. Drain and set aside.

3. Press the Sauté button and heat the sesame oil.
4. Cook the beef in the pot for 5 minutes or until browned.
5. Stir in the mushrooms, carrots, onion, and cabbage. Cook for 5 minutes or until softened.
6. Add the noodles. Top with the sauce and mix well. Cook for 1 more minute. Garnish with scallions and sesame seeds and serve immediately.

Refined Carrot And Bacon Soup

Servings:4
Cooking Time: 4 Minutes
Ingredients:
- 2 pounds carrots, peeled
- 4 cups broth
- ½ cup yellow onion, chopped
- ½ pack bacon cut into ¼ inch pieces
- ½ cup apple cider vinegar
- ½ cup white vinegar

Directions:
1. Set your Ninja Foodi to Saute mode and add butter, allow the butter to melt and add bacon and onion, Saute for a while. Slice 1 -2 heirloom carrots thinly and add them to a small bowl
2. Add vinegar to cover them, allow them to pickle
3. Chop the remaining carrots into inch long pieces
4. Add chopped carrots and broth to your Instant Pot
5. Lock up the lid and cook on HIGH pressure for 4 minutes. Perform a natural release
6. Use an immersion blender break down the carrots until you have a smooth mix
7. Stir in onions and bacon, salt and apple cider vinegar. Serve and enjoy!

Taco Meatballs

Servings: 4
Cooking Time: 11 Minutes
Ingredients:
- 2 cups ground beef
- 1 egg, beaten
- 1 teaspoon taco seasoning
- 1 tablespoon sugar-free marinara sauce
- 1 teaspoon garlic, minced
- 1/2 teaspoon salt

Directions:
1. Take a suitable mixing bowl and place all the ingredients into the bowl.
2. Stir in all the ingredients into the bowl. Mix together all the ingredients by using a spoon or fingertips. Then make the small size meatballs and put them in a layer in the air fryer rack.
3. Lower the air fryer lid.
4. Cook the meatballs for 11 minutes at 350 °F.
5. Serve immediately and enjoy.

Nutrition:
- InfoCalories: 205; Fat: 12.2g; Carbohydrates: 2.2g; Protein: 19.4g

Baked Ziti With Meat Sauce

Servings: 4
Cooking Time:32 Minutes
Ingredients:
- 1 tablespoon extra-virgin olive oil
- 2 pounds ground beef
- 2 (24-ounce) jars marinara sauce
- 1 cup water
- 1 cup dry red wine

- 1 (16-ounce) box ziti
- ½ teaspoon garlic powder
- ½ teaspoon sea salt
- 1 cup ricotta cheese
- 1 cup shredded mozzarella cheese
- ½ cup chopped fresh parsley

Directions:
1. Select Sear/Sauté and set to High. Select Start/Stop to begin. Allow the pot to preheat for 5 minutes.
2. Put the oil in the preheated pot, then add the ground beef and cook for 5 to 8 minutes, or until browned and cooked through.
3. Add the marinara sauce, water, wine, and ziti to the pot, stirring to combine. Season with the garlic powder and salt.
4. Assemble the Pressure Lid, making sure the pressure release valve is in the Seal position. Select Pressure and set to Low. Set the time to 2 minutes, then select Start/Stop to begin.
5. When pressure cooking is complete, allow the pressure to naturally release for 10 minutes, then quick release any remaining pressure by moving the pressure release valve to the Vent position. Carefully remove the lid when the pressure has finished releasing.
6. Stir in the ricotta, then evenly top the pasta with the mozzarella cheese.
7. Close the Crisping Lid. Select Broil, and set the time to 3 minutes. Select Start/Stop to begin. Cook for 3 minutes, or until the cheese is melted, bubbly, and slightly browned.
8. Top with the parsley and serve immediately.

Pork Chops With Seasoned Butter

Servings: 4
Cooking Time: 15 Minutes
Ingredients:
- ¼ cup butter, soft
- 2 tbsp. Dijon mustard
- 1 clove garlic, chopped fine
- Nonstick cooking spray
- 4 pork chops, 1 ¼-inch thick
- 4 slices bacon, thick-cut

Directions:
1. In a small bowl, combine butter, mustard, and garlic until thoroughly combine. Wrap in waxed paper and form into the shape of a stick of butter. Refrigerate until ready to use.
2. Spray the rack with cooking spray and add it to the pot.
3. Season chops with salt and pepper. Wrap a slice of bacon around each chop and secure with a toothpick. Place them on the rack.
4. Add the tender-crisp lid and set to broil. Cook chops 6-7 minutes, turn the chops over and cook another 5-6 minutes. Turn off the heat and let rest 3 minutes.
5. To serve, place the chops on serving plates. Slice the seasoned butter into 4 pieces and place one on each chop. Serve immediately.

Nutrition:
- InfoCalories 450,Total Fat 40g,Total Carbs 1g,Protein 33g,Sodium 362mg.

Beef And Turnip Chili

Servings: 6
Cooking Time: 30 Min
Ingredients:
- 1 pound turnips, peeled and cubed /450g
- 1 pound ground beef meat /450g
- 1 can whole tomatoes /840g

- 1 bell pepper; chopped
- 1 yellow onion; chopped
- 4 garlic cloves; minced
- 2 cups beef stock /500ml
- 2 tomatoes; chopped
- 1 tbsp chili powder /15g
- 1 tbsp olive oil /15ml
- 2 tbsp tomato puree /30ml
- ½ tsp ground turmeric /2.5g
- 2 tsp ground cumin /10g
- 1 tsp dried oregano /5g
- 1 pinch cayenne pepper
- salt to taste

Directions:
1. Warm oil on Sear/Sauté. Add in onion with a pinch of salt and cook for 3 to 5 minutes until softened. Stir in garlic, chili powder, turmeric, cumin, tomato puree, oregano, and cayenne pepper; cook for 2 to 3 minutes as you stir until very soft and sticks to the pot's bottom; add beef and cook for 5 minutes until completely browned. Mix in tomatoes, turnips, bell pepper, and beef stock.
2. Seal the pressure lid, choose Pressure, set to High, and set the timer to 15 minutes; press Start. When ready, release the pressure quickly.

Apricot Lemon Ham
Servings: 12
Cooking Time: 1 Hr
Ingredients:
- 5 pounds smoked ham /2250g
- ¾ cup apricot jam /98g
- ¼ cup water /62.5ml
- ½ cup brown sugar /65g
- Juice from 1 Lime
- ½ tsp ground cardamom /2.5g
- ¼ tsp ground nutmeg /1.25g
- 2 tsp mustard /10g
- freshly ground black pepper to taste

Directions:
1. Into the pot, add water and ham to the steel pot of a pressure cooker. In a bowl, combine jam, lemon juice, cardamom, pepper, nutmeg, mustard, and brown sugar; pour the mixture over the ham. Seal the pressure lid, choose Pressure, set to High, and set the timer to 10 minutes. Press Start.
2. When ready, release the pressure quickly. Transfer the ham to a cutting board; allow to sit for 10 minutes. Press Sear/Sauté.
3. Simmer the liquid and cook for 4 to 6 minutes until thickened into a sauce. Slice ham and place onto a serving bowl. Drizzle with sauce before serving.

Brisket Green Chili Verde
Servings:4
Cooking Time: 19 Minutes
Ingredients:
- 1 tablespoon vegetable oil
- ½ white onion, diced
- 1 jalapeño pepper, diced
- 1 teaspoon garlic, minced
- 1 pound (454 g) brisket, cooked
- 1 (19-ounce / 539-g) can green chile enchilada sauce
- 1 (4-ounce / 113-g) can fire-roasted diced green chiles
- Juice of 1 lime
- 1 teaspoon seasoning salt

- ½ teaspoon ground chipotle pepper

Directions:
1. Select SEAR/SAUTÉ and set temperature to HI. Select START/STOP to begin and allow to preheat for 5 minutes.
2. Add oil to the pot and allow to heat for 1 minute. Add the onion, jalapeño, and garlic. Sauté for 3 minutes or until onion is translucent.
3. Add the brisket, enchilada sauce, green chiles, lime juice, salt, and chipotle powder. Mix well.
4. Assemble the pressure lid, making sure the pressure release valve is in the SEAL position.
5. Select PRESSURE and set to HI. Set the time to 15 minutes. Select START/STOP to begin.
6. When cooking is complete, quick release the pressure by turning the pressure release valve to the VENT position. Carefully remove the lid when the unit has finished releasing pressure.

Chili Pork Roast And Tomatoes
Servings: 4
Cooking Time: 35 Minutes
Ingredients:
- 1 tablespoon olive oil
- 4 garlic cloves, minced
- 1 yellow onion, chopped
- 1½ pounds (680 g) pork roast
- 12 ounces (340 g) tomatoes, crushed
- 1 cup (250 mL) beef stock
- 2 tablespoons chili powder
- 1 tablespoon apple cider vinegar
- 1 teaspoon dried oregano
- A pinch of salt and black pepper

Directions:
1. Press the Sauté button and heat the olive oil.
2. Add the garlic and onion and sauté for 5 minutes, stirring occasionally.
3. Add the remaining ingredients to the cooking pot and stir.
4. Assemble pressure lid, making sure the pressure release valve is in the Seal position. Select Pressure and set to high . Set time to 30 minutes. Press Start to begin.
5. Once cooking is complete, do a natural pressure release for 10 minutes, then release any remaining pressure. Carefully open the lid.
6. Serve hot.

Roasted Zucchini And Summer Squash
Servings:4
Cooking Time: 25 Minutes
Ingredients:
- 2 medium zucchini, cut into ¼-inch-thick rounds
- 2 medium yellow summer squash, cut into ¼-inch-thick rounds
- ½ cup fresh flat-leaf parsley leaves
- 3 tablespoons peanut oil or vegetable oil
- Zest of 1 lemon
- 2 teaspoons kosher salt
- ½ teaspoon freshly ground black pepper

Directions:
1. Place the zucchini, yellow squash, parsley, oil, lemon zest, salt, and pepper into the Foodi's inner pot and stir to evenly coat the squash with the oil. Transfer the squash mixture to the crisping basket and place it in the inner pot. Set the Foodi to Air Crisp at 390ºF for 25 minutes, stirring occasionally, or until browned.
2. Serve warm.

Extremely Satisfying Beef Curry

Servings:4
Cooking Time: 20 Minutes
Ingredients:
- 2 pounds beef steak, cubed
- 2 tablespoons extra virgin olive oil
- 1 tablespoon Dijon mustard
- 2 and ½ tablespoons curry powder
- 2 yellow onions, peeled and chopped
- 2 garlic cloves, peeled and minced
- 10 ounces canned coconut milk
- 2 tablespoons tomato sauce
- Salt and pepper to taste

Directions:
1. Set your Ninja Foodi to "Saute" mode and add oil, let it heat up
2. Add onions, garlic, stir cook for 4 minutes. Add mustard, stir and cook for 1 minute
3. Add beef and stir until all sides are browned
4. Add curry powder, salt, and pepper, stir cook for 2 minutes
5. Add coconut milk and tomato sauce, stir, and cove
6. Lock lid and cook on HIGH pressure for 10 minutes
7. Release pressure naturally over 10 minutes. Serve and enjoy!

Crispy Roast Pork

Servings: 4
Cooking Time: 50 Min
Ingredients:
- 4 pork tenderloins
- ¾ tsp garlic powder /3.75g
- 1 tsp five spice seasoning /5g
- ½ tsp white pepper /2.5g
- 1 tsp salt /5g
- Cooking spray

Directions:
1. Place the pork, white pepper, garlic powder, five seasoning, and salt into a bowl and toss to coat. Leave to marinate at room temperature for 30 minutes.
2. Place the pork into the Foodi basket, greased with cooking spray, close the crisping lid and cook for 20 minutes at 360 °F or 183°C. After 10 minutes, turn the tenderloins. Serve hot.

Wine-glazed Roasted Cabbage

Servings:8
Cooking Time: 32 Minutes
Ingredients:
- 1 head green cabbage
- ½ cup, plus 1 tablespoon water
- 1 tablespoon extra-virgin olive oil
- Kosher salt
- Freshly ground black pepper
- 2 cups white wine
- ¼ cup minced red onion
- 1 cup heavy (whipping) cream
- ¼ cup minced fresh dill
- ¼ cup minced fresh parsley
- 2 tablespoons whole-grain mustard
- 1 tablespoon cornstarch

Directions:
1. Place the cabbage and ½ cup of water, stem-side down, in the pot.

2. With a knife cut an X into the top of the cabbage cutting all the way through to the bottom through the core. Assemble pressure lid, making sure the pressure release valve is in the SEAL position.
3. Select PRESSURE and set temperature to HI. Set time to 15 minutes. Select START/STOP to begin.
4. When pressure cooking is complete, quick release the pressure by turning the pressure release valve to the VENT position. Carefully remove lid when unit has finished releasing pressure.
5. Brush the cabbage with the olive oil and season with salt and pepper. Close crisping lid.
6. Select AIR CRISP, set temperature to 390ºF , and set time to 12 minutes. Select START/STOP to begin.
7. Once cooking is complete, open lid, lift out the cabbage, wrap with foil, and set aside. Leave any remaining water in the pot.
8. Select SEAR/SAUTÉ. Set temperature to HI. Select START/STOP to begin.
9. Add the white wine and onion and stir, scraping any brown bits off the bottom of the pot. Stir in the cream, dill, parsley, and mustard. Let simmer for 5 minutes.
10. In a small bowl, whisk together the cornstarch and the remaining 1 tablespoon of water until smooth. Stir it into the mixture in the pot. Cook until the sauce has thickened and coats the back of a spoon, about 2 minutes.
11. Pour half of the sauce over the cabbage. Cut the cabbage into 8 pieces and serve with remaining sauce.

Garlicky Rosemary Braised Lamb Shanks

Servings: 4
Cooking Time: 1 Hour
Ingredients:
- ½ tsp. sea salt
- ½ tsp. freshly ground black pepper
- 2 lamb shanks
- 2 tbsps. extra-virgin olive oil, divided
- 4 garlic cloves, minced
- 1 onion, chopped
- 2 celery stalks, chopped
- 2 carrots, chopped
- 1 (14-ounce, 397 g) can diced tomatoes, undrained
- 3½ cups beef broth
- 2 rosemary sprigs

Directions:
1. Preheat the pot by selecting Sear/Sauté and setting to High. Select Start/Stop to begin. Preheat it for 5 minutes.
2. While the pot is preheating, use salt and black pepper to season all sides of the lamb shanks.
3. In the preheated pot, add 1 tablespoon of oil and the seasoned lamb shanks. Cook for about 10 minutes total, until browned on all sides. Remove the lamb shanks and set aside.
4. Add the remaining 1 tablespoon of oil, the garlic and onion to the pot. Cook for 5 minutes, stirring occasionally. Add the celery and carrots, cook for another 3 minutes.
5. Stir in the rosemary, broth and tomatoes to the pot. Place the lamb shanks back to the pot. Assemble the Pressure Lid, set the pressure release valve to the Seal.
6. Select Pressure. Set the time to 30 minutes, then select Start/Stop to begin.
7. When pressure cooking is complete, move the pressure release valve to the Vent position to quick release the

pressure. Remove the lid when the pressure has finished releasing carefully.
8. Discard the rosemary sprigs and remove the lamb shanks. Shred the lamb coarsely.
9. Serve the lamb over the broth and vegetables.

Meatballs With Marinara Sauce

Servings: 6
Cooking Time: 35 Min
Ingredients:
- 1½ pounds ground beef /675g
- 1 egg
- 3 cups marinara sauce /750ml
- ⅓ cup warm water /88ml
- ¾ cup grated Parmigiano-Reggiano cheese /98g
- ½ cup bread crumbs /65g
- ½ cup capers /65g
- 2 tbsp fresh parsley /30g
- ¼ tsp dried oregano /1.25g
- ¼ tsp garlic powder /1.25g
- 1 tsp olive oil /5ml
- salt and ground black pepper to taste

Directions:
1. In a large bowl, mix ground beef, garlic powder, pepper, oregano, bread crumbs, egg, and salt; shape into meatballs. Warm the oil on Sear/Sauté. Add meatballs to the oil and brown for 2-3 minutes and all sides.
2. Pour water and marinara sauce over the meatballs. Seal the pressure lid, choose Pressure, set to High, and set the timer to 10 minutes. Press Start.
3. When ready, release the pressure quickly. Serve in large bowls topped with capers and Parmigiano-Reggiano cheese.

Baked Bacon Macaroni And Cheese

Servings:6
Cooking Time: 30 Minutes
Ingredients:
- 4 strips bacon, chopped
- 5 cups water
- 1 box elbow pasta
- 2 tablespoons unsalted butter
- 1 tablespoon ground mustard
- 1 can evaporated milk
- 8 ounces Cheddar cheese, shredded
- 8 ounces Gouda, shredded
- Sea salt
- Freshly ground black pepper
- 2 cups panko or Italian bread crumbs
- 1 stick (½ cup) butter, melted

Directions:
1. Select SEAR/SAUTÉ and set temperature to HI. Select START/STOP to begin. Let preheat for 5 minutes.
2. Add the bacon and cook, stirring frequently, for about 6 minutes or until crispy. Using a slotted spoon, transfer the bacon to a paper towel-lined plate to drain.
3. Add the water, pasta, 2 tablespoons of butter, and mustard. Assemble pressure lid, making sure the pressure release valve is in the SEAL position.
4. Select PRESSURE and set to LO. Set time to 0 minutes. Select START/STOP to begin.
5. When pressure cooking is complete, allow pressure to naturally release for 10 minutes. After 10 minutes, quick release remaining pressure by moving the pressure release valve to the VENT position. Carefully remove lid when unit has finished releasing pressure.
6. Add the evaporated milk, Cheddar cheese, Gouda cheese and the bacon. Season with salt and pepper. Stir well to melt the cheeses and ensure all ingredients are combined.
7. In a medium bowl, stir together the bread crumbs and melted butter. Cover the pasta evenly with the mixture. Close crisping lid.
8. Select AIR CRISP, set temperature to 360°F, and set time to 7 minutes. Select START/STOP to begin.
9. When cooking is complete, serve immediately.
Nutrition:
- InfoCalories: 721,Total Fat: 45g,Sodium: 1213mg,Carbohydrates: 44g,Protein: 35g.

Steak And Chips

Servings: 4
Cooking Time: 50 Min
Ingredients:
- 4 potatoes; cut into wedges
- 4 rib eye steaks
- 1 tbsp olive oil /15ml
- 1 tsp sweet paprika /5g
- 1 tsp salt; divided /5g
- 1 tsp ground black pepper /5g
- Cooking spray

Directions:
1. Put the Crisping Basket in the pot. Close the crisping lid. Choose Air Crisp, set the temperature to 390°F or 199°C, and set the time to 5 minutes. Press Start. Meanwhile, rub all over with olive oil. Put the potatoes in the preheated Crisping Basket and season with ½ tsp or 2.5g of salt and ½ tsp or 2.5g of black pepper and sweet paprika.
2. Close the crisping lid. Choose Air Crisp, set the temperature to 400°F or 205°C, and set the time to 35 minutes. Choose Start/Stop to begin baking.
3. Season the steak on both sides with the remaining salt and black pepper. When done cooking, remove potatoes to a plate.
4. Grease the Crisping Basket with cooking spray and put the steaks in the basket.
5. Close the crisping lid. Choose Air Crisp, set the temperature to 400°F or 205°C, and set the time to 8 minutes. Choose Start/Stop to begin grilling.
6. When ready, check the steaks for your preferred doneness and cook for a few more minutes if needed. Take out the steaks from the basket and rest for 5 minutes. Serve the steaks with the potato wedges and the steak sauce.

Korean-inspired Beef

Servings: 6
Cooking Time: 22 Minutes
Ingredients:
- ¼ cup low-sodium beef broth or Vegetable Broth
- ¼ cup low-sodium gluten-free tamari or soy sauce
- 2 tbsps. apple cider vinegar
- 2 tsps Sriracha sauce (optional)
- 2 tbsps. black molasses
- 1 tbsp. sesame oil
- 3 tbsps. minced garlic
- 1 tbsp. peeled and minced fresh chives
- 1 tsp. freshly ground black pepper

- 2 pounds top round beef, cut into thin, 3-inch-long strips
- 2 tbsps. cornstarch
- 1 tsp. sesame seeds
- 2 scallions, green parts only, thinly sliced

Directions:
1. Combine the broth, tamari, vinegar, Sriracha , black molasses, sesame oil, garlic, chives and pepper in a 2-cup measuring cup or medium bowl.
2. Incorporate the meat and broth mixture in the Ninja pressure cooker, stir to combine.
3. Close and lock the pressure cooker's cover. Set the valve to the closed position.
4. Cook for 10 minutes on high pressure.
5. When the cooking is finished, press Stop and release the pressure quickly.
6. Unlock and remove the cover after the pin has dropped.
7. Transfer the meat to a serving dish using a slotted spoon. Select Sauté/More from the menu.
8. To create a slurry, mix the cornstarch and 3 tablespoons cold water in a small bowl. Cook, stirring constantly, for approximately 2 minutes or until the sauce has thickened, whisking the cornstarch mixture into the liquid in the saucepan. Press the Stop button.
9. Drizzle the sauce over the meat and sprinkle with sesame seeds and scallions to finish.

Lamb Tagine

Servings:8
Cooking Time: 55 Minutes
Ingredients:
- 1 cup couscous
- 2 cups water
- 3 tablespoons extra-virgin olive oil, divided
- 2 yellow onions, diced
- 3 garlic cloves, minced
- 2 pounds lamb stew meat, cut into 1- to 2-inch cubes
- 1 cup dried apricots, sliced
- 2 cups chicken stock
- 2 tablespoons ras el hanout seasoning
- 1 can chickpeas, drained
- Kosher salt
- Freshly ground black pepper
- 1 cup toasted almonds, for garnish

Directions:
1. Place the couscous in the pot and pour in the water. Assemble pressure lid, making sure the pressure release valve is in the SEAL position.
2. Select PRESSURE and set to HI. Set time to 5 minutes. Select START/STOP to begin.
3. When pressure cooking is complete, quick release the pressure by turning the pressure release valve to the VENT position. Carefully remove lid when unit has finished releasing pressure.
4. Stir 1 tablespoon of oil into the couscous, then transfer the couscous to a bowl.
5. Select SEAR/SAUTÉ and set to MD:HI. Select START/STOP to begin. Let preheat for 3 minutes
6. Add the remaining 2 tablespoons of oil, onion, garlic, and lamb. Sauté for 7 to 10 minutes, stirring frequently.
7. Add the apricots, chicken stock, and ras el hanout. Stir to combine. Assemble pressure lid, making sure the pressure release valve is in the SEAL position.

8. Select PRESSURE and set to HI. Set time to 30 minutes. Select START/STOP to begin.
9. When pressure cooking is complete, quick release the pressure by turning the pressure release valve to the VENT position. Carefully remove lid when unit has finished releasing pressure.
10. Stir in the chickpeas.
11. Select SEAR/SAUTÉ and set to MD:LO. Select START/STOP to begin. Let the mixture simmer for 10 minutes. Season with salt and pepper.
12. When cooking is complete, ladle the tagine over the couscous. Garnish with the toasted almonds.

Nutrition:
- InfoCalories: 596,Total Fat: 21g,Sodium: 354mg,Carbohydrates: 65g,Protein: 39g.

Pork Pie

Servings:8
Cooking Time: 45 Minutes
Ingredients:
- 2 tablespoons extra-virgin olive oil
- 1 pound ground pork
- 1 yellow onion, diced
- 1 can black beans, drained
- 1 cup frozen corn kernels
- 1 can green chiles
- 2 tablespoons chili powder
- 1 box cornbread mix
- 1½ cups milk
- 1 cup shredded Cheddar cheese

Directions:
1. Select SEAR/SAUTÉ and set temperature to MED. Select START/STOP to begin. Let preheat for 3 minutes.
2. Add the olive oil, pork, and onion. Brown the pork, stirring frequently to break the meat into smaller pieces, until cooked through, about 5 minutes.
3. Add the beans, corn, chiles, and chili powder and stir. Simmer, stirring frequently, about 10 minutes.
4. In a medium bowl, combine the cornbread mix, milk, and cheese. Pour it over simmering mixture in an even layer. Close crisping lid.
5. Select BAKE/ROAST, set temperature to 360°F, and set time for 25 minutes. Select START/STOP to begin.
6. After 20 minutes, use wooden toothpick to check if cornbread is done. If the toothpick inserted into the cornbread does not come out clean, close lid and cook for the remaining 5 minutes.
7. When cooking is complete, open lid. Let cool for 10 minutes before slicing and serving.

Nutrition:
- InfoCalories: 491,Total Fat: 24g,Sodium: 667mg,Carbohydrates: 47g,Protein: 24g.

Barbecue Juicy Pork Chops

Servings: 4
Cooking Time: 100 Min
Ingredients:
- 4 bone-in pork chops
- 1½ cups chicken broth /375ml
- 1 tbsp freshly ground black pepper /15g
- 1 tbsp olive oil /15ml
- 4 tbsp barbecue sauce /60ml
- 3 tbsp brown sugar /45g
- 1 tbsp salt /15g

- 1½ tbsp smoked paprika /22.5g
- 2 tsp garlic powder /10g

Directions:

1. Choose Sear/Sauté and set to High. Choose Start/Stop to preheat the pot. In a small bowl, mix the brown sugar, salt, paprika, garlic powder, and black pepper. Season both sides of the pork with the rub. Heat the oil in the preheated pot and sear the pork chops, one at a time, on both sides, about 5 minutes per chop. Set aside.

2. Pour the chicken broth into the pot and with a wooden spoon, scrape the bottom of the pot of any browned bits. Place the Crisping Basket in the upper position of the pot. Put the pork chops in the basket and brush with 2 tbsps of barbecue sauce.

3. Seal the pressure lid, choose Pressure and set to High. Set the time to 5 minutes, then Choose Start/Stop to begin cooking. When the timer is done, perform a natural pressure release for 10 minutes, then a quick pressure release, and carefully open the lid.

4. Apply the remaining barbecue sauce on both sides of the pork and close the crisping lid. Choose Broil and set the time to 3 minutes. Press Start/Stop to begin. When ready, check for your desired crispiness and remove the pork from the basket.

Awesome Korean Pork Lettuce Wraps

Servings: 8
Cooking Time: 60 Minutes
Ingredients:

- ¼ cup of miso
- ¼ cup of soy sauce (Low Sodium)/Coconut Aminos
- 3 tablespoon of Korean red paste
- 1 teaspoon of ground sesame oil
- 1 teaspoon of ground black pepper
- 1 pork shoulder trimmed of excess fat
- Lettuce leaves
- Radishes
- Cucumbers
- Green onion

Directions:

1. Take a small bowl and add miso, soy sauce, ¼ cup of water Korean red paste, black pepper, and sesame oil. Mix well until smooth

2. Pour half of the sauce into your Ninja Foodi . Add pork and pour the rest of the sauce on top

3. Lock up the lid and cook on HIGH pressure for 1 hour. Release the pressure naturally

4. Shred the pork and serve in lettuce wraps with cucumbers, radish, green onion etc.

Asian Beef

Servings: 6
Cooking Time: 15 Minutes
Ingredients:

- 1/4 cup soy sauce
- 1/2 cup beef broth
- 1 tablespoon sesame oil
- 1/4 cup brown erythritol, packed
- 4 cloves garlic, minced
- 1 teaspoon hot sauce
- 1 tablespoon rice wine vinegar
- 1 tablespoon ginger, grated
- 1/2 teaspoon onion powder
- 1/2 teaspoon pepper

- 3 lb. boneless beef chuck roast, cubed
- 3 tablespoons corn starch dissolved in 1 teaspoon water

Directions:

1. Mix all the seasonings in a suitable bowl except the chuck roast and corn starch.

2. Pour the mixture into the Ninja Foodi. Stir in the beef. Seal the pot.

3. Select pressure. Cook at "HIGH" pressure for 15 minutes.

4. Do a quick pressure release. Stir in the corn starch.

5. Select sauté setting to thicken the sauce.

Nutrition:

- InfoCalories: 482; Fat: 16.6g; Carbohydrate: 8.4g; Protein: 70.1g

Beef Stroganoff

Servings:6
Cooking Time: 55 Minutes
Ingredients:

- 2 tablespoons unsalted butter
- 1 yellow onion, diced
- 4 cups cremini mushrooms, sliced
- 2 pounds beef stew meat, cut in 1- to 2-inch cubes
- 2 teaspoons freshly ground black pepper
- 2 sprigs fresh thyme
- 2 tablespoons soy sauce
- 2 cups chicken stock
- 1 package egg noodles
- 2 tablespoons cornstarch
- 2 tablespoons water
- ½ cup sour cream

Directions:

1. Select SEAR/SAUTÉ and set to MED. Select START/STOP to begin. Let preheat for 3 minutes.

2. Add the butter, onion, and mushrooms and sauté for 5 minutes.

3. Add the beef, black pepper, thyme, soy sauce, and chicken stock. Simmer for 2 to 3 minutes. Assemble pressure lid, making sure the pressure release valve is in the SEAL position.

4. Select PRESSURE and set to HI. Set time to 10 minutes. Select START/STOP to begin.

5. When pressure cooking is complete, quick release the pressure by turning the pressure release valve to the VENT position. Carefully remove lid when unit has finished releasing pressure.

6. Add the egg noodles. Stir well. Assemble pressure lid, making sure the pressure release valve is in the SEAL position.

7. Select PRESSURE and set to HI. Set time to 5 minutes. Select START/STOP to begin.

8. In a small bowl, mix the cornstarch and water until smooth.

9. When pressure cooking is complete, quick release the pressure by turning the pressure release valve to the VENT position. Carefully remove lid when unit has finished releasing pressure.

10. Stir in cornstarch until incorporated. Stir in the sour cream. Serve immediately.

Nutrition:

- InfoCalories: 448,Total Fat: 16g,Sodium: 605mg,Carbohydrates: 35g,Protein: 41g.

Chicken Pho

Servings: 4
Cooking Time:29 Minutes
Ingredients:
- 1 tablespoon extra-virgin olive oil
- 1 onion, diced
- 1½ teaspoons ground coriander
- ½ teaspoon ground cinnamon
- ¼ teaspoon ground cardamom
- ¼ teaspoon ground cloves
- 1 pound boneless, skinless chicken breasts
- 1 (1-inch) piece ginger, peeled and chopped
- 1 lemongrass stalk, trimmed and cut into 2-inch pieces
- ¼ cup fish sauce
- 2 cups chicken broth
- ¼ teaspoon sea salt
- 1 (16-ounce) package rice vermicelli, prepared according to package directions
- Lime wedges, bean sprouts, sliced jalapeño peppers, and/or fresh basil leaves, for garnish (optional)

Directions:
1. Select Sear/Sauté and set to Medium High. Select Start/Stop to begin. Allow the pot to preheat for 5 minutes.
2. Put the oil and onion in the preheated pot and cook for 3 minutes, stirring occasionally. Add the coriander, cinnamon, cardamom, and cloves to the pot and toast until fragrant, about 1 minute.
3. Add the chicken and cook to brown for 5 minutes.
4. Add the ginger, lemongrass, fish sauce, chicken broth, and salt to the pot. Assemble the Pressure Lid, making sure the pressure release valve is in the Seal position. Select Pressure and set to High. Set the time to 13 minutes, then select Start/Stop to begin.
5. When pressure cooking is complete, quick release the pressure by moving the pressure release valve to the Vent position. Carefully remove the lid when the pressure has finished releasing.
6. Remove and discard the ginger and lemongrass. Remove the chicken from the pot and use two forks to shred the meat.
7. Divide the rice noodles and shredded chicken among bowls and ladle some of the broth into each bowl. Let the soup sit for about 3 minutes to rehydrate the noodles. Garnish each bowl with toppings such as lime wedges, bean sprouts, jalapeño slices, and basil leaves (if using), and serve.

Cajun Red Beans And Rice

Servings:4
Cooking Time: 47 Minutes
Ingredients:
- For the Rice:
- 2 cups short-grain white rice, rinsed well
- ½ teaspoon kosher salt
- For the Beans:
- 3 tablespoons peanut oil or vegetable oil
- 3 celery stalks, chopped
- 1 medium yellow onion, diced
- 1 green bell pepper, seeded, ribbed, and diced
- 3 garlic cloves, minced
- 5 sprigs fresh thyme
- 2 dried bay leaves, or 1 fresh
- 3 tablespoons Cajun seasoning
- 1 smoked ham hock
- 1 pound (454 g) dried red kidney beans
- 1 teaspoon kosher salt
- Fresh thyme leaves, for garnish
- Black pepper, for garnish

Directions:
1. Make the Rice
2. Add the rice, 2 cups water, and the salt to the Foodi's inner pot. Lock on the Pressure Lid, making sure the valve is set to Seal, and set to Pressure on High for 3 minutes. When the timer reaches 0, allow the pressure to naturally release for 11 minutes, then quick-release any remaining pressure and carefully remove the lid. Transfer the rice to a large bowl. Wash and dry the inner pot.
3. Make the Beans
4. Add the oil to the inner pot, set the Foodi to Sear/Sauté on High, and heat the oil for 5 minutes. Add the celery, onion, and bell pepper and cook until beginning to soften, about 6 minutes, stirring often.
5. Add the garlic, thyme, bay leaves, and Cajun seasoning and cook until aromatic, about 3 minutes, stirring occasionally.
6. Add the ham hock, kidney beans, and 4 cups water and stir. Lock on the Pressure Lid, making sure the valve is set to Seal, and set the Foodi to Pressure on High for 30 minutes. When the timer reaches 0, allow the pressure to naturally release for 15 minutes, then quick-release any remaining pressure and carefully remove the lid. Stir in the salt. Add a ladleful of beans and broth to a bowl, top with a small scoop of rice, and serve with extra thyme and pepper.

Beef Meatballs With Roasted Tomatoes

Servings: 4
Cooking Time: 16 Minutes
Ingredients:
- 2 tablespoons avocado oil
- 1 pound (454 g) ground beef
- ½ teaspoon dried basil
- ½ teaspoon crushed red pepper
- ½ teaspoon ground cayenne pepper
- ½ teaspoon kosher salt
- ½ teaspoon freshly ground black pepper
- 2 (14-ounce / 397-g) cans fire roasted tomatoes

Directions:
1. Press the Sauté button and heat the avocado oil.
2. In a large bowl, mix the remaining ingredients, except for the tomatoes. Form the mixture into 1½-inch meatballs and place them in the cooking pot. Spread the tomatoes evenly over the meatballs.
3. Assemble pressure lid, making sure the pressure release valve is in the Seal position. Select Pressure and set to high . Set time to 16 minutes. Press Start to begin.
4. When timer beeps, perform a natural pressure release for 5 minutes, then release any remaining pressure.
5. Open the lid and serve.

Easy Burnt Ends

Servings:6
Cooking Time: 1 Hour, 50 Minutes
Ingredients:
- 3 pounds beef brisket, some (but not all) fat trimmed
- ¼ cup barbecue spice rub
- 1 cup water
- 2 cups barbecue sauce

Directions:

1. Season the brisket liberally and evenly with the barbecue spice rub.
2. Add the water, then place the brisket in the pot. Assemble pressure lid, making sure the pressure release valve is in the SEAL position.
3. Select PRESSURE and set to HI. Set time to 1 hour, 30 minutes. Select START/STOP to begin.
4. When pressure cooking is complete, quick release the pressure by moving the pressure release valve to the VENT position. Carefully remove lid when unit has finished releasing pressure.
5. Carefully remove the brisket from the pot and place on a cutting board. Let cool at room temperature for 10 minutes, or until brisket can be easily handled.
6. Cut the brisket into 2-inch chunks. Drain the cooking liquid from the pot. Place the brisket chunks in the pot. Add the barbecue sauce and stir gently so the brisket chunks are coated. Close crisping lid.
7. Select AIR CRISP, set temperature to 360°F, and set time to 20 minutes. Select START/STOP to begin.
8. When cooking is complete, open lid and serve.

Nutrition:

*   InfoCalories: 449,Total Fat: 14g,Sodium: 933mg,Carbohydrates: 32g,Protein: 48g.

Beef Jerky

Servings: 4
Cooking Time: 20 Minutes
Ingredients:

*   1/2-pound beef, sliced into 1/8-inch-thick strips
*   1/2 cup of soy sauce
*   2 tablespoons Worcestershire sauce
*   2 teaspoons black pepper
*   1 teaspoon onion powder
*   1/2 teaspoon garlic powder
*   1 teaspoon salt

Directions:

1. Add listed ingredient to a large-sized Ziploc bag, seal it shut.
2. Shake well, seal and leave it in the fridge overnight.
3. Lay strips on dehydrator trays, making sure not to overlap them.
4. Lock Air Crisping Lid and Set its cooking temperature to 135 °F, cook for 7 hours.

Nutrition:

*   InfoCalories: 62; Fat: 7g; Carbohydrates: 2g; Protein: 9g

Beef Satay With Peanut Sauce And Cucumber Salsa

Servings: 4
Cooking Time: 20 Minutes
Ingredients:

*   FOR THE BEEF
*   ½ tsp. kosher salt (or ¼ tsp. fine salt)
*   1 pound (455 g) skirt steak
*   1 tbsp. coconut oil or vegetable oil
*   1 tbsp. soy sauce
*   1 tbsp. freshly squeezed lime juice (from about ½ lime)
*   1½ tsps. Thai red curry paste
*   FOR THE CUCUMBER RELISH
*   ½ English (hothouse) cucumber
*   ¼ cup water

*   ½ cup rice vinegar
*   2 tbsps. sugar
*   1 tsp. kosher salt (or ½ tsp. fine salt)
*   1 serrano chile, cut into thin rounds (optional)
*   FOR THE SAUCE
*   1 tbsp. coconut oil or vegetable oil
*   1 tsp. finely minced garlic
*   1 tbsp. finely minced onion
*   2 tsps. Thai red curry paste
*   1 cup coconut milk
*   1 tsp. brown sugar
*   ⅓ cup water
*   ½ cup peanut butter
*   1 tablespoon freshly squeezed lime juice

Directions:

1. TO MAKE THE BEEF
2. Sprinkle the salt on both sides of the skirt steak. Place in a resealable plastic bag and set aside while you make the marinade.
3. Whisk together the coconut oil, soy sauce, lime juice and curry paste in a small bowl. Pour over the steak into the bag, seal, and squish the bag around to coat the steak. Set aside for 20 minutes.
4. TO MAKE THE CUCUMBER RELISH
5. Meanwhile, prepare the cucumber relish. Cut the cucumber into ¼-inch slices, then cut each slice into quarters.
6. Add the water, vinegar, sugar, and salt into a medium bowl, whisk them together until the sugar and salt dissolve. Add the cucumber pieces and serrano . Refrigerate until needed.
7. TO MAKE THE SAUCE
8. On your Foodi, preheat the inner pot by selecting Sear/Sauté. Press Start. Preheat for 5 minutes. Add the coconut oil and heat until shimmering. Stir in the garlic and onion. Cook and stir for 1 to 2 minutes, or until fragrant and slightly softened.
9. Add the curry paste, coconut milk, and brown sugar, and stir well.
10. Lock the Pressure Lid into place, set the valve to Seal. Select Pressure, adjust the cook time to 0.5 minute . Press Start.
11. When the cooking is complete, quick release the pressure. Open and remove the Pressure Lid carefully. Stir in the water.
12. Take the steak out from the marinade and place it on the Reversible Rack set to the upper position. Place the rack with the steak in the pot.
13. Close the Crisping Lid and select Broil. Adjust the cook time to 14 minutes. Press Start. After cooking for about 7 minutes, open the lid and flip the steak over. Close the lid and continue cooking.
14. After cooking, place the steak onto a cutting board or a wire rack set on a baking sheet and allow it to rest for a few minutes.
15. Meanwhile, stir the lime juice and peanut butter into the sauce. Taste and adjust the seasoning.
16. Cut the steak against the grain into thin slices, serve with the peanut sauce and cucumber relish on the side.

Turkey Potpie

Servings: 6
Cooking Time:33 Minutes
Ingredients:

- 4 tablespoons (½ stick) unsalted butter
- 1 onion, diced
- 2 garlic cloves, minced
- 2 pounds boneless turkey breasts, cut into 1-inch cubes
- 2 Yukon Gold potatoes, diced
- 1 cup chicken broth
- ½ teaspoon sea salt
- ½ teaspoon freshly ground black pepper
- 1 (16-ounce) bag mixed frozen vegetables
- ½ cup heavy (whipping) cream
- 1 store-bought refrigerated piecrust, at room temperature

Directions:
1. Select Sear/Sauté and set to Medium High. Select Start/Stop to begin. Allow the pot to preheat for 5 minutes.
2. Put the butter, onion, and garlic in the preheated pot and sauté until the onion is softened, about 3 minutes.
3. Add the turkey, potatoes, and broth to the pot. Season with the salt and black pepper. Assemble the Pressure Lid, making sure the pressure release valve is in the Seal position.
4. Select Pressure and set to High. Set the time to 10 minutes, then select Start/Stop to begin.
5. When pressure cooking is complete, quick release the pressure by moving the pressure release valve to the Vent position. Carefully remove the lid when the pressure has finished releasing.
6. Select Sear/Sauté and set to Medium High. Select Start/Stop to begin. Add the frozen vegetables and cream to the pot. Stir until the sauce thickens and bubbles, about 3 minutes.
7. Lay the piecrust evenly on top of the filling mixture, folding over the edges if necessary. Make a small cut in the center of the crust so that steam can escape during baking.
8. Close the Crisping Lid. Select Broil and set the time to 10 minutes. Select Start/Stop to begin.
9. When cooking is complete, remove the pot from the Ninja Foodi™ and it place on a heat-resistant surface. Let the potpie rest for 10 to 15 minutes before serving.

Cheesy Chicken Enchilada Casserole

Servings: 6
Cooking Time:34 Minutes
Ingredients:

- 1 tablespoon extra-virgin olive oil
- 1 yellow onion, diced
- 2 garlic cloves, minced
- 1 pound boneless, skinless chicken breasts
- 2 cups enchilada sauce
- ¼ teaspoon sea salt
- ¼ teaspoon freshly ground black pepper
- 1 (15-ounce) can black beans, drained and rinsed
- 1 (16-ounce) bag frozen corn
- 8 (6-inch) corn tortillas, each cut into 8 pieces
- 2 cups shredded Cheddar cheese, divided

Directions:
1. Select Sear/Sauté and set to Medium High. Select Start/Stop to begin. Allow the pot to preheat for 5 minutes.

2. Put the oil and onion in the preheated pot and cook for 5 minutes, stirring occasionally. Add the garlic and cook until fragrant, about 1 minute more.
3. Add the chicken and enchilada sauce to the pot, and season with the salt and black pepper. Stir to combine.
4. Assemble the Pressure Lid, making sure the pressure release valve is in the Seal position. Select Pressure and set to High. Set the time to 15 minutes, then select Start/Stop to begin.
5. When pressure cooking is complete, quick release the pressure by moving the pressure release valve to the Vent position. Carefully remove the lid when the pressure has finished releasing.
6. Shred the chicken with silicone tongs. Add the black beans, corn, tortilla pieces, and 1 cup of Cheddar cheese to the pot. Stir to combine.
7. Arrange the remaining 1 cup of cheese evenly on top of the casserole. Close the Crisping Lid. Select Broil and set the time to 5 minutes. Press Start/Stop to begin.
8. When cooking is complete, let the casserole sit for 5 minutes before serving.

Pot Roast With Broccoli

Servings: 4
Cooking Time: 35 Min
Ingredients:

- 2 lb. beef chuck roast /900g
- 1 packet onion soup mix
- 2 red bell peppers, seeded and quartered
- 1 yellow onion, quartered
- 1 cup chopped broccoli /130g
- 1 cup beef broth /250ml
- 3 tbsp olive oil; divided into 2 /45ml
- Salt to taste

Directions:
1. Season the chuck roast with salt and set aside. Select Sear/Sauté mode on the Foodi cooker. Add the olive oil, and once heated, add the chuck roast. Sear for 5 minutes on each side. Then, pour in the beef broth.
2. In a zipper bag, add broccoli, onions, peppers, the remaining olive oil, and onion soup. Close the bag and shake the mixture to coat the vegetables well. Use tongs to remove the vegetables into the pot and stir with a spoon.
3. Close the lid, secure the pressure valve, and select Pressure mode on High pressure for 18 minutes. Press Start/Stop.
4. Once the timer has stopped, do a quick pressure release, and open the pressure lid. Make cuts on the meat inside the pot and close the crisping lid.
5. Cook on Air Crisp mode for about 10 minutes, at 380 °F or 194°C, until nice and crispy. Plate and serve with the vegetables and a drizzle of the sauce in the pot.

Pork Medallions With Dijon Sauce

Servings: 4
Cooking Time: 10 Minutes
Ingredients:

- 1 lb. pork tenderloin, cut in 1-inch-thick slices
- ¼ tsp salt
- ¼ tsp pepper
- 1 tbsp. olive oil
- ¼ cup half-and-half
- 1 tbsp. Dijon mustard

Directions:

1. Place the pork slices between 2 sheets of plastic wrap and pound out to ¼-inch thick. Season with salt and pepper.
2. Add the oil to the cooking pot and set to sauté on med-high.
3. Add the pork and cook until browned on both sides, about 2-3 minutes per side. Transfer to a plate and keep warm.
4. Reduce the heat to low and add half and half and mustard stirring to combine. Cook 1-2 minutes until heated through.
5. Place pork medallions on serving plates and top with sauce. Serve immediately.
Nutrition:
- InfoCalories 165,Total Fat 6g,Total Carbs 2g,Protein 24g,Sodium 263mg.

Flank Steak With Bell Pepper Salsa
Servings: 6
Cooking Time: 30 Minutes
Ingredients:
- 2 tbsp. soy sauce, low sodium
- 4 tbsp. apple cider vinegar, divided
- 5 cloves garlic, chopped fine, divided
- 4 tbsp. olive oil, divided
- ¼ tsp pepper
- 2 lb. flank steak
- 1 green bell pepper, chopped fine
- 4 green onions, sliced thin
- 2 tbsp. fresh basil, chopped
- ¼ tsp red pepper flakes
- Salt & pepper to taste

Directions:
1. In a large bowl, combine soy sauce, 2 tablespoons vinegar, 4 cloves of garlic, 2 tablespoons oil, and pepper, mix well. Place the steak in the bowl and turn to coat. Let sit 20 minutes.
2. In a medium bowl, combine bell pepper, green onions, 1 clove garlic, basil, pepper flakes, remaining vinegar and oil, mix well. Salt and pepper to taste. Cover until ready to use.
3. Spray the rack with cooking spray and place in the cooking pot.
4. Lay the steak on the rack. Add the tender-crisp lid and set to broil. Cook steak 3-4 minutes per side, for rare, 5-6 minutes per side for medium rare, or to desired doneness.
5. Transfer meat to a cutting board and tent with foil. Let rest 10-15 minutes before slicing.
6. Slice against the grain and top with salsa to serve.
Nutrition:
- InfoCalories 161,Total Fat 10g,Total Carbs 2g,Protein 15g,Sodium 312mg.

The Authentic Beef Casserole
Servings:4
Cooking Time: 8 Hours
Ingredients:
- ½ cabbage, roughly sliced
- 1 onion, diced
- 3 cloves garlic, chopped
- 1 and ½ pounds ground beef
- 2 cups cauliflower rice
- 4 tablespoons Ghee
- 1 heaping tablespoon Italian seasoning
- ½ teaspoon crushed red pepper

- Salt and pepper to taste
- ½ cup fresh parsley, chopped
Directions:
1. Add the listed to your Ninja Foodi and give it a nice stir
2. Place lid and cook on SLOW COOK MODE for 7-8 hours until the beef is cooked
3. Stir in parsley and serve. Enjoy!

Stuffed Cabbage Rolls
Servings: 6
Cooking Time: 5 Hours
Ingredients:
- 12 cabbage leaves
- 3 ¼ tsp salt, divided
- 15 oz. tomato sauce
- 2 tbsp. honey
- 1 tsp paprika
- ½ tsp thyme
- 2 tbsp. lemon juice
- 2 tbsp. ketchup
- 1 tsp Worcestershire sauce
- 1 ¼ tsp pepper
- 1 cup long grain brown rice, cooked
- 1 egg, beaten
- ¼ cup milk
- ¼ cup onion, chopped fine
- 1 clove garlic, chopped fine
- 1 lb. lean ground beef

Directions:
1. Fill a large pot with water and add 2 teaspoons salt. Bring to a boil on high heat. Add cabbage leaves and boil 2 minutes. Transfer leaves to a plate and let cool.
2. In a medium bowl, whisk together tomato sauce, honey, spices, lemon juice, ketchup, Worcestershire, remaining salt, and pepper until smooth.
3. In a separate bowl, combine rice, egg, milk, onion, garlic, and beef. Stir in ¼ of the sauce and mix well.
4. Spoon ¼ cup of beef mixture into the center of each cabbage leaf. Roll up, tucking in the ends. Place in the cooking pot. Pour remaining sauce over the rolls.
5. Add the lid and set to slow cook in high. Cook 4-5 hours until cabbage is tender and filling is cooked through. Serve.
Nutrition:
- InfoCalories 282,Total Fat 10g,Total Carbs 25g,Protein 24g,Sodium 1732mg.

Pork And Cauliflower Dish
Servings:4
Cooking Time: 65 Minutes
Ingredients:
- 1 onion, chopped
- 4 cloves garlic, crushed and minced
- 4 cups cauliflower, chopped
- 2 ribs celery
- Salt and pepper to taste
- 3-pound pork roast
- 8 ounces mushrooms, sliced
- 2 tablespoons coconut oil
- 2 tablespoons ghee
Directions:
1. Add onion, garlic, cauliflower, celery to Ninja Foodi
2. Put pork roast on top. Season with salt and pepper

3. Add 2 cups of water. Lock lid and cook on HIGH pressure 60 minutes
4. Quick release pressure. Transfer roast to baking pan
5. Add pan to oven and bake for 5 minutes at 400 degrees F
6. Prepare gravy by transfer the remaining contents from the pot to a blender
7. Blend until smooth. Set your pot to Saute mode and add coconut oil and ghee
8. Add mushrooms and blended mixture. Cook for 5 minutes
9. Serve pot roast with mushroom gravy and enjoy!

Mongolian Beef And Broccoli
Servings: 4
Cooking Time:30 Minutes
Ingredients:
- 1 tablespoon extra-virgin olive oil
- 2 pounds flank steak, cut into ¼-inch-thick strips
- 4 garlic cloves, minced
- ½ cup soy sauce
- ½ cup water, plus 3 tablespoons
- ⅔ cup dark brown sugar
- ½ teaspoon minced fresh ginger
- 2 tablespoons cornstarch
- 1 head broccoli, trimmed into florets
- 3 scallions, thinly sliced

Directions:
1. Select Sear/Sauté and set to Medium High. Select Start/Stop to begin. Allow the pot to preheat for 5 minutes.
2. Put the oil and beef in the preheated pot and sear the beef strips on both sides, about 5 minutes total. Remove from the pot and set aside.
3. Add the garlic to the pot and sauté for 1 minute.
4. Add the soy sauce, ½ cup of water, the brown sugar, and ginger to the pot. Stir to combine. Return the beef to the pot.
5. Assemble the Pressure Lid, making sure the pressure release valve is in the Seal position. Select Pressure and set to High. Set the time to 10 minutes, then select Start/Stop to begin.
6. Meanwhile, in a small mixing bowl whisk together the cornstarch and remaining 3 tablespoons of water.
7. When pressure cooking is complete, quick release the pressure by moving the pressure release valve to the Vent position. Carefully remove the lid when the pressure has finished releasing.
8. Select Sear/Sauté and set to Medium Low. Select Start/Stop to begin. Add the cornstarch mixture to the pot, stirring continuously until the sauce comes to a simmer.
9. Add the broccoli to the pot, stirring to coat it evenly in the sauce, and cook for another 5 minutes.
10. Once cooking is complete, garnish with the scallions.

Tonkatsu Shoyu Ramen
Servings: 4
Cooking Time: 25 Minutes
Ingredients:
- 3 tbsps. vegetable oil
- 1 small (12-ounce, 340 g) pork tenderloin
- ½ tsp. kosher salt (or ¼ tsp. fine salt)
- 2 cups panko bread crumbs
- 4 cups Chicken Stock, or store-bought low-sodium chicken broth
- ⅓ cup all-purpose flour

- 1 large egg, beaten
- 1 tbsp. sesame oil
- 1 tbsp. soy sauce
- ½ tsp. granulated garlic
- 2 packages ramen noodles, seasoning packets discarded
- 2 scallions, chopped
- ½ cup frozen peas, thawed
- 1 medium carrot, peeled and grated
- ½ cup tonkatsu sauce

Directions:
1. Slice the tenderloin into about ⅓ inch thick pieces. Flatten each piece slightly with the heel of your hand, to about ¼ inch thick. Use salt to season on both sides of the slices. Set aside.
2. On your Foodi, preheat the inner pot by selecting Sear/Sauté. Press Start. Preheat for 5 minutes. Add the vegetable oil and heat until shimmering. When the pot is hot, add the panko and stir to coat with the oil. Cook for about 3 minutes, until the crumbs are a light golden brown, stirring. Place them onto a shallow dish to cool. Set aside.
3. Place the pot back to the base, select Sear/Sauté. Pour in the chicken stock to warm.
4. In a shallow bowl, add the flour. And in a separate shallow bowl, add the beaten egg. While the stock heats, dredge each pork piece in flour to coat completely. Pat off the excess. Then transfer it into the egg and turn to coat both sides. Place into the panko, pressing the pork into the panko to make sure it adheres. Put the tenderloin slices on the Reversible Rack set in the upper position and set the rack aside.
5. Add the sesame oil, soy sauce, and granulated garlic to the warm stock. Break up each block of noodles into 3 or 4 pieces and place them in the pot in a single layer as much as possible.
6. Lock the Pressure Lid into place,set the valve to Seal. Select Pressure, adjust the cook time to 0 minutes . Press Start.
7. When the cooking is complete, quick release the pressure. Open and remove the Pressure Lid carefully.
8. Stir in the scallions, peas, and carrot.
9. Put the rack with the pork in the pot in the upper position.
10. Close the Crisping Lid and select Broil. Adjust the cook time to 10 minutes. Press Start. After cooking for 5 minutes, open the lid. The cutlets should be browned and crisp. Turn them over and close the lid. Continue to cook until the second side is crisp. Serve with the tonkatsu sauce and a bowl of noodles and vegetables on the side.

Pork Teriyaki With Rice
Servings: 4
Cooking Time:24 Minutes
Ingredients:
- 1 cup long-grain white rice
- 1 cup water
- 1 head broccoli, trimmed into florets
- 1 tablespoon extra-virgin olive oil
- ¼ teaspoon sea salt
- ¼ teaspoon freshly ground black pepper
- 1 pork tenderloin, trimmed and cut into 1-inch pieces
- 1 cup teriyaki sauce
- Nonstick cooking spray
- Sesame seeds, for garnish

Directions:

1. Put the rice and water in the pot and stir to combine. Assemble the Pressure Lid, making sure the pressure release valve is in the Seal position. Select Pressure and set to High. Set the time to 2 minutes, then select Start/Stop to begin.

2. Meanwhile, in a large mixing bowl, toss the broccoli with the olive oil. Season with the salt and black pepper. In a medium mixing bowl, toss the pork with the teriyaki sauce until well coated.

3. When pressure cooking of the rice is complete, quick release the pressure by moving the pressure release valve to the Vent position. Carefully remove the lid when the pressure has finished releasing.

4. Place the Reversible Rack inside the pot over the rice, making sure the rack is in the higher position. Spray the rack with cooking spray. Place the pork pieces on the rack. Arrange the broccoli around the pork.

5. Close the Crisping Lid. Select Broil and set the time to 12 minutes. Press Start/Stop to begin.

6. After cooking is complete, check for your desired crispiness and remove the rack from the pot. Serve the pork and broccoli over the rice, garnished with sesame seeds.

Sausage & Roasted Red Pepper Linguine

Servings: 4
Cooking Time: 15 Minutes
Ingredients:
- 1 tbsp. extra virgin olive oil
- ¾ lb. Italian sausage
- 3 cloves garlic, chopped fine
- 1 cup roasted red bell peppers, chopped
- 1 tbsp. capers
- ½ cup black olives, pitted & halved
- 3 tomatoes, seeded & chopped
- ¼ cup fresh basil, chopped
- 1 lb. linguine, cooked & drained

Directions:
1. Add the oil to the cooking pot and set to sauté on medium heat.
2. Add sausage and break it up while it's cooking. When it starts to brown add the garlic and cook 1 minute more.
3. Stir in the peppers, capers, and olives and cook stirring 2 minutes.
4. Increase heat to high and add tomatoes and basil, cook 2 minutes more.
5. Add the pasta to the sausage mixture and toss to combine. Serve.

Nutrition:
- InfoCalories 203,Total Fat 9g,Total Carbs 23g,Protein 7g,Sodium 200mg.

Bacon & Blue Cheese Stuffed Burgers

Servings: 4
Cooking Time: 10 Minutes
Ingredients:
- Nonstick cooking spray
- 1 lb. lean ground beef
- 1/3 cup blue cheese, crumbled
- 4 slices bacon, cooked crisp & crumbled
- Salt & pepper to taste

Directions:
1. Spray the rack with cooking spray and add it to the cooking pot.
2. Divide the ground beef into 4 equal portions. Flatten each portion and top with blue cheese and bacon. Wrap ground beef around the cheese and bacon to cover them completely. Flatten into a patty and season with salt and pepper. Place the patties on the rack.
3. Add the tender-crisp lid and set to broil on 450°F. Cook burger patties 5-6 minutes per side, or to desired doneness. Serve on toasted buns with your favorite toppings.

Nutrition:
- InfoCalories 346,Total Fat 31g,Total Carbs 0g,Protein 15g,Sodium 311mg.

Pepper Crusted Tri Tip Roast

Servings: 6
Cooking Time: 45 Minutes
Ingredients:
- 1 tbsp. salt
- 1 tbsp. pepper
- 1 tbsp. garlic powder
- 1 tbsp. onion powder
- 1 tsp cayenne pepper
- 1 tbsp. oregano
- 1 tsp rosemary
- ½ tsp sage
- 3 lb. tri-tip roast
- Nonstick cooking spray

Directions:
1. In a small bowl, combine all the spices until mixed.
2. Place the roast on baking sheet and massage the rub mix into all sides. Cover and let sit 1 hour.
3. Lightly spray the cooking pot with cooking spray. Set to sear.
4. Add the roast and brown all sides. Add the tender-crisp lid and set to roast on 300°F.
5. Cook until meat thermometer reaches desired temperature for doneness, 120°F for a rare roast, 130°F for medium-rare and 140°F for medium, about 20-40 minutes.
6. Remove roast from cooking pot, tent with foil and let rest 10-15 minutes. Slice across the grain and serve.

Nutrition:
- InfoCalories 169,Total Fat 8g,Total Carbs 7g,Protein 19g,Sodium 2300mg.

The Epic Carne Guisada

Servings: 4
Cooking Time: 45 Minutes
Ingredients:
- 3 pounds beef stew
- 3 tablespoon seasoned salt
- 1 tablespoon oregano chili powder
- 1 tablespoon organic cumin
- 1 pinch crushed red pepper
- 2 tablespoons olive oil
- ½ medium lime, juiced
- 1 cup beef bone broth
- 3 ounces tomato paste
- 1 large onion, sliced

Directions:
1. Trim the beef stew as needed into small bite-sized portions
2. Toss the beef stew pieces with dry seasoning
3. Set your Ninja Foodi to Saute mode and add oil, allow the oil to heat up
4. Add seasoned beef pieces and brown them
5. Combine the browned beef pieces with rest of the
6. Lock up the lid and cook on HIGH pressure for 3 minutes. Release the pressure naturally . Enjoy!

Mean Cream Mushroom Garlic Chicken

Servings: 4
Cooking Time: 15 Minutes
Ingredients:

- 2 pounds chicken thighs
- 7 ounces Cremini mushrooms
- 2 teaspoons garlic, minced
- ½ cup chicken broth
- ½ cup whipping cream
- 1 teaspoon cayenne pepper
- 1 tablespoon lemon juice
- 1 tablespoon parsley, chopped
- 1 tablespoon olive oil
- Salt and pepper to taste

Directions:

1. Trim the stems of mushrooms. Wash and rinse chicken thighs under cold water
2. Pat dry with paper towels
3. Use kitchen scissors to trim excess skin and d fat from chicken thighs
4. Season both sides with salt and pepper, keep them on the side
5. Set your Ninja Foodi to Saute mode and add olive oil, let it heat up
6. Add chicken thighs and brown both sides. Scoop out excess fat and discard
7. Add garlic, whipping cream, mushrooms, broth, salt and pepper
8. Lock lid and cook on HIGH pressure for 10 minutes. Release pressure naturally over 10 minutes
9. Open the lid and set your pot to Saute mode. Add lemon juice and parsley. Serve and enjoy!

Spicy "faux" Pork Belly

Servings: 4
Cooking Time: 15 Minutes
Ingredients:

- 1 pound of pork belly, chopped
- 4 cups cauliflower, riced
- ½ a cup of bone broth
- ½ red onion, sliced
- ½ a cup of cilantro
- 2 green onion, sliced
- 1 tablespoon of lime juice
- 3 cloves garlic cloves, sliced
- 1 teaspoon turmeric
- 1 tablespoon oregano
- 1 tablespoon cumin
- ½ a teaspoon salt

Directions:

1. Add all of the to your Instant Pot except ¼ cup of cilantro
2. Lock up the lid and cook on HIGH pressure for 15 minutes
3. Release the pressure naturally over 10 minutes
4. Open the lid and serve with sprinkled cilantro leaves
5. Enjoy!

Beef Short Rib & Ale Stew

Servings: 8
Cooking Time: 3 Hours 30 Minutes
Ingredients:

- 4 slices bacon, thick cut
- ½ cup flour
- 2 tbsp. hot paprika
- 2 tsp smoked paprika
- 1 ½ tsp salt, divided
- 1 teaspoon pepper
- 4 lbs. beef short ribs, bone in & trimmed
- 1 onion, chopped
- 4 cloves garlic, chopped fine
- 12 oz. malty brown ale
- 14 ½ oz. whole peeled tomatoes, chopped & juices reserved
- 2 lbs. Yukon Gold potatoes, peel & cut in 1-inch pieces
- 2 large carrots, peel & cut in 1-inch pieces
- 1 lb. turnips, peel & cut in 1-inch pieces

Directions:

1. Add the bacon to the cooking pot and set to sauté on med-high heat. Cook until most of the fat has been rendered, about 5 minutes. Transfer bacon to a paper towel lined plate. Drain off all but 1 tablespoon of the fat.
2. In a large bowl, combine flour, both paprika, 1 teaspoon salt, and pepper, until well mixed. Coat the ribs on all sides.
3. Add the ribs to the pot, working in batches if needed, and brown on all sides, about 3-5 minutes per side. Transfer to a bowl.
4. Add the onions to the pot and season with ½ teaspoon salt. Cook, stirring occasionally, until translucent, about 4 minutes. Add the garlic and cook 1 minute more.
5. Stir in ale, scraping up brown bits from the bottom of the pot. Add tomatoes and crumble the bacon in the pot. Increase heat to high and bring to a boil.
6. Return the ribs to the pot. Add the lid and set to pressure cook on high. Set timer for 1 hour. When timer goes off, use quick release to remove the pressure.
7. Add the potatoes, turnips, and carrots, stir to combine. Replace the lid and pressure cook on high 20 minutes. When the timer goes off, use quick release again.
8. Remove the bones before ladling into bowls and serving.

Nutrition:

- InfoCalories 114,Total Fat 5g,Total Carbs 7g,Protein 9g,Sodium 119mg.

Paprika Pork And Brussels Sprouts

Servings: 4
Cooking Time: 30 Minutes
Ingredients:

- 2 tablespoons olive oil
- 2 pounds (907 g) pork shoulder, cubed
- 2 cups (500 mL) Brussels sprouts, trimmed and halved
- 1½ cups (375 mL) beef stock
- 1 tablespoon sweet paprika
- 1 tablespoon chopped parsley

Directions:

1. Press the Sauté button and heat the olive oil.
2. Add the pork and brown for 5 minutes. Stir in the remaining ingredients.
3. Assemble pressure lid, making sure the pressure release valve is in the Seal position. Select Pressure and set to high . Set time to 25 minutes. Press Start to begin.
4. Once cooking is complete, do a natural pressure release for 10 minutes, then release any remaining pressure. Carefully open the lid.
5. Divide the mix between plates and serve warm.

Chapter 10: Desserts

Baked Zucchini Bread

Servings: 6
Cooking Time: 40 Minutes
Ingredients:
- 2 eggs
- 8 tablespoons unsalted butter, melted
- 1⅓ cups sugar
- 1 teaspoon vanilla extract
- 1 teaspoon ground cinnamon
- ⅛ teaspoon ground nutmeg
- ½ teaspoon baking soda
- ¼ teaspoon baking powder
- ½ teaspoon sea salt
- 1½ cups all-purpose flour
- 1 cup grated zucchini
- Nonstick cooking spray

Directions:
1. Close the Crisping Lid. Preheat the unit by selecting Bake/Roast, setting the temperature to 325°F , and setting the time to 5 minutes. Select Start/Stop to begin.
2. Meanwhile, in a large mixing bowl, combine the eggs, butter, sugar, and vanilla. Add the cinnamon, nutmeg, baking soda, baking powder, and salt and stir to combine. Add the flour, a little at a time, stirring until combined.
3. Wring out the excess water from the zucchini and fold it into the batter.
4. Grease the Loaf Pan or another loaf pan with cooking spray and pour in the batter. Place the pan on the Reversible Rack, making sure the rack is in the lower position. Place the rack in the pot.
5. Close the Crisping Lid. Select Bake/Roast, set the temperature to 325°F , and set the time to 40 minutes. Select Start/Stop to begin.
6. When cooking is complete, remove the loaf pan from the pot and place it on a cooling rack. Allow the zucchini bread to cool for 30 minutes before slicing and serving.

Cherry Almond Bar Cookies

Servings: 9
Cooking Time: 15 Minutes
Ingredients:
- Butter flavored cooking spray
- ¼ cup dates
- 2 bananas
- 1 cup oats
- ½ cup cherries, dried, chopped
- ½ cup almond flour
- ½ cup almonds, chopped

Directions:

1. Place the rack in the cooking pot. Spray an 8x8-inch baking pan with cooking spray.
2. Place the dates in a food processor and pulse until they form a paste.
3. In a large bowl, mash the bananas with a fork.
4. Mix in remaining ingredients. Spread evenly in prepared pan.
5. Place the pan on the rack and add the tender-crisp lid. Set to bake on 325°F. Bake 15 minutes or until top is golden brown. Remove to wire rack to cool before cutting.

Nutrition:
- InfoCalories 177,Total Fat 5g,Total Carbs 30g,Protein 5g,Sodium 2mg.

Caramel Walnut Brownies

Servings: 4
Cooking Time: 60 Min+ Cooling Time
Ingredients:
- 2 large eggs, at room temperature
- 8 ounces white chocolate /240g
- 1 cup sugar /130g
- ½ cup caramel sauce/125ml
- ½ cup toasted walnuts /65g
- ¾ cup all-purpose flour /98g
- 8 tbsps unsalted butter /120g
- 2 tsp s almond extract /10ml
- A pinch of salt
- Cooking spray

Directions:
1. Put the white chocolate and butter in a small bowl and pour 1 cup or 250ml of water into the inner pot. Place the reversible rack in the lower position of the pot and put the bowl on top.
2. Close the crisping lid. Choose Bake/Roast; adjust the temperature to 375°F or 191°Cand the cook time to 10 minutes to melt the white chocolate and butter. Press Start. Check after 5 minutes and stir. As soon as the chocolate has melted, remove the bowl from the pot.
3. Use a small spatula to transfer the chocolate mixture into a medium and stir in the almond extract, sugar, and salt. One after another, crack each egg into the bowl and whisk after each addition. Mix in the flour until smooth, about 1 minute.
4. Grease a round cake pan with cooking spray or line the pan with parchment paper. Pour the batter into the prepared pan and place on the rack.
5. Close the crisping lid and Choose Bake/Roast; adjust the temperature to 250°F or 122°C and the cook time to 25 minutes. Press Start. Once the time is up, open the lid and check the brownies. The top should be just set. Blot out the butter that may pool to the top using a paper towel.

6. Close the crisping lid again and adjust the temperature to 300°F or 149°C and the cook time to 15 minutes. Press Start. Once the time is up, open the lid and check the brownies. A toothpick inserted into the center should come out with crumbs sticking to it but no raw batter.

7. Generously drizzle the caramel sauce on top of the brownies and scatter the walnuts on top. Close the crisping lid again and adjust the temperature to 325°F or 163°C and the cook time to 8 minutes; press Start.

8. When the nuts are brown and the caramel is bubbling, take out the brownies, and allow cooling for at least 30 minutes and cut into squares.

Apple Strudels

Servings: 8
Cooking Time: 25 Minutes
Ingredients:
- Butter flavored cooking spray
- 2 8 oz. whole grain puff pastry sheets
- 5 apples, cored, peeled & chopped
- ¼ cup raisins
- 1/8 cup pine nuts
- 1 tbsp. Stevia
- 1 tbsp. lemon zest
- ½ tsp cinnamon
- 1 egg

Directions:
1. Lightly spray the fryer basket with cooking spray.
2. Lay the puff pastry on a work surface and cut into 4 equal parts. Repeat with the second sheet.
3. In a large bowl, combine apples, raisins, pine nuts, Stevia, zest, and cinnamon and mix well. Spoon filling into center of each pastry piece. Fold over sides and roll up.
4. In a small bowl, whisk the egg. Place the pastries in the fryer basket in a single layer. Brush tops with egg.
5. Add the tender-crisp lid and set to air fry on 350°F. Bake 20-25 minutes or until puffed and golden brown. Serve immediately.

Nutrition:
- InfoCalories 376,Total Fat 23g,Total Carbs 17g,Protein 5g,Sodium 141mg.

Fried Oreos

Servings:9
Cooking Time: 8 Minutes
Ingredients:
- ½ cup complete pancake mix
- ⅓ cup water
- Cooking spray
- 9 Oreo cookies
- 1 tablespoon confectioners' sugar

Directions:
1. Close crisping lid. Select AIR CRISP, set temperature to 400°F, and set time to 5 minutes. Select START/STOP to begin preheating.
2. In a medium bowl, combine the pancake mix and water until combined.
3. Spray the Cook & Crisp Basket with cooking spray.
4. Dip each cookie into the pancake batter and then arrange them in the basket in a single layer so they are not touching each other. Cook in batches if needed.
5. When unit has preheated, open lid and insert basket into pot. Close crisping lid.
6. Select AIR CRISP, set temperature to 400°F, and set time to 8 minutes. Select START/STOP to begin.

7. After 4 minutes, open lid and flip the cookies. Close lid and continue cooking.
8. When cooking is complete, check for desired crispness. Remove basket and sprinkle the cookies with confectioners' sugar. Serve.

Nutrition:
- InfoCalories: 83,Total Fat: 2g,Sodium: 158mg,Carbohydrates: 14g,Protein: 1g.

Apple Cider

Servings: 6
Cooking Time: 45 Min
Ingredients:
- 6 green apples, cored and chopped
- 1/4 cup orange juice /62.5ml
- 3 cups water /750ml
- 2 cinnamon sticks

Directions:
1. In a blender, add orange juice, apples, and water and blend until smooth; use a fine-mesh strainer to strain and press using a spoon. Get rid of the pulp. In the cooker, mix the strained apple puree, and cinnamon sticks.
2. Seal the pressure lid, choose Pressure, set to High, and set the timer to 10 minutes. Press Start. Release the pressure naturally for 15 minutes, then quick release the remaining pressure. Strain again and do away with the solids.

Hearty Crème Brulee

Servings: 4
Cooking Time: 10 Minutes
Ingredients:
- 2 cups (500 mL) graham crackers, crushed
- 3 tablespoons brown sugar
- ¼ cup (63 mL) butter, melted
- Salt, to taste
- 2 (8-ounce / 227-g) cream cheese, softened
- ½ cup (125 mL) granulated sugar
- 2 large eggs
- 2 teaspoons vanilla extract
- ½ cup (125 mL) sour cream
- 2 tablespoons cornstarch
- 1 cup (250 mL) water
- 4 teaspoons white sugar

Directions:
1. Make the crust: Mix the crushed graham crackers with brown sugar, butter, and salt in a medium bowl. Spoon the mixture into 4 medium ramekins. Place in refrigerator for 15 minutes to harden.
2. In a bowl, stir the cream cheese and sugar until smooth. Whisk in eggs and vanilla until smooth. Fold in sour cream and cornstarch.
3. Remove ramekins from the refrigerator, then pour in the cream cheese mixture, and cover with foil.
4. Pour the water in the cooking pot, then place the reversible rack in pot, and place ramekins on top.
5. Assemble pressure lid, making sure the pressure release valve is in the Seal position. Select Pressure and set to high . Set time to 10 minutes. Press Start to begin.
6. When cooking is complete, allow a natural pressure release for 10 minutes, then release any remaining pressure.
7. Unlock the lid, carefully remove the ramekins and take off the foil. Allow to cool for 10 minutes and then chill further for 2 hours in the refrigerator.
8. Remove the ramekins from the refrigerator and sprinkle 1 teaspoon of sugar on each ramekin. Use a torch to caramelize the sugar until browned in color. Serve immediately.

Date Orange Cheesecake

Servings: 8
Cooking Time: 20 Minutes
Ingredients:
- Butter flavored cooking spray
- 2 cups water
- 2 lbs. ricotta cheese
- 4 eggs
- ¼ cup sugar
- ¼ cup honey
- Juice & zest of ½ orange
- ¼ tsp vanilla
- 1 cup dates, soak in warm water 20 minutes, chop fine

Directions:
1. Place the trivet in the cooking pot and add 2 cups water. Spray a deep, 8-inch springform pan with cooking spray.
2. In a large bowl, beat ricotta cheese until smooth.
3. In a medium bowl, beat eggs and sugar 3 minutes. Fold into ricotta cheese.
4. In a small saucepan, heat honey over low heat, do not let it get hot, just warm.
5. Whisk in orange juice, zest, and vanilla until combined. Whisk into cheese mixture until combined.
6. Fold in dates and pour into prepared pan. Cover with foil.
7. Place the cheesecake in the cooking pot and secure the lid. Set to pressure cooking on high. Set the timer for 20 minutes.
8. When timer goes off use natural release to remove the lid. Transfer cheesecake to wire rack to cool completely. Cover and refrigerate at least 4 hours before serving.

Nutrition:
- InfoCalories 343,Total Fat 17g,Total Carbs 32g,Protein 16g,Sodium 132mg.

Vanilla Hot Lava Cake

Servings: 8
Cooking Time: 40 Min
Ingredients:
- 1 ½ cups chocolate chips /195g
- 1 ½ cups sugar /195g
- 1 cup butter /130g
- 1 cup water /250ml
- 5 eggs
- 7 tbsp flour/105g
- 4 tbsp milk /60ml
- 4 tsp vanilla extract /20ml
- Powdered sugar to garnish

Directions:
1. Grease the cake pan with cooking spray and set aside. Open the Foodi, fit the reversible rack at the bottom of it, and pour in the water. In a medium heatproof bowl, add the butter and chocolate and melt them in the microwave for about 2 minutes. Remove it from the microwave.
2. Add sugar and use a spatula to stir it well. Add the eggs, milk, and vanilla extract and stir again. Finally, add the flour and stir it until even and smooth.
3. Pour the batter into the greased cake pan and use the spatula to level it. Place the pan on the trivet in the pot, close the lid, secure the pressure valve, and select Pressure on High for 15 minutes. Press Start/Stop.
4. Once the timer has gone off, do a natural pressure release for 10 minutes, then a quick pressure release, and open the lid.

5. Remove the rack with the pan on it and place the pan on a flat surface. Put a plate over the pan and flip the cake over into the plate. Pour the powdered sugar in a fine sieve and sift it over the cake. Use a knife to cut the cake into 8 slices and serve immediately (while warm).

Chocolate Rice Pudding

Servings: 8
Cooking Time: 20 Minutes
Ingredients:
- 2/3 cup brown rice, cooked
- 2 cans coconut milk
- ½ cup Stevia
- ½ tsp cinnamon
- 1/8 tsp salt
- 1 tsp vanilla
- ½ cup dark chocolate chips

Directions:
1. Set cooker to sauté on medium. Add milk, Stevia, cinnamon, and salt and bring to a simmer, stirring frequently.
2. Stir in rice and reduce heat to low. Cook 15 minutes, stirring occasionally, until pudding has thickened.
3. Turn off cooker and stir in vanilla and chocolate chips until chocolate has melted. Serve warm or refrigerate at least one hour and serve it cold.

Nutrition:
- InfoCalories 325,Total Fat 22g,Total Carbs 35g,Protein 3g,Sodium 62mg.

Baked Apples With Pecan Stuffing

Servings: 4
Cooking Time: 45 Minutes
Ingredients:
- 4 Fuji apples
- ½ cup pecans, chopped
- ¼ cup Stevia
- 2 tbsp. coconut oil, melted
- 1 tbsp. molasses
- ½ tsp cinnamon
- ½ cup water

Directions:
1. Hollow out the apples by carefully removing the core and seeds. Place in the cooking pot.
2. In a medium bowl, combine nuts, Stevia, oil, molasses, and cinnamon, mix well. Spoon into the apples, stuffing them fully.
3. Pour the water around the apples. Add the tender-crisp lid and set to bake on 350 °F. Bake 40-45 minutes. Let cool slightly before serving.

Nutrition:
- InfoCalories 329,Total Fat 17g,Total Carbs 49g,Protein 2g,Sodium 11mg.

Brown Sugar And Butter Bars

Servings: 6
Cooking Time: 55 Min
Ingredients:
- 1 ½ cups Water /375ml
- 1 cup Oats /130g
- ½ cup Brown Sugar /65g
- ½ cup Sugar /65g
- 1 cup Flour /130g
- ½ cup Peanut Butter, softened /65g

- ½ cup Butter, softened /65g
- 1 Egg
- ½ tsp Baking Soda /2.5g
- ½ tsp Salt /2.5g

Directions:
1. Grease a springform pan and line it with parchment paper. Set aside. Beat together the eggs, peanut butter, butter, salt, white sugar, and brown sugar. Fold in the oats, flour, and baking soda.
2. Press the batter into the pan. Cover the pan with a paper towel and with a piece of foil. Pour the water into the Foodi and add a reversible rack. Lower the springform pan onto the rack.
3. Seal the pressure lid, choose Pressure, set to High, and set the time to 35 minutes. Press Start. When ready, do a quick release. Wait for 15 minutes before inverting onto a plate and cutting into bars.

Cherry Pie

Servings: 6
Cooking Time: 45 Min
Ingredients:
- 1 9-inch double Pie Crust
- 4 cups Cherries, pitted /520g
- 1 cup Sugar /130g
- 2 cups Water /500ml
- 4 tbsp Quick Tapioca /60g
- ½ tsp Vanilla Extract /2.5ml
- ¼ tsp Almond Extract /1.25ml
- A pinch of Salt

Directions:
1. Pour water inside your cooker and add the reversible rack. Combine the cherries with tapioca, sugar, extracts, and salt, in a bowl. Place one pie crust at the bottom of a lined springform pan.
2. Spread the cherries mixture and top with the other crust. Lower the pan onto the reversible rack.
3. Seal the pressure lid, choose Pressure, set to High, and set the time to 18 minutes. Press Start. Once cooking is completed, do a quick pressure release. Let cool the pie on a cooling rack. Slice to serve.

Cranberry Cheesecake

Servings: 8
Cooking Time: 1 Hr
Ingredients:
- 1/3 cup dried cranberries /44g
- 1 cup water /250ml
- ½ cup sugar /65g
- 1 cup coarsely crumbled cookies/ 130g
- 1 cup mascarpone cheese, room temperature /130g
- 2 eggs, room temperature
- 2 tbsp sour cream /30ml
- 2 tbsp butter, melted /30ml
- ½ tsp vanilla extract /2.5ml

Directions:
1. Fold a 20-inch piece of aluminum foil in half lengthwise twice and set on the pressure cooker. In a bowl, combine melted butter and crushed cookies; press firmly to the bottom and about 1/3 of the way up the sides of a 7-inch springform pan. Freeze the crust while the filling is being prepared.
2. In a separate bowl, beat together mascarpone cheese and sugar to obtain a smooth consistency; stir in vanilla extract and sour cream. Beat one egg and add into the cheese mixture to combine well; do the same with the second egg.
3. Stir cranberries into the filling. Transfer the filling into the crust. Into the pot, add water and set the reversible rack at the bottom. Center the springform pan onto the prepared foil sling. Use the sling to lower the pan onto the reversible rack.
4. Fold foil strips out of the way of the lid. Close the crisping lid and select Bake/Roast; adjust the temperature to 250°F or 122°C and the cook time to 40 minutes. Press Start.
5. When the time is up, open the lid and let to cool the cheesecake. When, transfer the cheesecake to a refrigerator for 2 hours or overnight.
6. Use a paring knife to run along the edges between the pan and cheesecake to remove the cheesecake and set to the plate.

Vanilla Pound Cake

Servings: 8
Cooking Time: 45 Minutes
Ingredients:
- Nonstick cooking spray
- 1 cup butter, unsalted, soft
- 1 cup sugar
- 4 eggs
- 2 tsp vanilla
- ½ tsp salt
- 2 cups flour

Directions:
1. Add the rack to the cooking pot. Spray a loaf pan with cooking spray.
2. In a large bowl, on high speed, beat butter and sugar until fluffy.
3. Beat in eggs, one at a time, until combined. Stir in vanilla and salt.
4. Turn mixer to low and add flour a 1/3 at a time. Beat just until combined. Pour into prepared pan.
5. Place the pan on the rack and add the tender-crisp lid. Set to bake on 350°F. Bake 45-50 minutes or until cake passes the toothpick test.
6. Let cool in pan 15 minutes then invert onto a wire rack and let cool completely.

Nutrition:
- InfoCalories 389,Total Fat 18g,Total Carbs 49g,Protein 7g,Sodium 192mg.

Pecan Pie Bars

Servings: 16
Cooking Time: 25 Minutes
Ingredients:
- Butter flavored cooking spray
- 1/3 cup + 4 tbsp. butter soft
- ¾ cup Stevia brown sugar, packed, divided
- ¼ cup almond flour
- ¼ tsp salt
- ¼ cup maple syrup
- ¼ cup milk
- ¼ tsp vanilla
- 1 ½ cups pecans, chopped

Directions:
1. Place the rack in the cooking pot. Line an 8x8-inch baking pan with foil, leaving some overlap over the sides and spray with cooking spray.
2. In a medium bowl, beat 1/3 cup butter and ¼ cup Stevia until light and fluffy.

3. Add the flour and salt, beat until combined. Press evenly on the bottom of the prepared pan.
4. Place pan on the rack and add the tender-crisp lid. Set to bake on 350°F. Bake 10-13 minutes.
5. In a medium saucepan over medium heat, combine butter, remaining Stevia, syrup, and milk. Bring to a simmer, stirring occasionally. Cook 1 minute.
6. Remove butter mixture from heat and stir in vanilla and pecans. Pour evenly over crust. Bake another 10-12 minutes or until bubbling, center will still be soft.
7. Transfer to wire rack and cool completely. Once the bars are room temperature, cover and refrigerate until ready to serve.
Nutrition:
- InfoCalories 177,Total Fat 17g,Total Carbs 17g,Protein 2g,Sodium 84mg.

Milk Dumplings In Sweet Sauce
Servings: 20
Cooking Time: 30 Min
Ingredients:
- 2 ½ cups Sugar /325g
- 6 cups Milk /1500ml
- 6 cups Water /1500ml
- 3 tbsp Lime Juice /45ml
- 1 tsp ground Cardamom /5g

Directions:
1. Bring to a boil the milk, on Sear/Sauté, and stir in the lime juice. The solids should start to separate. Pour milk through a cheesecloth-lined colander. Drain as much liquid as you can. Place the paneer on a smooth surface. Form a ball and divide into 20 equal pieces.
2. Pour water in the Foofi and bring to a boil on Sear/Sauté. Add in sugar and cardamom and cook until dissolved. Shape the dumplings into balls, and place them in the syrup.
3. Seal the pressure lid and choose Pressure, set to High, and set the time to 5 minutes. Press Start. Once done, do a quick pressure release. Let cool and refrigerate for at least 2 hours.

Butterscotch Almond Brownies
Servings: 12
Cooking Time: 30 Minutes
Ingredients:
- Butter flavored cooking spray
- ½ cup butter, soft
- 1 ½ cups Stevia brown sugar
- 4 eggs
- 1 ½ tbsp. vanilla
- ¾ cup flour
- 1 ½ tsp baking powder
- ¾ cup almonds, chopped

Directions:
1. Place the rack in the cooking pot. Spray an 8x8-inch baking pan with cooking spray.
2. In a large bowl, beat butter and Stevia together until smooth.
3. Add eggs and vanilla and mix well. Stir in remaining ingredients and spread in prepared pan.
4. Place the pan on the rack and add the tender-crisp lid. Set to bake on 350°F. Bake 25-30 minutes or until brownies pass the toothpick test.
5. Transfer to wire rack to cool before serving.
Nutrition:

- InfoCalories 147,Total Fat 11g,Total Carbs 36g,Protein 3g,Sodium 74mg.

Blackberry Crisp
Servings: 6
Cooking Time: 45 Minutes
Ingredients:
- 6 cups blackberries
- 2 tbsp. sugar, divided
- 1 tbsp. cornstarch
- 1 cup oats
- ½ cup almond flour
- ½ cup almonds, chopped
- 1 tsp cinnamon
- ¼ tsp salt
- ¼ cup coconut oil, melted

Directions:
1. Add the rack to the cooking pot. Spray an 8-inch baking dish with cooking spray.
2. In a large bowl, add the blackberries, 1 tablespoon sugar, and cornstarch, toss to coat. Pour into prepared dish.
3. In the same bowl, combine oats, flour, nuts, cinnamon, salt, coconut oil, and remaining sugar, mix well. Pour over berries.
4. Place the dish on the rack. Add the tender-crisp lid and set to bake on 350°F. Bake 30-35 minutes or until top is golden brown. Transfer to wire rack to cool before serving.
Nutrition:
- InfoCalories 282,Total Fat 13g,Total Carbs 38g,Protein 6g,Sodium 100mg.

Steamed Lemon Pudding
Servings: 6
Cooking Time: 90 Minutes
Ingredients:
- Nonstick cooking spray
- ¾ cup butter, unsalted, soft
- 1 cup caster sugar
- 2 eggs
- 2 cups flour
- 1 tsp baking powder
- Zest & juice from 2 lemons

Directions:
1. Lightly spray a 1 liter oven-safe bowl with cooking spray.
2. Add the butter and sugar to the bowl and beat until light and fluffy.
3. Add the eggs, one at a time, beating well after each addition.
4. Stir in the flour and baking powder until combined.
5. Fold in the lemon zest and juice and mix until smooth. Cover lightly with foil.
6. Pour 1 ½ cups water into the cooking pot and add steamer rack.
7. Place the bowl on the rack, secure the lid. Set to steam on 212°F. Cook 90 minutes, or until pudding is cooked through.
8. Remove the pudding from the cooker and let sit 5 minutes before inverting onto serving plate.
Nutrition:
- InfoCalories 446,Total Fat 17g,Total Carbs 66g,Protein 7g,Sodium 33mg.

Steamed Blackberry Pudding

Servings: 6
Cooking Time: 50 Minutes
Ingredients:
- Butter flavored cooking spray
- 1 ½ cups water
- 5 ¼ tbsp. butter, soft
- 8 tbsp. caster sugar
- Zest of 1 lemon
- 2 eggs
- 1 cup flour
- 4 tbsp. milk
- 4 tbsp. honey
- 1 ½ cups blackberries

Directions:
1. Spray 6 ramekins with cooking spray. Pour the water in the cooking pot and add the steamer rack.
2. In a large bowl, beat butter, sugar, and lemon zest until light and fluffy.
3. Beat in eggs, flour, and milk until combined. Stir in 2 tablespoons honey.
4. Drizzle the remaining honey in the bottoms of the ramekins. Add blackberries and pour the pudding mixture over them.
5. Tent the ramekins with foil, leave some space for puddings to rise while cooking. Place the ramekins on the steamer rack.
6. Add the lid and select steam function. Cook 40-50 minutes, or until puddings pass the toothpick test. Transfer to wire rack to cool slightly.
7. To serve, invert onto serving plates and top with whipped cream if desired, or just eat them plain.

Nutrition:
- InfoCalories 318,Total Fat 12g,Total Carbs 48g,Protein 5g,Sodium 109mg.

Tres Leches Cake

Servings:8
Cooking Time: 38 Minutes
Ingredients:
- 1 box of yellow cake mix
- Cooking spray
- 1 can evaporated milk
- 1 can sweetened condensed milk
- 1 cup heavy (whipping) cream

Directions:
1. Close crisping lid. Select BAKE/ROAST, set temperature to 400°F, and set time to 43 minutes. Select START/STOP to begin. Let preheat for 5 minutes.
2. Prepare the cake batter according to the box instructions.
3. Grease a Ninja Multi-Purpose Pan or a 1½-quart round baking dish with cooking spray. Pour the batter into the pan. Place the pan on Reversible Rack, making sure rack is in the lower position.
4. Once unit has preheated, open lid and place rack with pan in pot. Close lid, and reduce temperature to 315°F. Cook for 38 minutes.
5. In a medium bowl whisk together the evaporated milk, condensed milk, and heavy cream.
6. When cooking is complete, remove rack with pan from pot and let cool for 10 minutes.
7. Remove pan from the rack. Using a long-pronged fork, poke holes every inch or so across the surface of the cake.

Slowly pour the milk mixture over the cake. Refrigerate for 1 hour.
8. Once the cake has cooled and absorbed the milk mixture, slice and serve. If desired, top with whipped cream and strawberries.

Nutrition:
- InfoCalories: 644,Total Fat: 28g,Sodium: 574mg,Carbohydrates: 89g,Protein: 12g.

Pumpkin Spice Bread Pudding

Servings: 8
Cooking Time: 5 Hours
Ingredients:
- Butter flavored cooking spray
- 1 ¼ cups almond milk, unsweetened
- ¾ cups pumpkin puree, sugar free
- ½ cup honey
- 1 egg
- 4 egg whites
- ½ tsp cinnamon
- ¼ tsp ginger
- 1/8 tsp allspice
- 1/8 tsp cloves
- 5 cups whole grain bread, cubed

Directions:
1. Lightly spray the cooking pot with cooking spray.
2. In a large bowl, whisk all ingredients, except bread, until smooth and combined.
3. Place the bread in the cooking pot and pour the liquid mixture over it, stir gently.
4. Add the lid and set to slow cooking on low. Cook 4-5 hours or until bread pudding passes the toothpick test. Let cool slightly before serving.

Nutrition:
- InfoCalories 155,Total Fat 2g,Total Carbs 30g,Protein 6g,Sodium 162mg.

Blueberry Peach Crisp

Servings: 8
Cooking Time: 40 Minutes
Ingredients:
- 1 cup blueberries
- 6 peaches, peeled, cored & cut in ½-inch pieces
- ½ cup + 3 tbsp. flour
- ¾ cups Stevia, divided
- ½ tsp cinnamon
- ¼ tsp salt, divided
- Zest & juice of 1 lemon
- 1 cup oats
- 1/3 cup coconut oil, melted

Directions:
1. Place the rack in the cooking pot.
2. In a large bowl, combine blueberries, peaches, 3 tablespoons flour, ¼ cup Stevia, cinnamon, and 1/8 teaspoon salt, toss to coat fruit. Stir in lemon zest and juice just until combined. Pour into an 8-inch baking dish.
3. In a medium bowl, combine oats, ½ cup Stevia, coconut oil, remaining flour and salt and mix with a fork until crumbly. Sprinkle over the top of the fruit.
4. Place the dish on the rack and add the tender-crisp lid. Set to bake on 350 °F. Bake 35-40 minutes until filling is bubbly and top is golden brown. Serve warm.

Nutrition:
- InfoCalories 265,Total Fat 11g,Total Carbs 44g,Protein 6g,Sodium 74mg.

Simple Cinnamon Donuts

Servings: 4
Cooking Time: 10 Minutes
Ingredients:
- ⅔ cup all-purpose flour, plus additional for dusting
- 3 tablespoons granulated sugar, divided
- ½ teaspoon baking powder
- ¼ teaspoon, plus ½ tablespoon cinnamon
- ¼ teaspoon sea salt
- 2 tablespoons cold unsalted butter, cut into small pieces
- ¼ cup plus 1½ tablespoons whole milk
- Cooking spray

Directions:
1. In a medium bowl, mix together the flour, 1 tablespoon of sugar, baking powder, ¼ teaspoon of cinnamon, and salt.
2. Use a pastry cutter or two forks to cut in the butter, breaking it up into little pieces until the mixture resembles coarse cornmeal. Add the milk and continue to mix together until the dough forms a ball.
3. Place the dough on a lightly floured work surface and knead it until a smooth ball forms, about 30 seconds. Divide the dough into 8 equal pieces and roll each piece into a ball.
4. Place the Cook & Crisp Basket in the pot. Close crisping lid. Select AIR CRISP, set temperature to 350ºF , and set time to 3 minutes. Press START/STOP to begin.
5. Once preheated, coat the basket with cooking spray. Place the dough balls in the basket, leaving room between each. Spray them with cooking spray. Close crisping lid.
6. Select AIR CRISP, set temperature to 350ºF , and set time to 10 minutes. Press START/STOP to begin.
7. In a medium bowl, combine the remaining 2 tablespoons of sugar and ½ tablespoon of cinnamon.
8. When cooking is complete, open lid. Place the dough balls in the bowl with the cinnamon sugar and toss to coat. Serve immediately.

Nutty Baked Pears

Servings: 2
Cooking Time: 25 Minutes
Ingredients:
- 2 pears, halved
- 1 tsp cinnamon
- ¼ cup walnuts, chopped
- 2 tsp maple syrup

Directions:
1. Place the rack in the cooking pot. Line a small baking sheet with parchment paper.
2. Cut a small slice off the back of the pears so they lie flat. Use a teaspoon or melon baller to scoop out the seeds. Place the pears, cut side up, on prepared baking sheet.
3. Sprinkle pears evenly with cinnamon and fill the middles with walnuts. Drizzle with maple syrup.
4. Place the pears on the rack and add the tender crisp lid. Set to bake on 375°F. Bake 20-25 minutes until pears are tender and the tops are lightly browned. Serve immediately.
Nutrition:
- InfoCalories 228,Total Fat 10g,Total Carbs 34g,Protein 3g,Sodium 3mg.

Bacon Blondies

Servings:6
Cooking Time: 35 Minutes
Ingredients:
- 6 slices uncooked bacon, cut into ¼ slices

- 1½ cups unsalted butter, at room temperature, plus additional for greasing
- 1 cup dark brown sugar
- 2 cups all-purpose flour
- Ice cream, for serving

Directions:
1. Grease the Ninja Multi-Purpose Pan with butter.
2. Select SEAR/SAUTÉ and set to HI. Select START/STOP to begin. Let preheat for 5 minutes.
3. Place the bacon in the pot. Cook, stirring frequently, for about 5 minutes, or until the fat is rendered and bacon starts to brown. Transfer the bacon to a paper towel-lined plate to drain. Wipe the pot clean of any remaining fat and return to unit.
4. In a medium bowl, beat the butter and brown sugar with a hand mixer until well incorporated. Slowly add in the flour and continue to beat until the flour is fully combined and a soft dough forms. Next, fold the cooked bacon into the dough.
5. Press the dough into the prepared pan. Place pan on Reversible Rack, ensuring it is in the lower position. Lower rack into pot. Close crisping lid.
6. Select BAKE/ROAST, set temperature to 350°F, and set time to 25 minutes. Select START/STOP to begin.
7. After 20 minutes, open lid and check for doneness by sticking a toothpick through the center of the dough. If it comes out clean, remove rack and pan from unit. If not, close lid and continue cooking.
8. When cooking is complete, remove rack and pan from unit. Let the blondies cool for about 30 minutes before serving with ice cream, if desired.
Nutrition:
- InfoCalories: 771,Total Fat: 54g,Sodium: 453mg,Carbohydrates: 60g,Protein: 12g.

Crispy Coconut Pie

Servings: 8
Cooking Time: 1 Hour
Ingredients:
- 3 eggs
- 1 ½ cup Stevia
- 1 cup coconut, grated
- ½ cup butter, melted
- 1 tbsp. vinegar
- 1 tsp vanilla
- 1/8 tsp salt
- 1 9" pie crust, raw

Directions:
1. In a large bowl, beat the eggs.
2. Add remaining ingredients and mix well. Pour into pie crust.
3. Use a foil sling to carefully place the pie in the cooking pot. Add the tender-crisp lid and set to bake on 350°F. Bake 1 hour or until top is nicely browned and crisp.
4. Transfer to a wire rack to cool before serving.
Nutrition:
- InfoCalories 427,Total Fat 22g,Total Carbs 45g,Protein 3g,Sodium 304mg.

Key Lime Pie

Servings: 8
Cooking Time: 15 Minutes
Ingredients:
- 1 cup water
- Butter flavored cooking spray

- ¾ cup graham-cracker crumbs
- 3 tbsp. butter, unsalted, melted
- 1 tbsp. sugar
- 14 oz. sweetened condensed milk
- 4 egg yolks
- ½ cup fresh key lime juice*
- 1/3 cup sour cream
- 2 tbsp. key lime zest, grated

Directions:
1. Place the trivet in the cooking pot and add the water. Spray a 7-inch springform pan with cooking spray.
2. In a small bowl, combine cracker crumbs, butter, and sugar, mix well. Press evenly on the bottom and up sides of the pan. Freeze 10 minutes.
3. In a large bowl, beat egg yolks until they are light yellow.
4. Slowly beat in condensed milk until thickened.
5. Slowly beat in lime juice until smooth. Stir in sour cream and zest until combined. Pour into crust. Cover tightly with foil and place on the trivet.
6. Secure the lid and set to pressure cooking on high. Set timer for 15 minutes. When timer goes off, use natural release to remove the lid. Pie is done when the middle is set, if not done, cook another 5 minutes.
7. Transfer to wire rack and remove foil to cool. Wrap with plastic wrap and refrigerate at least 4 hours before serving.

Nutrition:
- InfoCalories 246,Total Fat 11g,Total Carbs 32g,Protein 6g,Sodium 92mg.

Simple Cheesecake

Servings: 12
Cooking Time: 1 Hour 10 Minutes
Ingredients:
- 1 cup almond flour
- 4 tbsp. butter, unsalted, melted
- ½ tsp cinnamon
- 16 oz. cream cheese, soft
- ½ cup Stevia
- 1 tsp vanilla
- 1 tsp fresh lemon juice
- 2 eggs, room temperature
- 1 cup water

Directions:
1. In a large bowl, combine almond flour, butter and cinnamon and stir just until combined. Press on the bottom of a 7-inch springform pan. Refrigerate.
2. In a separate large bowl, beat cream cheese, Stevia, and vanilla until smooth. Slowly beat in lemon juice.
3. Beat in eggs, one at a time, beat well after each addition. Pour into chilled crust.
4. Cover tightly with foil and wrap another piece of foil around the sides and bottom.
5. Add 1 cup of water to the cooking pot and add the trivet. Place the cheesecake on the trivet. Add the lid and set to pressure cook on high. Set the timer for 40 minutes.
6. When the timer goes off, use natural release to remove the pressure. Remove from the cooking pot and let cool completely. Once it has reached room temperature, refrigerate overnight.

Nutrition:
- InfoCalories 232,Total Fat 22g,Total Carbs 5g,Protein 5g,Sodium 154mg.

Chocolate Cake

Servings: 16
Cooking Time: 30 Minutes
Ingredients:
- Butter flavored cooking spray
- 8 Eggs
- 1 lb. semi-sweet chocolate chips
- 1 cup butter

Directions:
1. Place the rack in the cooking pot. Line the bottom of an 8-inch springform pan with parchment paper. Spray with cooking spray and wrap foil around the outside of the pan.
2. In a large bowl, beat eggs until double in size, about 6-8 minutes.
3. Place the chocolate chips and butter in a microwave safe bowl. Microwave at 30 second intervals until melted and smooth.
4. Fold 1/3 of the eggs into chocolate, folding gently just until eggs are incorporated. Repeat two more times.
5. Pour the batter into the prepared pan. Pour 1 ½ cups water into the cooking pot. Place the cake on the rack.
6. Add the tender-crisp lid and set to air fry on 325°F. Bake 25-30 minutes or until center is set.
7. Transfer to wire rack to cool. When cool, invert onto serving plate, top with fresh berries if desired. Slice and serve.

Nutrition:
- InfoCalories 302,Total Fat 25g,Total Carbs 15g,Protein 5g,Sodium 130mg.

Rhubarb, Raspberry, And Peach Cobbler

Servings:6
Cooking Time: 40 Minutes
Ingredients:
- 1 cup all-purpose flour, divided
- ¾ cup granulated sugar
- ½ teaspoon kosher salt, divided
- 2½ cups diced fresh rhubarb
- 2½ cups fresh raspberries
- 2½ cups fresh peaches, peeled and sliced into ¾-inch pieces
- Cooking spray
- ¾ cup brown sugar
- ½ cup oat flakes (oatmeal)
- 1 teaspoon cinnamon
- Pinch ground nutmeg
- 6 tablespoons unsalted butter, sliced, at room temperature
- ½ cup chopped pecans or walnuts

Directions:
1. Select BAKE/ROAST, set temperature to 400°F, and set time to 30 minutes. Select START/STOP to begin. Let preheat for 5 minutes.
2. In a large bowl, whisk together ¼ cup of flour, granulated sugar, and ¼ teaspoon of salt. Add the rhubarb, raspberries, and peach and mix until evenly coated.
3. Grease a Ninja Multi-Purpose Pan or a 1½-quart round ceramic baking dish with cooking spray. Add the fruit mixture to the pan.
4. Place pan on Reversible Rack, making sure the rack is in the lower position. Cover pan with aluminum foil.
5. Once unit has preheated, place rack in pot. Close crisping lid and adjust temperature to 375°F. Cook for 25 minutes.

6. In a medium bowl, combine the remaining ¾ cup of flour, brown sugar, oat flakes, cinnamon, remaining ¼ teaspoon of salt, nutmeg, butter, and pecans. Mix well.

7. When cooking is complete, open lid. Remove the foil and stir the fruit. Spread the topping evenly over the fruit. Close crisping lid.

8. Select BAKE/ROAST, set temperature to 400°F, and set time to 15 minutes. Select START/STOP to begin. Cook until the topping is browned and the fruit is bubbling.

9. When cooking is complete, remove rack with pan from pot and serve.

Nutrition:

• InfoCalories: 476,Total Fat: 19g,Sodium: 204mg,Carbohydrates: 76g,Protein: 6g.

Ninja Pear Wedges

Servings: 3
Cooking Time: 15 Min
Ingredients:

• 2 Large Pears, peeled and cut into wedges
• 3 tbsp Almond Butter /45g
• 2 tbsp Olive Oil /30ml

Directions:

1. Pour 1 cup of water in the Foodi. Place the pear wedges in a steamer basket and then lower the basket at the bottom. Seal the pressure lid, and cook for 2 minutes on High pressure.

2. When the timer goes off, do a quick pressure release. Remove the basket, discard the water and wipe clean the cooker. Press the Sear/Sauté and heat the oil. Add the pears and cook until browned. Top them with almond butter, to serve.

Mixed Berry Cobbler

Servings: 4
Cooking Time: 40 Min
Ingredients:

• 2 bags frozen mixed berries
• 1 cup sugar /130g
• 3 tbsps arrowroot starch /45g
• For the topping
• 1 cup self-rising flour /130g
• ⅔ cup crème fraiche, plus more as needed /177ml
• 1 tbsp melted unsalted butter /15ml
• 1 tbsp whipping cream /15ml

• 5 tbsps powdered sugar; divided /75g
• ¼ tsp cinnamon powder /1.25g

Directions:

1. To make the base, pour the blackberries into the inner pot along with the arrowroot starch and sugar. Mix to combine. Seal the pressure lid, choose Pressure; adjust the pressure to High and the cook time to 3 minutes; press Start. After cooking, perform a quick pressure release and carefully open the lid.

2. To make the topping, in a small bowl, whisk the flour, cinnamon powder, and 3 tbsps of sugar. In a separate small bowl, whisk the crème fraiche with the melted butter.

3. Pour the cream mixture on the dry ingredients and combine evenly. If the mixture is too dry, mix in 1 tbsp of crème fraiche at a time until the mixture is soft.

4. Spoon 2 to 3 tbsps of dough on top over the peaches and spread out slightly on top. Brush the topping with the whipping cream and sprinkle with the remaining sugar.

5. Close the crisping lid and Choose Bake/Roast; adjust the temperature to 325°F or 163°Cand the cook time to 12 minutes. Press Start. Check after 8 minutes; if the dough isn't cooking evenly, rotate the pot about 90 , and continue cooking.

6. When ready, the topping should be cooked through and lightly browned. Allow cooling before slicing. Serve warm.

Chocolate Soufflé

Servings: 2
Cooking Time: 25 Min
Ingredients:

• 2 eggs, whites and yolks separated
• 3 oz. chocolate, melted /90ml
• ¼ cup butter, melted /32.5ml
• 2 tbsp flour /30g
• 3 tbsp sugar /45g
• ½ tsp vanilla extract /2.5ml

Directions:

1. Beat the yolks along with the sugar and vanilla extract. Stir in butter, chocolate, and flour. Whisk the whites until a stiff peak forms.

2. Working in batches, gently combine the egg whites with the chocolate mixture. Divide the batter between two greased ramekins. Close the crisping lid and cook for 14 minutes on Roast at 330 °F or 166°C.

Recipes Index

Printed in Great Britain
by Amazon

37101822R00059